DATE DUE FOR RETURN

LEGACIES OF WEST INDIAN SLAVERY

DUAL LEGACIES IN THE CONTEMPORARY CARIBBEAN

LEGACIES OF WEST INDIAN SLAVERY

Lectures and conference papers given during the
William Wilberforce 150th anniversary celebrations
at the University of Hull, July 1983

OUT OF SLAVERY
Abolition and After
Edited by Jack Hayward

ABOLITION AND ITS AFTERMATH
The Historical Context 1790–1916
Edited by David Richardson

DUAL LEGACIES IN THE CONTEMPORARY CARIBBEAN
Continuing Aspects of British and French Dominion
Edited by Paul Sutton

THE CARIBBEAN IN EUROPE
Aspects of the West Indian Experience in Britain,
France and The Netherlands
Edited by Colin Brock

DUAL LEGACIES IN THE CONTEMPORARY CARIBBEAN: CONTINUING ASPECTS OF BRITISH AND FRENCH DOMINION

Edited by
PAUL SUTTON
University of Hull

FRANK CASS

First published 1986 in Great Britain by
FRANK CASS & CO. LTD
Gainsborough House, 11 Gainsborough Road,
London E11 1RS, England

and in the United States of America by
FRANK CASS & CO. LTD
c/o Biblio Distribution Centre
81 Adams Drive, P.O. Box 327, Totowa, N.J. 07511

Copyright © 1986 Frank Cass & Co. Ltd

British Library Cataloguing in Publication Data

Dual legacies in the contemporary Caribbean
continuing aspects of British and French
dominion.—(Legacies of West Indian slavery)
1. Caribbean Area—Social conditions—1945.
I. Sutton, Paul   II. Series
909'.09821   HN192.5

ISBN 0-7146-3262-7

$\subset$

345508

Typeset by Williams Graphics, Abergele, Clwyd
Printed and bound in Great Britain by
A. Wheaton & Co. Ltd, Exeter

For
LORRAINE

CONTENTS

Preface   ix
Acknowledgements   xi
Contributors   xii

Introduction: The Past in the Present
Paul Sutton   1

The Post-War Decline of the Sugar Economy in
  the Commonwealth Caribbean
Ramesh Ramsaran   33

Sugar in Barbados and Martinique: A Socio-
  economic Comparison
Michael Sleeman   62

The Sugar Protocol of the Lomé Conventions
  and the Caribbean
Paul Sutton   89

Citizenship and Parliamentary Politics in the
  English-Speaking Caribbean
Anthony Maingot   120

The Political Economy of Independence of the
  Former Associated States of the Commonwealth
  Caribbean
Tony Thorndike   141

Guyane: A Département Like the Others?
Frank Schwarzbeck   171

An Economic Policy for Martinique
Jean Crusol   188

The Social and Political Thought of Aimé Césaire
and C.L.R. James: Some Comparisons
John La Guerre 201

Cultural Dualism and Political Domination in Haiti
David Nicholls 223

Contemporary Educational Issues in the
Commonwealth Caribbean
Colin Brock 240

Index 259

PREFACE

This volume is the second of the three-volume edition of the proceedings of an international conference on Legacies of West Indian Slavery held at the University of Hull in July 1983 to commemorate the sesquicentenary of the abolition of slavery in the British Empire. Its focus is on the contemporary Caribbean and the omnipresent legacies of slavery that continue to mark everyday life in the region. To catalogue these in any detail would be a monumental task, so pervasive and lasting have been their influence throughout the archipelago. The concerns of this volume are therefore necessarily limited to only part of a complex whole, though they do focus on what are self-evidently among the most important and tangible legacies from the era of slavery presently manifest in the Caribbean: the problem of a declining cane sugar industry; the difficulties of decolonization in a politically fragmented and island divided region; and the ever present dialectic between metropolitan and creole culture. In each of these areas similarities and differences within a common theme are identified and the acknowledged and unacknowledged weight of the past is assessed.

The volume also seeks to advance the comparative method in Caribbean studies. Given the diversity of the region this might be taken as a statement of the obvious. Yet, it is surprising how little cross-national research or writing there is, particularly with respect to the lingering European presence in the region. An attempt has therefore been made to address an omission by explicit reference to the two most significant colonial traditions still extant, the British and the French. Various chapters focus on both the shared experiences and the differential responses engendered by these two powers, incidentally raising new questions and agendas for research as they also yield insights on patterns of persistence and change.

The genesis of this volume in a Conference necessarily

requires a double acknowledgement: to those who made the Conference possible and to those who subsequently assisted in the preparation of the book. Among the former my thanks first go to those who provided the finance: the British Council, the British Academy and, above all, the Commonwealth Foundation. The Commonwealth Foundation's generosity, without which the Conference might well have been still-born, allowed a number of Commonwealth contributors to present papers, three of which are included in this volume. Second, I wish to thank all who helped in the organization of the Conference and in particular Jack Hayward, David Richardson and Colin Brock. Each of them rendered invaluable assistance and working with them is a pleasure I often recall. Third, I wish to pay particular tribute to C. L. R. James who was Guest of Honour at the Conference and to Ivar Oxaal who acted as his host. The presence of such a distinguished 'man of letters' and West Indian revolutionary made the Conference for everyone an extra-special event. Finally, special thanks go to the secretaries in the Department of Politics and particularly to Janet Braim whose administrative skills and personal charm made light of the many difficulties and quite extraordinary duties such a conference brings.

After the Conference the book. Pride of place here must go to Melanie Bucknell who typed and retyped parts of the manuscript and responded to a mountain of correspondence. There must have been days when the book appeared more a distant possibility than an attainable goal. That it was realized in the end is in no small measure due to her cheerful patience and unflagging energy to see it through to the finish. Thanks also go to Tony Payne who commented on the entire manuscript. His suggestions, always valued, provided a sure guide in those instances where one's own judgement is sometimes uncertain. Errors and omissions are mine alone.

Throughout the preparation of the Conference and the book the one constant has been the support of my wife. The toll on time which should rightfully have been hers was immense yet always willingly given. As a small token of appreciation and recompense this book is dedicated to her.

Paul Sutton

ACKNOWLEDGEMENTS

Frank Schwarzbeck's chapter originally appeared in a shortened version in English in *Caribbean Review* Vol. 13, No. 2, 1984.

David Nicholls' chapter also appears in his *Haiti in Caribbean Context: Ethnicity, Economy and Revolt* (St Antony's: Macmillan, 1985).

CONTRIBUTORS

Paul Sutton is Lecturer in Politics at the University of Hull.

Ramesh Ramsaran is Senior Lecturer in International Relations at the University of the West Indies in Trinidad.

Michael Sleeman, formerly of the University of Surrey, is now a Teacher at Ruseas High School in Jamaica.

Anthony Maingot is Professor of Sociology and Director of the Graduate Programme in International Studies at Florida International University.

Tony Thorndike is Head of the Department of International Relations and Politics at North Staffordshire Polytechnic.

Frank Schwarzbeck, formerly of the University of Hamburg, is now with the United Nations Development Programme in Rwanda.

Jean Crusol is Lecturer in Economics at the Université des Antilles et de la Guyane, Martinique.

John La Guerre is Senior Lecturer in Government at the University of the West Indies in Trinidad.

David Nicholls, formerly at Exeter College, Oxford University, is now Vicar at Littlemore, Oxford.

Colin Brock is Lecturer in Education at the University of Hull.

Introduction:
The Past in the Present

PAUL SUTTON

A legacy is also an inheritance. It necessarily requires both a giver and a receiver; and it may be welcome or unwelcome, sought or imposed, according to context. These considerations should not be forgotten in any survey such as the one being undertaken here, which seeks to relate a given phenomenon in the past, chattel slavery, with its consequences in the present. More so when that past seems somewhat remote in time and so much appears to have transpired in the meantime to lend it distance. And yet, appearances are not essences and much contemporary Caribbean social science has emphatically confirmed the past within the present, even to the point of suggesting that in reality very little has changed at all. Three examples can suffice.

In the discipline of economics the most widely discussed school of thought in the Caribbean in recent years has been the structuralist/dependency approach. As quintessentially expressed in the writings of Lloyd Best and George Beckford, the plantation economy – pure, modified and further modified[1] and in its institutional nexus[2] – has profoundly shaped the character of Caribbean social reality and imparted to it an associated underdevelopment bias. The legacy, accordingly, is all pervasive and almost entirely negative. From their point of view it is unwelcome and imposed and ought to be rejected, or at the very least 'engineered', to effect greater reward to the Caribbean people who are its hapless victims. In the discipline of sociology it is the plural society thesis of M. G. Smith which has been at the centre of a hotly contested debate. In this interpretation ethnicity, not class, is the dominant structuring variable in the Caribbean, with the position of any group in the social order determined largely by the position it occupied under slavery.[3] Of course, later developments, particularly the experience of indenture, are admitted as distorting the picture, but not to the extent of making it unrecognisable. Smith's 'framework' thus continues to influence many current studies on the Caribbean, so attesting again to the presumed durability of norms originally fashioned under slavery but now permeating all groups. Finally, within the discipline of politics there is considerable emphasis on familiarity with the past as an aid to understanding the present in the Caribbean. Gordon Lewis, who is today the most highly regarded of the region's political scientists, has in numerous writings, theoretical and empirical and covering the wide spectrum of Caribbean politics, made this very plain.[4] He has also, in his work, drawn attention to the heterogeneity as well as the homogeneity of political legacies in the Caribbean; and has pointed out that they exhibit both a negative and a positive side. Thus while the old colonial order must be condemned and the new order of political independence be sustained, it is inevitable that the latter contains elements of the former, and is conditioned accordingly.

If the social scientists are to be believed, it follows that the proper starting point for an understanding of the contemporary Caribbean is an appreciation of Caribbean history. That history, by common agreement, is one powerfully shaped by the sugar plantation, negro slavery and imperial domination, to determine in its combination a distinctive socio-cultural area[5] which in turn serves as the basis for the most satisfying definition of the geographical boundaries of the region.[6] That is, the Caribbean archipelago to include all the islands of the Caribbean Sea from the Bahamas in the North to Trinidad in the South plus the mainland 'extensions' of Guyana, Suriname and Guyane on the South American mainland and Belize on the Central American mainland. It also imposes a paradox on the Caribbean recently expressed by Franklin Knight as 'a fragmented nationalism'. He writes that while 'the sum of the common experiences and understandings of the Caribbean outweigh the territorial and insular differences or peculiarities' it is also true that 'the separate political identities are as patently strong as they are inescapable'.[7] In other words, the Caribbean is a nation divided from itself. On current estimates it embraces some

32 million people divided into 16 separate states and 11 dependent territories over which four 'external' powers continue to exercise 'legitimate' interests (and which in turn serve as 'home' to several million more persons of Caribbean origin).

The concerns of this book focus on but a part of this complex whole. It identifies two of the external traditions – the British and the French – and three of the legacies – the economic, political and cultural. It proceeds on the basis that what are being compared are directly comparable and that the subjects under consideration are self-evidently among the most important tangible legacies from the era of slavery presently manifest in the Caribbean – sequentially, sugar and what to do about it; the consequences of political fragmentation for political decolonization; and cultural adaptation for nationhood.

THE PROBLEM OF SUGAR

In 1965 the Commonwealth Caribbean recorded an all-time high in sugar production of 1,321,800 tons. In 1982 it produced a mere 820,480 tonnes, less than two-thirds of this. A decline in the fortunes of the sugar industry, evident in some cases since well before the Second World War, has apparently set in and now seems irreversible. Thus one hundred and fifty years after Emancipation had called into question the existence of the industry its final demise appears near.

However, as Ramsaran points out, the decline is by no means even. While in Barbados, Jamaica and Trinidad the sugar industry is in dire straits and in Guyana and St. Kitts is at best stagnating, in Belize it is buoyant. There sugar has been the largest contributor to the economy since the 1960s and as of 1983 plans for limited expansion in plant capacity in the two sugar factories were under serious consideration. However, Belize's exceptionality and historical marginality to the Commonwealth Caribbean sugar industry only serve to underline the prevailing trend which has set the region on a downward path as far as sugar as a profitable export crop is concerned.

The reasons for this are many and varied and of a short, medium and long-term economic nature. They are also well known and focus on inefficient field and factory operations (poor cultivation, harvesting, transportation and refining of cane) and inadequate levels of investment (into research in cane varieties, mechanization of harvesting and replacement of technically obsolescent and sub-optimum factories). The consequences have been costs of production close to or in excess of prices received. One study, for example, estimated average costs of production in 1975 to have been about £150 per ton f.o.b. for Jamaica and Trinidad, £130 per ton f.o.b. for Barbados and £115 per ton f.o.b. for Guyana as against a guaranteed price under the Sugar Protocol of the Lomé Convention of about £158 per ton c.i.f. for 1975–76.[8] Since then costs of production have risen steeply compared to guaranteed price, to the extent that in Trinidad in 1982 Ramsaran can cite a cost of production of T.T. $3,700 per ton as against a price of T.T. $850. In these circumstances continued sugar production clearly makes little economic sense though it may continue for what are regarded as sound political and social reasons.

Overwhelmingly, these centre on sugar as a provider of employment for the middle-aged, elderly and less educated rural populace for whom comparable alternatives are not readily available. This 'welfare' aspect of the sugar industry is one that governments in search of votes have quite naturally stressed and which, in turn, has inexorably led to a policy of government intervention in and eventually acquisition of the industry in most instances. However, once in control governments everywhere have fallen prey to inertia so that, in effect, neither the condition of the sugar workers[9] nor the productivity of the industry as a whole has improved. Ramsaran establishes that the reasons for this lie not in the sugar industry *per se* but in the wider context of the policies for economic development adopted by all post-war Commonwealth Caribbean governments. In this the stress has been on industrial development to the detriment of agricultural development. Land reform has not been seriously pursued as a priority and the consequences have been an ever escalating food import bill for the region. It therefore follows that it is not the abandonment of sugar cane cultivation which should be advocated (however tempting), but its rationalisation within a wider agricultural and regional programme of agricultural diversification. Ramsaran's conclusion here echo those of the World Bank:

The evidence suggests ... that other crops need not be directly substituted for sugar to any significant degree in the short or the medium term, since there is no real competition between sugarcane and other crops for the use of inputs such as land and labour. In the longer run, sugar industry policy should be designed to complement the region's new import substitution initiatives.[10]

In short, the immediate economic policies seem relatively clear. Whether there is the political will to achieve them, however, remains another matter.

Sleeman's study of sugar in Barbados and Martinique brings this point into sharp focus. He begins with the proposition that the sugar industry in both islands is atypical in regard to the Caribbean as a whole, yet they are directly comparable the one to the other. The historical evidence he marshalls to argue this is both overwhelming and convincing. It also converges in the emergence in both countries of an 'agri-business bourgeoisie' who have dominated the fortunes of the sugar industry this century. The result is that the recent history of the sugar industry is, in each case, properly speaking, the history of the development of this class. And it is to the differential response of the 'agri-business bourgeoisie' to specific situations that the decline of sugar production in Barbados and its virtual abandonment in Martinique can ultimately be traced.

To situate the outcome so squarely in class analysis provides a number of insights which are otherwise all too easily overlooked. The first, quite simply, is that the sugar industry, by virtue of its historic significance, is connected to Caribbean society in myriads of ways. To isolate it as purely an economic or social or political issue is to do a serious injustice to the complexity of the question and to ignore the fact that it is precisely its interconnectedness that makes the problem of sugar so intractable. Secondly, the identification of the same class in Barbados and Martinique as providing the 'key' to sugar underlines the value of cross-national comparative analysis in the Caribbean. This is much discussed yet rarely attempted, especially as regards direct comparison between the French and Commonwealth Caribbean experiences. Finally, by locating his study in class Sleeman develops an analysis which is both flexible and dynamic, thereby avoiding the static approaches of pluralist and plantation society frameworks which though they may describe never adequately explain Caribbean social reality.[11]

As regards the differential outcome for the sugar industry in each island perhaps the most important conclusion is the element of choice. In Barbados this would appear to have been more constrained than in Martinique, so that while a pattern of diversification away from sugar is evident, it is essentially uneven and incomplete. By contrast, in Martinique we have witnessed the destruction of the sugar industry in little more than a decade in a manner suggestive of deliberate abandonment in the face of more profitable alternatives. Why this has occurred when in Martinique the 'agri-business bourgeoisie' hold no formal political power while in Barbados they constitute an important element of that power remains in itself an intriguing question the answer to which is far from agreed.[12] In the meantime, in both islands, the 'agri-business bourgeoisie' continues to be transformed by economic processes into a commercial bourgeoisie and to be subject to the continuing haemorrhage of emigration. The ultimate demise of this class may therefore be anticipated and with it, presumably, the end of the sugar industry in Barbados unless the government directly intervenes to maintain it.

If it does move in this direction it will, of course, confront issues which are not purely local. The case of Martinique is here instructive. The demise of sugar production in that island is above all the final consequence of full integration under increasingly unfavourable economic conditions of *Départements d'Outre Mer* (DOM) sugar into the French metropolitan sugar market. How much so may be gauged from the fact that in the sugar year 1974/75 the estimated cost of production of raw sugar in the Caribbean DOM, estimated as 301.7 EUA per tonne, was well in excess of the intervention (guaranteed) price for raw sugar at only 227.1 EUA per tonne.[13] The continued production of cane sugar in the DOM was therefore possible only by negotiating additional premiums from the EEC and direct subsidies from France. Ironically, in so doing, the cost of DOM sugar has been increased beyond that of comparable African, Caribbean and Pacific (ACP) sugar to the level at which French sugar cane refiners in Marseille, Bordeaux and Nantes are now switching to cheaper ACP sugar, leaving in effect a sizeable surplus of subsidised DOM sugar fit only for re-export on the world market. A more unsatisfactory state of affairs for all concerned could scarcely be imagined.

Yet, as I establish in my contribution, this is symptomatic of the EEC sugar regime as a whole and of the ACP Sugar Protocol in particular. Without the Protocol it is abundantly clear that the Commonwealth Caribbean sugar industry would be under even more severe pressure to curtail production. Even with the Protocol, however, continued production is not certain. While, for example, Barbados 'benefits' if not prospers under present arrangements, it is significant that the highest cost producer in the Commonwealth Caribbean has all but given up production. Trinidad and Tobago has recently informed the EEC Commission that it cannot deliver the 12,000 tonnes of sugar outstanding; that it could not deliver a further quota of 13,500 tonnes in the 1984/85 delivery period; and that it did not wish either to ask for a supplementary delivery period or to invoke *force majeure*. Under the terms of the Protocol its quota has thus been reduced to 43,500 tonnes (63% of original quota).[14] The reaction to this default by other Commonwealth Caribbean producers is not known but is unlikely to have been positive even if they do stand to gain some immediate advantage through the redistribution of Trinidad's shortfall among themselves.

What, then, is the future for export sugar in the French and Commonwealth Caribbean? With regard to the former it is now confined to Guadeloupe and subject to a protracted crisis from which it may not recover.[15] With regard to the latter I have argued in my chapter that an organization of cane sugar exporting countries going beyond the Commonwealth Caribbean is a necessary step to secure markets. Set alongside Ramsaran's conclusions as to the viability of the industry, the way forward would therefore appear to be that advocated by Vincent Mahler several years ago:

The solution for sugar exporters is ... not an abrupt and complete disengagement from sugar cultivation but joint action to coordinate production and rationalize the historically chaotic world market. The problem, after all, is not sugar itself but the low and unstable prices it has traditionally commanded.[16]

Yet, logical as this proposal seems, it must be qualified by the admission that the record over the last few years does not give many grounds for optimism. The major attempt to regulate the international sugar market *via* the International Sugar Agreement has recently collapsed amid mutual recrimination. The inevitable consequence is that the international sugar market as a whole is now that much more competitive, with the natural concomitant that the value of 'regional protection' is further enhanced. For the Commonwealth Caribbean this confirms the utility of the Protocol whatever misgivings may privately be expressed. The same might be said about United States sugar quotas *via* the Caribbean Basin Intiative. In the final analysis, however, these are only partial solutions, able at best to ameliorate the ailing sugar industry but not to halt its decline. To arrest this a combination of national and international action at the broadest level is a vital necessity. If it is to be realized, another legacy of plantation slavery will need to be redressed – political fragmentation and uneven political decolonization.

THE PROBLEM OF DECOLONIZATION

England began its permanent colonization of the Caribbean with the founding of settlements in St. Kitts and Barbados in 1624. It completed it in 1862 when Britain formally added British Honduras (Belize) to its long list of territorial acquisitions in the region. The French began their colonization at approximately the same time as England, but as a result of the French Revolution and the Napoleonic Wars its presence was considerably reduced by 1815 to Martinique, Guadeloupe (including outlying islands) and Guyane (French Guiana). While the French have maintained these territories the British have relinquished hold over theirs, until now responsibility formally remains for only a scattering of islands the total population of which is 55,276 persons enjoying a GDP of approximately US $148.7 million. The comparable figures for the French possession are 696,000 and US $2590 million.[17]

Yet if the British presence is 'materially' minimal, and its general influence in the region is waning, its 'subjective' presence remains massive. Maingot draws attention to one specific, though vital aspect of this – the adoption of the 'Westminster model' as the system of government in all Commonwealth Caribbean countries. Without exception, familiarity with the Westminster system has been the medium through which independence has been granted and everywhere the formal mechanisms of the model are associated with 'good government'. The Commonwealth Caribbean is therefore a rich depository of constitutional forms clustering around the basic model, and those few countries which have rejected its precepts (Grenada under Bishop) or abused them (Guyana under Burnham) have been subject to much opprobrium and on occasion censure.[18]

While the Westminster model clearly remains 'valued', the main question, however, is whether it is 'valid'. Critics, who in the past have included Maingot, have tended to focus on the lack of congruence between institutions autochthonously derived from one social system which are transplanted to another that is radically different. Hence his endorsement, as a constitutional commissioner for Trinidad and Tobago in the early 1970s, of the general conclusion of that body that 'the Westminster model in its purest form as set out in our present Constitution is not suitable to the Trinidad and Tobago society';[19] and also his support for the Draft Constitution which was proposed which, whilst not fundamentally departing from the Westminster model, nevertheless recommended sweeping changes in a number of areas, among the most important of which was the electoral system. This is an issue to which Maingot returns in his chapter. Specifically, he is concerned to demonstrate, through the examples of Jamaica, Trinidad and Tobago and Grenada, that the electoral system as presently constituted in the Commonwealth Caribbean is in no sense 'neutral' but a prime determinant of characteristic features of the contemporary political life of each. Thus in Jamaica the polarization between the Jamaica Labour Party (JLP) and the People's National Party (PNP) is not primarily ideologically derived, as is generally thought, but is the consequence of the application of the first-past-the-post electoral system in which now one party and now the other is favoured at the polls, thereby encouraging the government of the time to draw the conclusion that it has a popular mandate for change, either to the right or the left. Likewise, in Trinidad and Tobago he argues that the characteristic ethnic division at the polls between those of African descent voting for the People's National Movement (PNM) and those of East Indian descent favouring other parties, is historically derived from the first-past-the-post system as applied in 1956 and consciously manipulated by the PNM ever since, to the electoral disadvantage of class or other non-ethnic based political groupings in the country. Finally, in Grenada the case is advanced that had the system of elections been 'fairer' in 1972 the New Jewel Movement (NJM) might not have emerged in the form in which it did and following the 1976 elections might not have been able to exploit the cynicism about parliamentary politics in the country to quite the same effect.

These claims are very large indeed and there are few analysts of Caribbean politics who would want to share them in their entirety. Nevertheless, Maingot has made a substantial point in returning the debate to the question of institutions which historically dominated the study of Caribbean politics but which, of late, have received scant consideration.[20] Similarly, his concern to draw a distinction between constitution-making as identity-building and constitution-making as modernization introduces some neglected normative questions into the discussion and invites the conclusion that what is at fault in the Commonwealth Caribbean is not the Westminster model itself but the failure of West Indians to fully appreciate its intrinsic value and to work it more effectively. In advancing this thesis, curiously enough, Maingot endorses a view not much different from that held by the late Dr Eric Williams of Trinidad who in one of his last conference addresses to the PNM discussed at length the merits and deficiencies of the Westminster model and enjoined his party to cleave closely to it.[21] All the signs are that they will follow his advice and that others in the Commonwealth Caribbean, for whatever reason, will do the same. Experimentation with other participatory forms, as happened in Grenada under the NJM,[22] is thus most unlikely in the near future despite the need for change.

The pitfalls of experimentation in constitutional forms are a prime concern of Thorndike's chapter. 'Associated statehood', as it was applied to the Eastern Caribbean, was a novel departure from the established practice of British decolonization. Normally, the policy of Britain was for its colonies to emerge into independence following the grant of internal self-government and with a short tutelary period thereafter. However, in the case of the smaller Commonwealth Caribbean island territories decolonization was to stop at internal self-government (i.e. full control of internal affairs), Britain retaining responsibility for external affairs (i.e. foreign affairs and defence). This constitutional innovation was considered, if not a permanent solution to the problem of the Eastern Caribbean, then at least one sufficient in itself to provide a framework for the development of these islands for the foreseeable future. Britain therefore refused to accept quadrennial review of the 'associated statehood' concept and following its implementation in the Caribbean in 1967 informed the U.N. that since the territories affected were now self-governing, it would no longer transmit information about them to the appropriate UN committee. With regard to the arrangements themselves it was resolved that in the case of a dispute between Britain and an 'associated state' the status could be terminated by either party. For Britain this would take the form of unilateral legal action and for the 'associated state' the establishment of a mandate for independence *via* constitutional procedures involving obtaining a two-thirds majority in both a referendum and the local House of Assembly.[23] Since this was notoriously difficult to achieve in the 'super-heated' political climate of each island, it was presumed that the option of independence in the immediate future was an unlikely outcome.

Yet, within a decade of 'associated statehood' being established, one island, Grenada, had moved to independence, and among the others, as Thorndike has reported elsewhere,[24] a sample survey of the political and commercial elite established a 69% opinion in favour of independence within the next ten years. The failure of 'association' was thus complete, the reasons for which were both economic and political, with a conjoint emphasis on the lack of progress that the status brought. The history of the smaller Caribbean islands, in Thorndike's words, was one of 'disadvantage' and 'dependency', manifest in psychological as well as material ways, engendering everywhere a feeling of 'inadequacy'. A limited constitutional advance, almost self-evidently, could not redress such a legacy. For this to be achieved it required at the minimum an international personality and at the maximum a revolution. The Eastern Caribbean was to experience both.

The minimalist solution was essentially a technical one. Its characteristic focus was on the economic and administrative advantages of independence as contrasted with the disadvantages of 'associated statehood'. The so-called *McIntyre Report*[25] published in March 1975 set out the main points. Although its principal recommendation 'that the Leeward and Windward islands should proceed to independence and enter into a scheme for constitutional association for the purpose of functioning as a single entity in their relations with other states and with international bodies' was not acceptable to island politicians, the thrust of its analysis found favour among many policy influentials and the logic of its arguments seemed inescapable. Especially attractive were those which maintained that political independence was a pre-requisite for economic development. Accordingly a shift of opinion occurred from independence 'whether' to independence 'when' and a policy was fashioned to take note of island differences by seeking independence on a singular *ad hoc* basis. In November 1978 Dominica became the first to tread this road followed in short order by St. Lucia in February 1979 and St. Vincent in November of the same year. With the Windward islands now independent (in each case by asking the British government to release them rather than by referendum) it was but a matter of time before the Leewards followed the same pattern and same course with independence for Antigua and Barbuda being achieved on 1 November 1981 and for St. Kitts–Nevis on September 19, 1983.

Even as the majority of the 'associated states' were preparing for independence, however, Grenada was demonstrating the perils independence could bring. Under Gairy's inefficient and arbitrary rule the island had sunk economically and politically to a low from which it was rescued in a dramatic and unprecedented fashion by the coup/insurrection of the NJM on 13 March 1979. In power, the NJM set about vigorously challenging those aspects of dependence, especially the psychological and functional, which the minimalist approach left untouched. This was a tremendous step forward of which Thorndike is rightly laudatory and supportive. The transformations being wrought in Grenada directly contradicted the assumption that small size in itself is a powerful independent constraint on the policies of a state; and the achievements of the revolution were tangible enough to attract favourable comment from a wide range of institutions and persons familiar with the development difficulties of Caribbean states.[26] It is therefore doubly tragic that the revolution should have ended in the way it did since, on the one hand, there is now no way of knowing whether revolution is a viable long-term means of economic and social development for the smaller Caribbean islands and, on the other, even assuming that it were, now little prospect of it being realized as long as the US and other Eastern Caribbean governments remain implacably opposed to non-capitalist and extra-parliamentary strategies of change.

The Eastern Caribbean is therefore set for the moment within a framework of possibility determined by a ruling philosophy of pragmatic conservatism. A more British approach, sterotypically, could scarcely be imagined. Yet this is not the legacy of Britain alone: it is also the legacy of France in its Caribbean DOM. In reviewing the political economy of these territories since the Second World War one is immediately struck by the force of the *status quo*. In the politics of the Fifth Republic this is manifest in the overwhelming vote for the 'conservative' candidate (as regards the status of the *départements*) in the presidential elections of 1965, 1968 and 1981. Indeed, as if to underline the point, the massive swing to the right in the 1981 elections in the DOM as compared to 1974 is attributable, above all, to apprehension over anticipated changes in the administration of the DOM favoured by the socialists and bitterly opposed by the 'conservatives'.[27] Likewise, the progressive integration of the Caribbean DOM into the economy of mainland France, which has accelerated since 1958, has introduced major distortions into the Antillean economies and has promoted neither structural change nor acceptable employment opportunities for significant sectors of the population. Consequently, and despite the relative surface prosperity of the islands, emigration to mainland France has continued in recent years, particularly among the young.

In the light of this the arguments for change presented by both Schwarzbeck and Crusol are understandable even if at present they constitute minority positions. This is especially so in the case of Schwarzbeck who advocates, by implication, independence for Guyane. His case, essentially, rests on the distinctiveness of that country which, in socio-economic terms, makes it very unlike France though very much like the rest of the Caribbean. When this is set alongside the fact that France has given little to Guyane in the past, and seems incapable of developing it in the present, then the future for the country as an independent state in closer association with the Caribbean, and especially the Commonwealth Caribbean, logically follows.

Unfortunately, as Schwarzbeck amply demonstrates in his historical remarks, logic has rarely entered into calculations concerning Guianese interests. The errors of the past are repeated in the present. The bizarre schemes of settlement of yesteryear therefore find an echo in the 1970s in attempts to settle Hmong refugees from Laos in the country. And a geographical remoteness which just over a hundred years ago marked the territory as a site for a notorious penal colony has in the last decade specified it as a site for a space centre. French interests continue to predominate and while there are political movements for greater autonomy and for independence they secure only limited support. The prospects for weakening the ties with France are therefore slight. This is frankly recognized by the 'separatists' themselves, one of whose leaders, Ian Hamel, has recently remarked: 'As separatists we are all totally superfluous. If we were really ever to gain ground, Paris would in no time shove a hundred thousand white settlers into the country so that every plebiscite could be passed irreproachably.'[28]

Guyane's status as a département 'unlike the others' thus seems assured for the present, especially as long as Paris is prepared to meet the cost. This it is willing to do, not least because the overwhelming proportion of public revenues spent in maintaining the local economy are returned to mainland France *via* private transactions. Guyane is therefore not a significant economic burden, as Schwarzbeck points out, though distortion of its economy inevitably results and local costs are incurred. This is felt, above all, in the productive sector, which remains undeveloped largely because the chief resource, tropical timber, lies unexploited, even when there is a rational complementarity of interests involved between France, Guyane and the EEC.[29] Local costs are also directly borne by the youth of the country who remain subject to high levels of unemployment or, correspondingly, dependent on employment opportunities within the local French administration, thereby reinforcing the association with France. In fact, wherever one looks in Guyane all avenues lead to Paris; and attachment to French culture provides the amalgam within which the more blatant contradictions are resolved. An observation that *French* Guiana is 'out of place and out of time' (as are the Falkland islands) is for this reason not likely to carry much weight, and for the same emotional reason that the Falkland islands remain British, Guyane will remain French for as long as France wishes it.

The same conclusion appears at first sight to also hold for the French Antilles. The politics of the Gaullists and Giscardiens have been based on the axiom that departmentalization has both permanently resolved the status issue and created the only basis by which economic and social progress can be realized. As established already, this view at present enjoys majority support in the islands. In recent years, though, it has also been under an increasingly strident intellectual attack, not least from the French mainland itself, which has resulted in reformist proposals being advanced under the Mitterrand presidency. As originally formulated, these would have permitted greater local control over the economy and enhanced local accountability to the electorate. In his contribution Crusol sets out both their form and their rationale, with particular emphasis on their economic aspect. He graphically depicts failures of the past about which no French government should be complacent; though more interestingly, and unusual for an academic, he proposes an alternative. The obvious questions that should therefore be asked are whether his proposals are practical in a two-fold sense: likely to realize economic development and likely to be politically feasible.

On the broad question of economic development Crusol is strongly influenced by the structuralist/dependency school of political economy which emerged in the Commonwealth Caribbean in the 1960s. Like them he identifies Martinique as a plantation economy and his objective echoes theirs in seeking to replace the present extraverted underdevelopment of the Caribbean islands with an internal dynamic of development.[30]

Predictably, strategy and means also follow familiar lines with policy principally directed toward removing internal obstacles to development by reform and revising external obstacles by negotiation, the whole accompanied by recommendations for diversification toward tourism, industrial development and longer-term Caribbean and Latin American economic integration. Intellectually, there is little to quarrel with here except for the arresting fact that nowhere in the Caribbean has such a policy yet met with success, except obliquely in Cuba where it has involved revolution and where the weakness of the economy is an acknowledged fact of life. The case Crusol presents therefore remains to be verified in practice and while there is, of course, no inherent reason why Martinique might not provide an exception to prove the rule, equally there is no overwhelming reason, as the argument is set out here, why it should.

Limitations are also evident in the political sphere. Crusol is a strong supporter of Mitterrand's decentralization proposals and to a considerable degree his advocacy of an internal dynamic for economic development depends on the acceptance and extension of local i.e. Martiniquan decision-making. Unfortunately, the reactions to the Mitterrand proposals do not give grounds for optimism in this direction. Within Martinique opposition to them has come from the *Conseil Général* (the local council) and in mainland France a determined campaign against the plan approved by the National Assembly on 1st October 1982 saw them rejected at first by the Senate and then declared unconstitutional by the Constitutional Council on 3rd December 1982. The proposals have therefore had to be amended[31] and a spirit of compromise toward the DOM has been attempted by the replacement of Mitterrand's radical and ideological Secretary of State for the DOM-TOM, Henri Emmanuelli, with the more pragmatic and cautious Georges Lemoine. In the meantime the centrepiece of the reforms, an elected *Conseil Régional*, has been in place since February 1983, though its exact competence, especially in regard to the continuing *Conseil Général*, has yet to be determined, and in Martinique the majority for the government is only slight.[32] Some measure of reform has therefore been achieved, though it is by no means as sweeping or as decisive as Crusol wishes, and as the recent elections for the European Parliament unequivocally demonstrate, opinion within the DOM continues strongly to favour departmentalization and the *status quo*.[33]

However, despite the above objections, one is left with the impression that the approach offered by Crusol is likely to be more attractive to France, and hence more realizable, than that proposed by Schwarzbeck. Crusol, after all, only seeks a change of status within an existing relationship (at least in the short term) whereas Schwarzbeck rejects it. Moreover, whereas Martinique and Guadeloupe, separately or together, exhibit an economy at least comparable to many other Eastern Caribbean islands, Guyane is an exception in every regard. In short, there is a qualitative difference between the Antillean and the South American DOM, pointing toward a greater autonomy presently being possible in the former than in the latter. All this betokens an approach by the French to their Caribbean territories which recognizes subtle distinctions between them. The weight of French colonial tradition, with its emphasis on centralization and assimilation, is however likely to militate against this. And here it stands in direct contrast to the British tradition with its emphasis on devolved government and local adaptation. Arguably, and unanswerably if judged by results, the British model has permitted a more workable decolonization in the region than the French, even if Britain remains perplexed as to what to do about its very smallest colonies. None of this, of course, is to deny the observation that at the end of the day both Britain and France have ended up at the same place − bequeathing legacies that are conservative in essence, if not downright reactionary. That they have done so by different means, however, is significant and attests to variability, particularly in the sphere of culture, which is one of the more persistent and most remarked upon legacies of colonialism in the region.

CULTURE AND IDENTITY

Caribbean society is multi-racial, multi-religious, multi-lingual, and multi-cultural. It is divided by island; stratified by colour and class; and subject to ceaseless in and out migration. There is in consequence little sense of community, though there is an emerging Caribbean identity and, more arguably, an evolving Creole consciousness. In the twentieth century this latter force has been expressed, above all, in a desire for nationhood and a promotion of a view of the region as *sui generis* i.e. unique in its own right. Two of the most outstanding intellectuals contributing to the trend have been C. L. R. James from Trinidad and Aimé Césaire from Martinique. No study of ideas in the contemporary Caribbean would be complete without them and in his chapter La Guerre addresses the complex and difficult task of a direct comparison of their social and political thought, stressing some similarities as well as several significant differences.

Taking the latter first, La Guerre identifies polarities between the thought of each on race and class. He correctly argues that for James race can be considered for most purposes as subordinate to the Marxist category of class in explaining historical events, whereas for Césaire race is *supra* class in the colonial milieu. Likewise, he plausibly develops a thesis of differences between them on colonial liberation, with James arguing that colonial revolution is but part of world revolution, the achievement of which is the historic task of the 'common man', whereas for Césaire colonial revolution is an end to the colonial condition, which is specific to time and place and possessed of its own internal logic. In a nutshell, James is more 'Marxist' in treating these questions than is Césaire who is, without insisting on the point, more 'idealist'. How may this be explained given that both hail from the Caribbean and have had parallel, and convergent, concerns?

In his conclusion La Guerre suggests that the differences between James and Césaire are at root the differences between the activist (James) and the artist (Césaire). This is a useful distinction; but one which should not be taken too far. Césaire is an activist in his own right. He is the leader of the Parti Progressiste Martiniquais (PPM), a party he founded in 1958 to promote the status of autonomy for Martinique, and he has been Mayor of Fort-de-France and a member of the French National Assembly since 1945. Indeed, on this account Césaire must be considered more successful than James whose own party, the Workers and Farmers Party in Trinidad, founded in 1965, was electorally unsuccessful and short-lived. By the same token James must also be considered an artist in his own right. Among his voluminous writings are a novel, many short stories, some literary criticism, as well as several philosophical treatises, including one dealing at length with Hegel and his contemporary significance. Césaire's output is unquestionably more literary in character, though scarcely more distinguished either in the general or the particular. In fact, both Césaire and James are demonstrably artist *and* activist – a combination of talents frequently to be encountered in the Caribbean and the hallmark, almost, of their identity as Caribbean intellectuals.[34]

If the distinction of artist and activist holds only weakly, another comparative point made by La Guerre carries greater weight. This is to view James and Césaire as products of Empire: extraordinary men whose lives have been deeply shaped by the respective cultures and practices of a colonialism to which they were arbitrarily assigned at birth. James frankly admits this. In *Beyond a Boundary* he writes that had he been born French or German or African he would have thought differently. But he is British: 'I knew best the British way of life, not merely in historical facts but in instinctive responses. I have acquired them in childhood and, without these, facts are merely figures'.[35] Following this through he can declare that 'Thackeray, not Marx, bears the heaviest responsibility for me',[36] whilst in his passion for cricket (which, of course, he shares with his compatriots from the Commonwealth Caribbean) is revealed, for many people, his quintessential 'Englishness'. Césaire is similarly identifiably 'French'. His rejection of French culture in developing the concept of negritude is a reaction to France and its policy of assimilation which, in its very negativity, carries within it powerful currents of French literary and philosophical thought: romanticism, surrealism, idealism and even racism (an 'antiracial racialism' as Senghor, the co-founder of negritude, would have us believe).[37] The common cause that Césaire finds is, accordingly, first and foremost with other black men of French culture and his desire, with them, is 'to assimilate but not be assimilated'.[38] In this instance political practice reflects theory. The vision of autonomy put forward by the PPM is one which seeks to remain indissolubly attached to France even as it achieves a transformation of the present relationship to permit a greater expression of Martiniquan identity. Césaire is quite explicit on this question and for the last twenty-five years it has served as the main point of departure between himself and those in Martinique favouring independence.[39] By contrast, for James, echoing British colonial practice, the imperative of independence for the colonies was never in doubt, only the pace and form of advance. It was this, in part, which identified him as a revolutionary in Britain in the 1930s when he was actively associated with the International African Service Bureau; as today it continues to single him out as a continuing revolutionary in his commitment and support for fundamental change in Africa, the Commonwealth Caribbean and elsewhere.[40]

The characteristic features of the French and British Empires, the distinction between 'French Cartesianism' and 'British Empiricism', therefore explain a great deal about the difference between Césaire and James. But what of their similarities? La Guerre suggests they agree on a great deal, both about the nature of racism and colonial liberation as well as the prominence of these themes for twentieth century man. He also demonstrates, throughout his chapter, that they have common cause in the celebration of the revolution in Saint Domingue and a fascination with its leader, Toussaint L'Ouverture. For both men he is the forerunner of the nationalist leaders of today as the lessons of the Haitian revolution and its sequel are held to anticipate the problems facing the new nations of the Third World. In a word, Haiti is symbolic: it demonstrates that racial equality is unconditional and that liberty is synonymous with political independence for subject peoples. While the latter truth might, with some justification, be claimed by the American revolution, the former is unique to Haiti. On this all historians agree and for this Haiti can justly claim as much recognition for its contribution to the progress of humanity as can the United States. It is, of course, a sad commentary on our times that this goes by largely unacknowledged.

The reasons that it does so are not difficult to find. For most of its history Haiti has been treated with disdain. During the nineteenth century it was isolated and inward looking: a peasant society developing slowly, in the words of Sidney Mintz, towards 'a traditionalism of unusual firmness and persistence'.[41] The US occupation from 1915 to 1934, while promising much changed very little, and it was only after the Second World War, and particularly with the advent to power of Duvalier in 1957, that anything 'qualitatively different' appeared in the offing. In the event, the changes wrought by Duvalier *père* were confined mainly to the political arena although the 'extraordinary' methods he used to achieve them earned him a notoriety abroad and excited, for the first time in many years, an interest in the country at large. Among the curious, by his own admission, was David Nicholls. His writings over the last decade or so have done much to dispel ignorance about Haiti and set the Duvalier phenomenon in context. It is, as he has explained elsewhere, to be understood neither as totalitarian nor fascist but 'as a further development of that post-colonial pattern which emerged in nineteenth century Haiti and from which the country has not entirely freed itself'.[42] A proper understanding of Haiti, in other words, is *via* an appreciation of its past manifest in the present. In his contribution Nicholls develops two aspects of this argument by way of a commentary on language and religion, with a particular emphasis on 'European' values and modes of behaviour transposed to Haiti and transformed in part within it by the encounter with the 'African' experience. The result has been the present 'dualistic' configuration of Haitian culture.

The coexistence of the French and Creole languages are particularly good examples of this. In Haiti everyone speaks Creole and a minority also speaks French. Yet it is French that is the official language with Creole manifestly subordinate to it, not even constituting the favoured medium of instruction in the primary schools of the country.[43] Why this is so is obviously a complex question, but the thrust of Nicholls' analysis points in one direction: politics. Mastery of French and Creole, the prerogative of the elite, is an instrument of political domination of the peasantry and to some extent the urban masses in a country where primary school education is itself a privilege. It is clear, therefore, that despite the fact that in recent years there has been a significant switch to Creole in hitherto French speaking situations, as well as a measure of positive evaluation of its functional potentiality for develop-ment,[44] any attempt at its formal legitimation is likely to meet resistance and even reversal unless equivalent alternative forms of cultural domination can be assured. Ironically, one such possibility has occurred of late in the popularity of English as opposed to French. The status of the latter, it almost goes without saying, remains vigorously defended by France, which has sought to strengthen its cultural presence in Haiti through the establishment of an Institut Pédagogique National to train primary school teachers and opposed the propagation of the phonetic spelling of Creole utilizing the Laubach–McConnell method in favour of an etymological orthography closer to the French language. Notwithstanding all this, English as a technical and business language continues to make headway among the elite (especially as commercial links with the United States are strengthened and the entrepreneurial activities of US investors widened) and a not inconsiderable section of the masses. This last aspect arises from the fact that hundreds of thousands of Haitians have been obliged to flee the successive Duvalier regimes to the United States, there to acquire necessarily some familiarity with English. Should they return in any number it is a reasonable speculation that the question might not be French counterposed to Creole but Creole counterposed to English!

Religion also demonstrates a duality between Catholicism and Voodoo. Again this is not absolute since the majority practise both and adherents of Voodoo are found across class lines i.e. among the mulatto elite as well as overwhelmingly among the peasantry and the urban lower classes. Indeed, Voodoo appears to correspond to the social fabric of the nation in a way that Catholicism does not and it is for this reason that it has been championed in the last fifty years by those who have wanted to assert a specific Haitian identity. Among these was Duvalier *père* who in numerous ways before 1957 made his support for Voodoo well known, as after that date he bound its leading practitioners to him by adroit use of government patronage and the manipulation of symbols. Thus he assured himself both of acceptance by the peasantry and a base from which to attack his enemies among whom was the hierarchy of the Catholic Church. In a vigorous campaign lasting from 1959 to 1966 he reduced considerably the power of this body and forced an indigenization upon them which, he wrote was 'for me the reflection of the struggles of the nation for its independence and sovereignty'.[45] More to the point he extracted from Mgr Ligondé, the first native archbishop of Port-au-Prince who was enthroned in 1966, the assurance 'of our entire collaboration in the political, economic and social domain'[46] and from that moment until the visit of the Pope in March 1983 relations with the Church were, from the point of view of the regime, tolerable if not especially cordial. In fact, a greater threat to its power and to Voodoo has come, as Nicholls points out, from the spread of protestant sects linked with the interests of the United States. Protestantism, according to one authority on Voodoo 'admits no compromise or tolerance of Vodoun [and] has remained immune to the syncretizing which had blended African and Catholic rituals from the beginning of the French rule of Haiti'.[47] The result is that a protestant convert is likely to abandon tradition with all that that implies for a political system which is by its nature conservative. In short, protestantism provides opportunities for new patterns of socialization as well as new channels for external domination. Precisely how this works and how subversive it might be is indicated by the example of 'a Creole text on Haitian history prepared by the Protestant Literacy Committee in which it is said that when the US marines landed in Haiti on July 28, 1915, to start the occupation of the country, most people were happy to see them and that the occupation was good for the country'.[48] Not only is this not true, but the image drawn from it of a benevolent United States is, to say the least, highly questionable. No one doubts that Haiti faces serious problems: what one can doubt is whether the United States, or protestantism, has the capacity to solve them in the interests of the majority of Haitians.

To assert this is again to go to the core of what Haiti has stood for in the non-Hispanic Caribbean. This is the twin achievement, after much struggle, of a distinctive national identity and a measure of cultural homogeneity greater than that prevailing elsewhere in the region. Haitians *are* Haitians in a way, for example, that Surinamers are not yet fully Surinamese or Jamaicans not yet one people. Haiti demonstrates that a sense of nationhood can be realized even under the most difficult conditions. It is in this context that education assumes an importance. Haiti's path to nationhood was that of violence. In the Commonwealth Caribbean this has been decisively eschewed and the task of making a nation has been assigned to the education system. Almost universally Commonwealth

Caribbean leaders have placed their hopes for nationhood in the spread of Enlightenment values among the population through education.[49] It follows that both the form and content of education are crucially important to the region's future and it is to these issues that Colin Brock's chapter is in good part directed.

The first impression gained is of the omnipresent influence of metropolitan models and modes of validation. Throughout the Commonwealth Caribbean the system reflects the philosophy of the British Education Acts of 1870 and 1944 modified according to local circumstance. An attempt has therefore been made to provide elementary education for all and, following independence, secondary education for as many as possible, without discrimination of race, class or creed. Within this broad pattern of equality of opportunity for everyone an emphasis has been placed on selectivity by formal academic achievement with the aim of promoting an intellectual cohort capable of benefitting from and contributing to university education. The apex of the system is therefore occupied by the University of the West Indies (UWI) which, befitting the generality of the model, is regarded as the regional institution *par excellence*.

Consistent with the above structure are expected levels of educational attainment and appropriate specialization at specified ages. Children enter primary schools at age five or six and after five or six years' schooling take an examination to determine whether they will have the opportunity to pursue an academically oriented education or be obliged to follow a technical one. If they follow the former, which is the more highly regarded by society, they will eventually sit 'O' Level examinations, which have until recently been validated in England, and if successful take 'A' Level examinations, also validated in England, usually at age sixteen and age eighteen respectively. If they follow the latter, which is the lot of the overwhelming majority, they may, according to circumstance, have another chance at an academic education at a later stage, although the chances are that they will not. The education they receive will therefore be technical in emphasis and designed to correspond to the perceived needs of the labour market. On leaving at the age of fifteen a student may have qualified for a school certificate which, in itself, is indicative of merit and achievement, but is not so regarded by society at large since it is locally oriented and locally validated. Only those with suitable qualifications, usually two 'A' Levels, can enter the UWI where, according to campus, specialization in undergraduate degrees over the whole range of university education can be followed. Again external validation plays a part, though a diminishing one, in determining that the system meets prevailing 'metropolitan' standards. Postgraduate education may be provided at the UWI though the majority favour pursuit of this at universities in Britain, Canada and the USA.

The pattern set out here has, as Brock points out, significant local variations. In Jamaica in the late 1970s, for example, the number of children in all age (5 – 15) elementary schools modelled on the British pattern of a century before were twice the number in primary schools and nearly twice the number in all the secondary schools combined. Government schools coexist alongside a thriving private sector in which an estimated 20% of school enrolment lies and which in recent years has also exhibited a strong post-secondary and vocational aspect. Discrimination on the basis of class, 'unintended' but none the less real, thus enters the system so that by the age of eleven a child attending a private preparatory school in Jamaica has a much greater chance of passing the entrance examination to the academic stream of the secondary school than one from a government school. Should he or she fail, a variety of private education is further available which is designed almost solely to provide the 'paper qualifications' so much sought after as a sign of status and employability.[50] In short, the Jamaican educational system mirrors Jamaican society and is responsive to it. As an agent of change it is, at best, uncertain, and at worst, totally ineffective, particularly with regard to any challenge to the dominance of the children of the elite in the secondary sector.[51]

Yet, of course, it is precisely in this sector, and more particularly in the junior secondary school, as Brock emphasizes, that hopes for change were concentrated. Trinidad and Tobago can here serve as an example. In 1972 the government embarked on a major scheme of educational expansion which sought a wider and better provision of secondary education through the division of the sector into a two-tier system of junior and senior secondary schools and for curriculum changes based on this pattern. Junior secondary schools would offer a general course of academic and practical subjects as the basis for later specialization in senior secondary schools or other educational establishments. Within a few years, however, it was clear that major difficulties had arisen. Parents and denominational bodies responsible for selective secondary school education were procrastinating over change and resisting innovation, particularly in regard to curriculum development favouring the up-grading of technical subjects at the expense of formal academic teaching.[52] The government were therefore obliged to announce a review of their educational plan and to restrain the reorganization and restructuring of the system in general. As of 1980 this was still not complete and one private study was to report that differentiation by social class in secondary schooling in Port-of-Spain was very evident, with pupils from middle and upper middle class homes predominating in assisted (private) secondary schools (the majority of pupils having attended private primary schools) whereas in the new government junior and senior secondary schools the overwhelming proportion of pupils came from working class manual households.[53] As in Jamaica, then, the education system faithfully replicates the social order and prospects for change have been successfully co-opted or contained. The conclusion must therefore be at one with Brock who argues that up to this moment in time the junior secondary school constitutes a 'lost opportunity' for new awareness and relevant educational need.

Of what the latter might realistically consist is a very large and controversial question. It is so because at root it is a matter of identity – of what the Caribbean people are and what they might become. In the determination of this three levels of relationship are evident, each with a well developed conscious expression: the metropolitan and the psychology of dependence; the regional and the assertion of creole culture; and the local in which both parochial and national sentiments are intertwined, as well as those of race and class. To ignore any one level or expression in the general study of the contemporary Caribbean is at present to be unduly selective and dismissive. Yet, this aside, there is undeniably a direction to events. The metropolitan link is being weakened (or at least multilateralized); pan-Caribbean identity is being actively developed (despite the absence of institutional form); while the vibrant promotion of the particular is very much in evidence, leading to the emergence of new integrative as well as disintegrative forces in society, the economy and the state. If the measure is change, then the future would appear to lie more with the region and within it, than with the outside world. Whether the outside world, which in the past has done so much to define the Caribbean, will encourage, or even permit this, on terms germane to the region itself, is, of course, another question.

SUMMARY REMARKS

The subjects discussed in this volume thus attest directly to the power of the past in conditioning the present in the Caribbean. To some extent, the same might be said of almost any society. In the Caribbean, though, it has a particular sharpness which serves to emphasize its significance and to make the Caribbean a very distinctive region in the Americas and beyond. It is so, as C. L. R. James has incisively argued, because of the sugar plantation and negro slavery; because a seventeenth century colonial system survives in the present; and because local culture is borrowed and adapted, not indigenous.[54] None of this, however, is to imply that the Caribbean is not changing. It is, but differentially.

In the sugar industry it is fair to conclude there has been the least change. The crisis that currently attends the industry in the non-Hispanic Caribbean is at least two hundred years in the making and solutions to it are almost as old. In the light of this the temptation to abandon sugar altogether is strong. Yet this is not the answer, as the contradictory directions of Cuban sugar policy in the last 25 years have shown. Instead, the future appears to lie in a will to tackle the question and to make changes in economy and society at large which will redefine the place of sugar in a region with which it has virtually become synonymous – no longer master but servant of its interests.

The colonial system in its seventeenth century form is coming to an end. Britain seeks only to tidy away the bits and pieces as does the Netherlands. This leaves France and the US. The former is encumbered of its own making and can easily undo what it has done without great loss to itself and arguably with much advantage to the region. The same simple solution is not open to the US. It entered the Caribbean in the age of imperialism not mercantilism and its domination has been both more thorough and more modern because of it. While not quite transforming the colonial system it 'inherited' it has done much to dynamize it, though in a selective and uneven manner, so emphasizing differences within as well as between territories of the region. How, or if, the Caribbean will live with this is anyone's guess though in parting one observation might be permitted: in London, Paris and the Hague governments will not fall because of what happens in the Caribbean; in Washington DC they just might and, of course, the converse of this for the Caribbean is that they do.

Finally, there is the question of culture and identity. Here it can be argued that change has gone the farthest. This might surprise some readers given the alleged backwardness of the region encapsulated in Naipaul's famous phrase, 'the Third World's third world'. He has a point and such an acute observer should not be summarily dismissed. Yet, typically, he has also missed much. If there is a psychological dependence to be found there is also a tradition of transformation and the undisputed fact that the Caribbean peoples are in many ways 'modern' peoples. Witness the ease as well as the pain with which they migrate to and settle in the most modern metropolitan centres. As such, it can be argued the Caribbean peoples are in advance of change in the Third World, not astern it. This is a conclusion which Sidney Mintz, the most distinguished social anthropologist of the region, has reached, and one which I would want to echo. I can do no better than end my remarks with a quote from his remarkable volume of essays which captures this particular essence and simultaneously portrays the complexity of the present:

Until we are able to deal with populations that are at once backward and modern, racist and anti-racist, European and anti-European we shall have no success in decomposing the nature of Caribbean national identity. These folk are, in their own distinctive ways, very much peoples of the future. The inability of Western observers to detect this strikes the writer as strong evidence of our own equally undetected anachronism in a world we made without knowing it.[55]

NOTES

1. See Lloyd Best and Kari Levitt, 'Character of Caribbean Economy' in George Beckford (ed.), *Caribbean Economy: Dependence and Backwardness* (Kingston, 1975).
2. George Beckford, *Persistent Poverty: Underdevelopment in Plantation Economies of the Third World* (Oxford, 1972).
3. See, in particular, M. G. Smith, *The plural society in the British West Indies* (Berkeley, 1965).
4. See, in particular, Gordon Lewis, *The Growth of the Modern West Indies* (London, 1968).
5. The best exposition is by Sidney Mintz, 'The Caribbean as a socio-cultural area' *Journal of World History*, Vol. 9, No. 4, 1966.
6. For such a definition stressing 'legacies' see W. G. Demas 'Foreword' in Richard Millett and W. Marvin Will (eds.), *The Restless Caribbean: changing patterns of international relations* (New York, 1979).
7. F. W. Knight, *The Caribbean: The Genesis of a Fragmented Nationalism* (New York, 1978), pp. x–xi.
8. Figures from Ian Smith, 'Can the West Indies' Sugar Industry Survive?', *Oxford Bulletin of Economics and Statistics*, Vol. 38, No. 2, 1976, p. 136. The price received, reflecting the then acute sugar shortage in Britain, was, in fact, £260 per ton. The following year it dropped to £188 per ton c.i.f.
9. See, for example, Rev. Idris Hamid (compiler), *The World of Sugar Workers* (Papers Presented at the International Sugar Workers' Conference, July, 1977, Trinidad) (Caribbean Ecumenical Programme, 1978).
10. Sidney E. Chernick, *The Commonwealth Caribbean: the integration experience* (Report of a mission sent to the Commonwealth Caribbean by the World Bank) (Baltimore and London, 1978), pp. 140–1.
11. For an elaboration of this see Susan Craig, 'Sociological Theorizing in the English-Speaking Caribbean: A Review' in Susan Craig (ed.), *Contemporary Caribbean: A Sociological Reader* (Vol. 2) (Trinidad, 1982).
12. For two parallel analyses to Sleeman, supportive in some respects but critically different in others, see R. Achéen and F. R. Faux, 'The French West Indies: A Socio-Historical Interpretation' and C. Karch, 'The Growth of the Corporate Economy in Barbados: Class/Race Factors, 1890–1977' in S. Craig (ed.), *Contemporary Caribbean: A Sociological Reader* (Vol. 1) (Trinidad, 1982).
13. Figures from J. Lucay Maillot, 'L'intégration du sucre des départements d'Outre-Mer dans le C.E.E.' in *L'Insertion des Départements d'Outre Mer dans la Communauté Economique Européenne* (Centre de Documentation et de Recherches Européennes, Université de Bordeaux, 1977). The intervention price for raw sugar from cane is derived from the intervention price for white sugar from beet. While the latter is fixed having regard to the cost of production the former clearly is not.
14. *The Courier*, No. 88, Nov.–Dec. 1984, p. vi.
15. See, in particular, E. Edinval, 'Conséquences de l'intégration du secteur sucrier dans la C.E.E.: L'example de la Guadeloupe' in *L'Insertion des Départements d'Outre-Mer dans la Communauté Economique Européenne.*

16. Vincent A. Mahler, 'Britain, the European Community, and the developing Commonwealth: dependence, interdependence, and the political economy of sugar', *International Organization*, Vol. 35, No. 3, 1981, p. 491.

17. Figures compiled from A. J. Payne, *The International Crisis in the Caribbean* (London, 1984), pp. 167–70.

18. For details in respect of Grenada see *ibid*. pp. 148–9.

19. Constitution Commission of Trinidad and Tobago, *Report of the Constitution Commission*, (Trinidad: 1974) para. 51.

20. Maingot's concern to effect this has received support from elsewhere in the profession. See, in particular, the review essay by Aaron Segal, 'Collecting the Caribbean: the not-so-hidden politics of explanation', *Caribbean Review*, Vol. 13, No. 2, 1984.

21. See Eric Williams, 'The Party's Stewardship, 1956 to 1980' in his *Forged from the Love of Liberty: selected speeches of Dr. Eric Williams* (Port-of-Spain, 1981), especially pp. 423–32.

22. For a celebration of these forms see People's Revolutionary Government of Grenada, *Is Freedom We Making: the new democracy in Grenada* (Government Information Service, Grenada, n.d.).

23. The case of Anguilla also demonstrated that an 'associated state' could revert to colonial status. For a legal and political examination of 'associated statehood' see M. Broderick, 'Associated Statehood: A New Form of Decolonization', *International and Comparative Law Quarterly*, Vol. 17, No. 2 (1968) and T. Thorndike, 'Associated Statehood: Quo Vadis' in B. Ince (ed.), *The Caribbean Yearbook of International Relations 1977* (Leiden and Trinidad, 1980).

24. Tony Thorndike, 'Associated Statehood and the Eastern Caribbean: The Search for Independence' (Paper presented to the Political Studies Association Conference, Sheffield, April 1979).

25. A. McIntyre, V. Lewis, P. Emmanuel, *The Political Economy of Independence for the Leeward and Windward Islands*. (A report of a committee of the Constitution Commission of St. Vincent, St. Lucia and St. Kitts–Nevis–Anguilla) (23 Feb. 1975, mimeo).

26. See, in particular, Anthony Payne, Paul Sutton and Tony Thorndike, *Grenada: Revolution and Invasion* (London, 1984), chapter 2.

27. The 1974 election was exceptional in that the conservative candidate, Giscard D'Estaing, only narrowly won Martinique and Guyane (57% and 53% of the votes cast) and lost to Mitterrand in Guadeloupe (receiving only 44% of the votes cast). The status of the DOM was not a major issue in this election. By contrast, in the 1981 election, and against the trend in mainland France, Mitterrand lost to Giscard D'Estaing in the Caribbean DOM receiving only 19% of the votes cast in Martinque, 22% of those cast in Guadeloupe and 34% of those cast in Guyane. Figures from *Latin American Regional Reports: Caribbean*, RC-81-05, 12 June 1981.

28. Cited in Gerhard Drekonja-Kornat, 'On the Edge of Civilization', *Caribbean Review*, Vol. 13, No. 2, 1984, pp. 26–7.

29. Wood and paper pulp is the second largest deficit item in EEC trade after petroleum. Security of supply from Guyane, technically within the boundaries of the EEC, is therefore an important consideration and of significant advantage to France in its dealings with other member states.

30. For an extended discussion of this distinction see Jean Crusol, *Economies Insulaires de la Caraïbe: Aspects théoriques et pratiques du développement* (Paris: 1980).

31. The original proposals were for a single assembly to be elected in each of the DOM, instead of a departmental and regional assembly as elsewhere, on the

grounds that in the DOM the *Département* and the *Région* were identical. It also proposed that the new body be given considerable powers in economic, social, cultural and environmental affairs and that it be elected by proportional representation. As amended, the opposition has won the constitutional argument that the DOM should not be treated differently from *départements* in mainland France but lost the political since the *Conseils Régionaux* have been elected by proportional representation.

32. In a turnout of 61% of the electorate, *départmentalistes* won 46% of the vote, those in favour of the reforms 49%, with *indépendentistes* winning just under 5%. Figures calculated from *Information Caraïbe* No. 449, 27 February 1983.

33. In Martinique in a turnout of only 30% of the electorate the list headed by Simone Veil (conservatives) won 59% of the vote as against 28% for the list headed by Jospin (socialists) and 6% for the communists. The conservatives and socialists won similar percentages in Guadeloupe and Guyane though in both the turnout was very low, at 14% and 24% respectively. Figures calculated from *Information Caraïbe* No. 514, 24 June 1984.

34. For an elaboration of this view see, in particular, Gordon K. Lewis, *Main Currents in Caribbean Thought: the historical evolution of Caribbean society and its ideological aspects, 1492–1900* (Baltimore and London: 1983), p. 329 and ff.

35. C. L. R. James, *Beyond a Boundary* (London: 1963), p. 152.

36. *Ibid.* p. 47.

37. Léopold Sédar Senghor, 'What is Negritude?' in P. E. Sigmund (ed.), *The Ideologies of the Developing Nations* (New York: revised edition, 1967), p. 249.

38. *Ibid.* p. 250.

39. The intellectual basis of this is discussed in R. D. E. Burton, 'Nationalist Ideologies in Contemporary Martinique', *Caribbean Societies*, Vol. 1 (Collected Seminar Papers, No. 29), Institute of Commonwealth Studies, University of London, 1982.

40. A useful survey of James which stresses this theme is 'C. L. R. James: His Life and Work', *Urgent Tasks*, No. 12, 1981.

41. Sidney Mintz, *Caribbean Transformations* (Chicago: 1974), p. 270.

42. David Nicholls, *From Dessalines to Duvalier: race, colour and national independence in Haiti* (Cambridge: 1979), pp. 213–14.

43. In September 1979 a law was passed which recognized the predominance of Creole in Haiti and allowed the use of it in the schools as both instrument and object of teaching. Whether this has come to anything is not known, though in this regard it is important to take into consideration the lethargy of Haitian public administration. The constitution of 1964 (Article 35) stipulated: 'the law will determine the cases and circumstances in which the use of Creole can be permitted and recommended in order to safeguard the material and moral interests of the citizens who do not speak French very well'.

44. For a useful discussion of this see Pierre-Michael Fontaine, 'Language, Society and Development: Dialectic of French and Creole Use in Haiti', *Latin American Perspectives*, Vol. 8, No. 1, 1981.

45. Cited in Nicholls, *From Dessalines to Duvalier*, p. 227.

46. *Ibid.* p. 226.

47. Rémy Bastien, 'Vodoun and Politics in Haiti' in R. Frucht (ed.), *Black Society in the New World* (New York: 1971), p. 305.

48. Fontaine, 'Language, Society and Development', p. 43.

49. For an elaboration of this theme see W. Bell, 'New States in the Caribbean: a Grounded Theoretical Account' in S. N. Eisenstadt and S. Rokkan (eds.), *Building States and Nations* (Beverley Hills: 1973).

50. The figures and arguments set out here have been developed at length in Judith Ennew, 'A Comparison of the Jamaican and British Education Systems', Paper presented to the Fifth Annual Conference of the Society for Caribbean Studies, England, May 1981.
51. See, in particular, Errol Miller, 'Education and Society in Jamaica' in P. Figueroa and G. Persaud (eds.), *Sociology of Education: a Caribbean Reader* (Oxford: 1976).
52. See Eric Williams, 'Education and Decolonization in Trinidad and Tobago', Address to the Caribbean Union Conference, 1974, reproduced in part in Williams, *Forged From the Love of Liberty*.
53. Information taken from Judith Foreman, 'Secondary Education, Gender and Development in Trinidad and Tobago', Paper presented to the Seventh Annual Conference of the Society for Caribbean Studies, England, March 1983.
54. C. L. R. James, 'From Toussaint L'Ouverture to Fidel Castro' in *The Black Jacobins* (New York: 1963, revised edition).
55. Mintz, *Caribbean Transformations*, p. 328.

The Post-War Decline of the Sugar Economy in the Commonwealth Caribbean

RAMESH RAMSARAN

Ever since the introduction of sugar cane into the Commonwealth Caribbean in the seventeenth century, sugar has been an important factor not only in the economies of these countries, but in their politics and culture as well. Indeed, in a very real sense, the modern history of these countries is the history of sugar in the Caribbean. So pervasive has been the influence of sugar on the socio-economic organisation that although sugar cane may eventually disappear from the landscape completely, its legacies will continue to be felt for a very long time in every facet of Caribbean life.

The sugar industry in the Caribbean has been in decline for many years. In some of the islands where the cane was originally introduced, sugar is no longer produced on a commercial scale. In other countries of the region where the industry still forms part of the economic fabric, there are questions surrounding its continued existence in the light of the increasing gap between costs of production and prices received in international markets.

The factors leading to the present situation have both internal and external origins. At the internal level domestic policies have contributed significantly to the diminution or disappearance of the sugar industry in the Commonwealth Caribbean (which was the mainstay of most of these economies under British colonialism). With the attainment of political independence, the governments of these countries felt the need to reduce their dependence on an industry developed in a particular colonial context, subject to great variation in fortune and dependent for survival on the retention of certain colonial arrangements.

The development strategies adopted, accordingly, did not ascribe any critical role to the sugar industry in the transformation process. Whatever strength or importance the industry still possesses is derived in a large measure from the weaknesses or performance of the new sectors. Sugar has been allowed to linger with few decisions of a positive nature in terms of re-organisation or research designed to enhance the well being of an industry whose viability calls for constant care. These problems have been reinforced by developments in the international sugar market over which the countries of the Commonwealth Caribbean, as small inefficient producers, have been able to exercise little or no control.

This chapter is an attempt to put these various factors in perspective. In the first part I give a preview of the early growth of the sugar industry in the Commonwealth Caribbean and outline the declining position of the sugar industry in the economies of the major regional sugar producers who still produce sugar on a commercial scale. In the second part I examine some of reasons, at the domestic level, which bear on the present state of the industry, and in the third I discuss the structure of the international sugar market and its implications for the Caribbean. Finally, some thoughts on the future of the industry are advanced.

SUGAR AND THE NATIONAL ECONOMY

Although there is some evidence of sugar cane being grown in certain of the Commonwealth Caribbean countries in the sixteenth century, commercial production did not begin on a significant scale until the second half of the seventeenth century. Table 1 gives some indication of the growth of sugar production in the region in the period between 1698 and 1928. Towards the end of the eighteenth century, all the territories had apparently been introduced to sugar, although the level of production varied widely from one country to another. Almost a century later, production had increased in most territories as the annual averages for the period 1877–86 show.

Available data shown in Table 1 indicate that while by 1928 sugar production had declined or disappeared in places like Montserrat, Dominica, Grenada, Nevis, Tobago and

TABLE 1

Sugar Production, 1698–1928

Metric Tons, tel quel

Countries	1698–1700[a]	1780	1800	1824–33[a]	1877–86[a]	1928
Antigua	3,033	1,812	5,976	8,346	10,431	19,984
Barbados	n.a.	3,491	6,181	15,075	47,000	64,152
Dominica	n.a.	3,379	2,484	2,518	2,891	–
Grenada	n.a.	8,803	6,719	10,941	–	–
Guyana	n.a.	2,438	n.a.	56,831	90,148	117,976
Jamaica	4,609[b]	59,600[c]	71,200	69,560	21,916	63,528
Montserrat	1,198	1,542	1,905	1,152	1,781	–
Nevis	2,406	1,071	2,174	2,492	11,827	19,754
St Kitts	d.	8,948	6,487	4,896		
St Lucia	n.a.	1,243	679	3,587	6,304	4,832
St Vincent	n.a.	5	8,231	12,311	7,550	1,554
Tobago	n.a.	n.a.	7,000[e]	5,285	3,518	–
Trinidad	n.a.	n.a.	7,000[f]	12,519	54,960	82,600

n.a. not available
a. average for period.   b. Average for 1699–1700
c. 1788
d. In 1687 production in St Christophe, the then French part of St Kitts amounted to 1,524 tons; the earliest recorded figure for the English part of the island is 134 tons in 1704
e. 1810   f. 1809

Source: International Sugar Council, *The World Sugar Economy, Structure and Policies*, Vol. II, 1963, pp. 8–9; *Report of the West Indian Sugar Commission*, London, H.M.S.O., 1930.

St Vincent,[1] there were substantial increases in Antigua, Barbados, Guyana, Jamaica, St Kitts and Trinidad. By this time sugar and by-products were accounting for over 80% of the domestic exports of Antigua, Barbados, and St Kitts, and for a fairly substantial proportion of the export trade of St Lucia, Guyana, Jamaica and Trinidad. For the region as a whole sugar and by-products accounted for 35% of domestic exports. If Jamaica and Trinidad and Tobago were excluded, the proportion would rise to 70%. The importance of the industry to the region at this time can also be seen in the number of people directly employed. As a proportion of the total population the figure varied from 3% in Jamaica to over 33% in St Kitts. If the dependents of those directly engaged in the industry were taken into account these proportions would be considerably higher. For instance, in Barbados, it was estimated that over half

TABLE 2

Selected Data on the Sugar Industry in the late 1920's

	Total Area	Cultivable[1]	Area Under Cane	No. of Persons Directly Employed[2]		Sugar[3] as a % of Domestic
				No.	% of Pop.	
	(acres)	(acres)	(acres)			Exports
Antigua	68,980	36,430 (19,454)	16,480	9,000	31	97
Barbados	106,470	67,682 (67,682)	35,000	34,000	20	95
Guyana	57,266,874	154,868 (154,868)	57,625	50,000	16	60
Jamaica	2,848,160	1,157,586 (270,240)	43,605	30,000	3	19
Nevis	32,000	24,000 (4,600)	350	n.a.	n.a.	n.a.
St Kitts	41,851	29,000 (18,000)	12,000	6,000	33	86
St Lucia	152,320	85,400 (22,000)	4,300	6,900	12	45
St Vincent	85,120	n.a.	–	–	–	9
Trinidad	1,267,236	(314,086)	32,874	40,000	10	20

– nil or negligible

n.a. not available

1. Figures in brackets indicate the number of acres actually under cultivation.
2. Figures do not reflect the number of persons dependent on the industry.
3. Including by-products.

Source: Report of the West Indian Sugar Commission, London, H.M.S.O., 1930.

the population was dependent on the industry, while almost the entire populations of St Kitts and Antigua depended on sugar for a livelihood.[2]

Barbados

Sugar production began in Barbados in the 1640s, and remained the dominant activity until the 1960s.[3] Barbados in this period was the arch-example of a mono-crop society. Available data indicate that, even as late as 1950, sugar contributed some 42% of GDP.[4] By 1960, however, this figure had fallen to between 20 and 30% and by 1980 to less than 10% (see Table 3). These figures, it should be noted, include the processing of sugar and molasses (which tend to be included in the manufacturing sector in Table 3). As a percentage of domestic exports, sugar (and

TABLE 3

Barbados: Selected Sugar Statistics

	1946	1970	1972	1974	1976	1978	1980	1982
Acres of Canes Reaped ('000 hectares)	16.2	20.2	17.8	16.8	15.9	15.8	16.1	15.8
Canes Milled ('000 tonnes)	1,123	1,456	1,060	956	919	895	1,205	766
Canes Per Hectare ('000)	69.3	72.1	59.7	57.0	57.8	56.4	74.9	48.5
Sugar Produced ('000 tonnes)	136.0	157.5	112.8	110.7	103.6	101.0	135.0	88.0
Tonnes Cane Per Tonne Sugar	8.2	9.2	9.4	8.6	10.0	8.9	9.0	8.6
Sugar Value (Current Price B$mn)*		34.8	33.3	46.8	47.2	51.6	115.0	71.5
Sugar Value as a % of GDP		9.3	7.7	7.3	6.1	5.5	7.9	3.2
Exports of Sugar ('000 tonnes)	99.7	145.3	99.2	98.3	65.0	86.4	119.3	89.0
Average Export Price (B$)		214.5	279.5	579.3	608.2	722.5	896.0	776.3
*Total Export Earnings (B$mn)		29.4	27.1	52.2	55.5	62.5	106.0	71.0
Production Costs Per Tonne (B$)		228.3	309.2	409.1	663.2	663.4	756.0	1,220

* made-up of sugar, fancy molasses and vacuum pan

Source: Barbados *Economic Report*, Various Issues; Barbados Statistical Service, *Abstract of Statistics*, Various Issues.

by-products) amounted to over 90% in the 1950s. In recent years the contribution of the sugar sector has fallen to around 20 to 30%. In terms of the contribution to overall foreign exchange earnings, sugar now ranks behind tourism and the manufacturing sector. In 1980 the respective contributions were sugar 10.3% (66% in 1950), manufacturing 17.8% (6% in 1950) and tourism 40.7% (15% in 1950).[5]

These developments correspond with a long-term declining trend in sugar production. The volume of sugar produced increased from about 79,000 tonnes in 1948 to 208,000 tonnes in 1957. In 1970 the figure was 157,000 tonnes, in 1980 135,000 tonnes and in 1982 88,000 tonnes (see Table 3).

Guyana

The cultivation of sugar cane in Guyana began with the Dutch East India Company, and the first consignment of sugar was despatched to Holland in 1661.[6] It is estimated that sugar cane growing (and the production of rum, sugar and molasses) contributed almost 30% to GDP in 1952. By 1980 the figure had dropped to less than 20%. In 1952 sugar and by-products accounted for 56% of the value of total domestic exports as compared to 51% in 1960 and 35% in 1980 (see Table 4). The main foreign exchange earner for Guyana is now bauxite and alumina which accounted for almost half of the value of domestic exports in 1980.

TABLE 4

Commonwealth Caribbean: Composition of GDP (at Current Factor Cost) 1950–80 (Percentages)

Sectors	Barbados			
	1955	1960	1970	1980
Sugar[a]	23.4	21.3	9.9	6.4
Other Agriculture[b]	11.8	6.7	4.8	3.4
Manufacturing	19.2[c]	8.3	10.1	10.9
Construction	7.3	9.8	10.0	7.2
Mining & Refining[d]	e	e	e	e
Distribution	10.6	23.0	26.0	21.8
Government	8.7	9.8	15.6	4.0
Tourism	e	e	e	12.0
Other	19.0	21.1	23.6	34.3
Total	100.0	100.0	100.0	100.0
Sugar Exports[f] as a % of Total Domestic Exports	93	93	60	37

Sectors	Guyana			
	1952	1960	1970	1980
Sugar[a]	13.6	17.6	12.4	14.8
Other Agriculture[b]	18.8	14.0	11.0	12.9
Manufacturing	14.7	5.3	8.2	8.1
Construction	d	9.5	7.9	6.7
Mining & Refining[d]	8.6	11.0	20.4	16.5
Distribution	13.0	14.1	11.4	8.6
Government	10.2	9.7	13.2	18.7
Tourism	d	d	d	d
Other	21.1	18.8	15.5	13.7
Total	100.0	100.0	100.0	100.0
Sugar Exports[f] as a % of Total Domestic Exports	56	51	31	35

Table 4 contd.

Sectors	Jamaica			
	1950	1962	1970	1980[h]
Sugar[a]	g	3.5	1.3	0.7
Other Agriculture[b]	30.4	8.5	6.8	7.6
Manufacturing	11.3	13.7	13.6	15.5
Construction	7.6	10.8	11.7	5.9
Mining & Refining[d]	–	9.6	15.2	14.3
Distribution	15.1	16.0	14.2	19.6
Government	6.0	7.1	8.4	14.7
Tourism	d	d	d	d
Other	29.6	30.8	28.8	21.7
Total	100.0	100.0	100.0	100.0
Sugar Exports[f] as a % of Total Domestic Exports	51	26	11	6

Sectors	Trinidad and Tobago			
	1952	1960	1970	1980
Sugar[a]	g	g	2.9[j]	0.7[j]
Other Agriculture[b]	17.9	12.5	3.0	1.6
Manufacturing	16.3	17.2	9.1	6.0
Construction	i	i	5.7	7.4
Mining & Refining[d]	28.6	30.4	21.5	42.0
Distribution	e	e	16.1	9.8
Government	e	e	8.4	7.6
Tourism	d	d	d	d
Other	37.2	39.9	33.3	24.9
Total	100.0	100.0	100.0	100.0
Sugar Exports[f] as a % of Total Domestic Exports	10	8	10	1

Table 4 contd.

Sectors	Belize		St Kitts–Nevis	
	1954	1979	1953[k]	1978
Sugar[a]	1.1	g	48.2[l]	g
Other Agriculture[b]	40.7	25.2	12.0	18.5
Manufacturing	3.9	13.3	0.2	14.8
Construction	9.6	6.1	5.7	6.2
Mining & Refining[d]	–	0.3	–	–
Distribution	11.8	17.7	12.8[m]	11.7
Government	12.8	11.7	8.5	20.8
Tourism	d	d	d	d
Other	20.1	25.4	12.6	28.0
Total	100.0	100.0	100.0	100.0
Sugar Exports[f] as a % of Total Domestic Exports	1.8[n]	60.0[o]	94.7	73.0[p]

Notes to Table 4

a. This tends to refer only to cultivation. Manufacturing or processing of sugar and by products is usually included in manufacturing.
b. Including forestry and fishing.
c. Processing of sugar and molasses contributed 11.5%.
d. Including quarrying.
e. Included in 'other'. With the exception of Barbados, for recent years 'tourism' is not available separately for the other countries.
f. Including rum and molasses.
g. Included in 'other Agriculture'.
h. At market prices.
i. Included in manufacturing.
j. Includes sugar commodities and distilleries.
k. St Kitts–Nevis–Anguilla.
l. Includes sugar milling.
m. Include finance.
n. 1953.
o. Average for recent years.
p. 1979.

Source: Official Publications; CARICOM Secretariat, *National Accounts Statistics*, 1970–1980. J. Bethel, 'A National Accounts Study of the Economy of Barbados', *Social and Economic Studies*, June 1960; C. O'Loughlin, 'The Economy of British Guiana, 1954–56, A National Accounts Study', *SES*, March, 1959; C. O'Loughlin, 'The Economy of St Kitts, Nevis–Anguilla', *SES*, December 1959; Ione Marshall, 'The National Accounts of British Honduras', *SES*, June, 1962.

While sugar production in Guyana varies from year to year, production levels have been kept at fairly high levels, enabling the country to meet its quota commitment under the Sugar Protocol of the Lomé Conventions. Production increased from 198.8 thousand tonnes in 1950 to 339.8 thousand tonnes in 1960. The average for the five year period 1978–82 was around 300 thousand tonnes.

Jamaica

Though Jamaica is recorded as producing sugar in 1527, significant production did not begin until after the island was taken over by England in 1650. Since then sugar has remained an important part of the agricultural sector and of the economy generally. Before the emergence of bauxite mining in the 1950s, agriculture was the predominant activity in the Jamaican economy. Between 1830 and 1930 the contribution of agriculture to GDP was consistently in excess of 40%.[7] In 1938 it was still as high as 36%. Sugar was the main crop until the turn of the century, when it was overtaken by bananas. The reasons cited for the decline in this period were the labour problems associated with Emancipation, increasing competition from beet sugar and the loss of protection in the British market resulting from the Sugar Duties Act of 1846.[8] With the re-establishment of the preferential markets in the post-war period, sugar regained its ascendency in the agricultural sector, but became increasingly overshadowed by bauxite and tourism, both as an income generator and a foreign exchange earner. In 1953 the sugar industry contributed about 9% to GDP. By 1962 this figure had fallen to 6% and in 1981 to about 1%. While sugar (and by-products) contributed over 50% to domestic export earnings in 1950, by 1980 this had fallen to about 6%.

The decline in earnings (as in the case of the other territories) is a reflection of the trend in both prices and production. Production of sugar increased from about 101.6 thousand tonnes in 1940 to 431.2 thousand tonnes in 1960. In 1971 the corresponding figure was 373,000 tonnes. Since then a declining trend has set in. In 1981 only 193,000 tonnes were produced.

Trinidad and Tobago

There is speculation that some sugar was produced in these islands by the Spaniards and the Dutch prior to British acquisition. The industry, however, did not assume commercial dimensions until the British took over Tobago in 1763 and Trinidad in 1797.[9] Data available for recent years indicate that sugar production increased from 52,000 tonnes in 1927 to 250,000 tonnes in 1961. Since then production has fluctuated from year to year within a declining long-term trend. The 1982 output of 79,000 tonnes was comparable to the level of 1945.[10]

The agricultural sector in Trinidad and Tobago contributed about 20% to GDP in the early 1950s. The actual contribution of sugar to GDP before 1966 is not available. In this latter year the industry's contribution to GDP amounted to TT$40 million at current prices (TT$46 million at 1970 prices) or 3.2% of GDP. In 1976 the contribution in current dollars was estimated to be around TT$135 million (TT$40.6 million in 1970 dollars) or 2.4% of GDP. In real terms therefore the contribution to GDP fell over this period.[11] The indications are that the sugar industry's contribution to GDP may have since declined even further. In 1980, agriculture as a whole contributed TT$81 million (at 1970 prices), or 2.8% to GDP. Of this figure, sugar was responsible for TT$33 million or 1.1% of GDP. In recent years oil has been contributing around 40% to GDP.

With respect to foreign exchange earnings, sugar and by-products accounted for 10% of total domestic earnings in 1952 and 40% of non-oil domestic exports. In 1980 earnings from the export of sugar and related products came to around TT$74 million or 1% of total domestic exports, or 14% of domestic exports excluding oil and related products.

Other Commonwealth Caribbean Countries

Sugar cane was introduced in the Leeward and Windward Islands in the mid-seventeenth century, but with the exception of Grenada and the Grenadines, where production reached 8,941 tons in 1762, no significant industry was established in the Windward Islands until the British took possession in 1763. The first recorded figure for exports from St Vincent was 36 tons in 1766, while for St Lucia it was 313 tons in 1779.[12]

As indicated earlier, sugar cane cultivation has virtually disappeared as an activity in several of the islands where it once flourished. Before the Second World War these included Nevis, Montserrat, Dominica and Tobago. After the war Antigua, St Lucia, St Vincent and Grenada which once produced sugar on a commerical scale have now virtually ceased production. Table 5 give some indications of the volume of production during the 1950s. In the case of Antigua, production reached a peak of 34.8 thousand tonnes in 1952, but by 1960 this had fallen to 20.3 thousand tonnes. Production in St Lucia reached 11.0 thousand tonnes in 1956, but declined steadily thereafter. Between 1950 and 1958, production in Grenada averaged about 2.2 thousand tonnes per annum, before ceasing. When the Mt. Bentick Estates Limited in St Vincent closed down in 1962, production of sugar was in the region of three to four thousand tonnes. In the face of growing unemployment and foreign exchange problems, intentions to revive the sugar industry in places like St Lucia, St Vincent and Antigua have been expressed from time to time, but with little positive result. Antigua, in particular, has met with economic disaster in recent years in trying to resurrect the sugar industry for the domestic market only. Early reports indicate that St Vincent will fare no better.

In the case of St Kitts, however, sugar remains the most

TABLE 5
Production of Sugar, 1950–82

'000 tonnes

Territory	1950	1955	1960	1970	1975	1980	1982
Antigua	31.6	20.0	20.3	–	–	–	–
Barbados	160.8	173.8	156.2	155.0	95.0	135.0	88.0
Guyana	198.9	254.0	339.8	311.0	300.0	270.0	287.0
Grenada	1.7	2.5	–	–	–	–	–
Jamaica	276.0	403.0	431.2	364.2	349.4	223.1	236.2
St Kitts	41.9	50.2	50.5	23.8[a]	24.8	33.9	34.6
St Lucia	10.6	10.8	5.5	–	–	–	–
St Vincent	2.8	4.5	3.6	–	–	–	–
Trinidad	148.9	195.9	221.4	212.7	157.5	109.2	78.7

a. 1973
– includes nil or negligible production

Sources: Federal Ministry of Trade and Industry, *Sugar Statistics*, 1962. Central Bank of Barbados, *Annual Statistical Digest*, 1982.

important sector in the economy, though its importance has been declining in recent years. The agricultural sector as a whole (which sugar dominates) now contributes about 20% to GDP, as compared to over 40% in the 1950s. Sugar exports now account for about 50 to 70% of domestic exports as compared to 90% up to the mid-1970s. Though sugar production has been declining, the industry still employs about a third of the labour force. While there has been some success in the initiation of certain types of manufacturing industries geared towards the regional market, these are largely assembly type activities heavily dependent on foreign inputs. Their net foreign exchange earnings capacity tends to be small or negligible.

Belize emerged as a sugar producer around the middle of the nineteenth century, and by 1880 production had reached 3,000 tonnes. The indications are that production had virtually ceased by the Second World War. The industry was resumed after the war and by 1954 production reached 2,452 tonnes, making the industry's contribution to GDP in that year about 1%. By 1970 sugar production had increased to 67.9 thousand tonnes and to a peak of 115.3 thousand tonnes in 1977/78. Since the 1960s, the sugar industry has contributed around 20% to GDP on average, and earns more than half of the country's foreign exchange. In terms of labour absorption, there are some 5,000 farmers engaged in cane farming, while the two factories employ about 1,100 people. Some 5,000 people are required to reap the crop.

DOMESTIC FACTORS AFFECTING THE DECLINE OF SUGAR IN THE COMMONWEALTH CARIBBEAN

The present policy towards the sugar industry in the Caribbean is influenced not only by historical experience, but also by prevailing social and economic conditions. Sugar was introduced into the Caribbean at a time when there was an expanding demand in Europe for sugar from the cane which was found to grow so well on the flat rich plains of many of the Caribbean islands. The British West Indies, as one writer remarked, were developed as exploitation colonies, or as adjuncts of a larger economic system based in Europe.[13] Sugar cane growing required large amounts of labour, which it was argued could not be satisfied by the immigration of free European workers because of climatic conditions. The sugar industry, almost from its inception, was thus organised on forced labour, first the native population, and then imported slaves from Africa and later indentured labour from Asia.[14]

While the riches have now largely gone out of sugar cane cultivation, the sugar plantations in the Caribbean were until recent years almost completely owned by foreigners.[15] In order to maintain a certain level of profits, wages in the industry were kept low. In fact, the sugar industry in the Caribbean has been associated with the lowest wages and worst working conditions in the various economies, even though every study or report done on the sugar industry over the years has recognised sugar work as very arduous. Improving the lot of the sugar worker has been a constant struggle which in later years became part of the broader agitation against colonialism and exploitation. With the attainment of political independence a primary objective was to reduce dependence on sugar by encouraging new manufacturing industries which, it was widely felt, would lead the way to modernisation and development. Industrialisation was also needed to overcome structural weaknesses in the respective economies. In trying to promote this objective incentives were offered in the form of tax holidays, duty free importation of raw materials and equipment, accelerated depreciation allowances, factory sites and protection from foreign competition.

The industrial sector that emerged from this policy has been disappointing on several fronts. Firstly, the sector has relied heavily on imported inputs (raw materials and capital goods) to the extent that little effort has been made to develop and use local materials where this was possible. The largely assembly type nature of the manufacturing sector means that local value added tends to be small. The kind of inter-sectoral linkages which were initially envisaged have failed to materialise. This feature, combined with the fact that the sector has tended to be internally oriented, means that the net foreign exchange earnings capacity of the sector tends to be small or non-existent. A high proportion of the enterprises set up behind the high protective walls reflect arrangements between local business cliques and foreign entrepreneurs whose main concern has been to capture or control the local market, or to get access to raw materials and in some cases cheap labour. In the highly protective environment of the Caribbean, exporting is apparently not necessary to make money. With respect to the creation of employment opportunities, the manufacturing sector has been extremely disappointing in a situation where not only have there been natural increases in the labour force, but where employment has been declining in traditional activities. One of the major reasons explaining the low employment potential of the sector can be attributed to the capital intensive nature of the technology being used, which itself is the result of the kind of policy framework embraced. Some of the incentives offered have unwittingly tended to make capital less expensive in relation to labour in a situation where there is a surplus of labour. The fact, too, that there have been few guidelines or much direction governing the use of technology, has resulted in the wholesale importation of production processes designed for a situation where there was a relative scarcity of labour. There has been little pressure to adapt technology to the local environment.

As can be seen in Table 6, in the early post-war years agriculture still employed a substantial proportion of the labour force in the Commonwealth Caribbean. For the region as a whole the proportion was 44%. In Barbados the proportion was around 30%, as compared to over 40% in Guyana, Jamaica, and Belize, over 25% in Trinidad and Tobago and over 50% in the Windward and Leewards. The figures relating to manufacturing include the labour force engaged in the processing of rum and molasses. Export agriculture was the predominant activity in this period. While by 1970 the share of the labour force in all the territories had fallen, the rates of decline were different. In 1970, 16% of Barbados' working population was in agriculture, as compared to 29% for Guyana and Jamaica, 16% for Trinidad and Tobago, 36% for Belize, and 34% for St Kitts–Nevis. Although data on the agricultural labour force is not available for all the territories for recent years, the indications are that the proportions engaged in agriculture have since fallen further.

In terms of actual numbers, Table 7 gives some indications of the decline of the agricultural labour force in the post-war period. In almost all the territories the number of people engaged in agricultural pursuits has been falling. While I do not have

TABLE 6

Percentage Distribution of Working Population, 1943–46 and 1970

Sectors	Barbados		Guyana		Jamaica		Trinidad and Tobago		Belize	
	1943–46	1970	1943–46	1970	1943–46	1970	1943–46	1970	1943–46	1970
Agriculture[1]	29.3	16.2	46.2	29.0	47.2	29.4	27.6	15.7	40.9	35.6
Mining & Refining[2]	–	0.4	a	4.9	a	1.5	a	5.2	–	0.1
Manufacturing	13.1	14.6	15.6	15.0	8.6	14.4	16.8	13.4	11.0	14.6
Construction	8.6	12.7	5.0	4.5	7.0	6.9	10.1	9.4	5.4	9.3
Commerce	13.6	14.4	8.2	10.8	8.2	8.8	8.8	12.7	8.5	8.4
Services	24.0	30.5	16.8	28.1	17.0	24.8	22.8	30.0	20.3	23.1
Other	11.4	11.2	8.2	7.7	88.0	14.2	13.9	13.6	13.9	8.9
Total	100.0	100.0	100.0	100.0	100.0	100.0	100.0	100.0	100.0	100.0

1. includes, forestry and fishing
a. includes quarrying
2. included in 'manufacturing'

Sources: G. W. Roberts, 'Movements in Population and the Labour Force', in G. E. Cumper, *The Economy of the West Indies*, I.S.E.R., 1960; Norma Abdullah, *The Labour Force in The Commonwealth Caribbean, A Statistical Analysis*, I.S.E.R., St Augustine 1977.

TABLE 7

Movements in the Agricultural[1] Labour Force[2] 1891–1970

Countries	1891	1943–46	1960	1970
Antigua	12,700	8,500	n.a.	2,449
Barbados	45,000	26,800	22,439	13,658
Belize	n.a.	n.a.	10,529	11,207
Dominica	11,400	12,400	11,693	7,738
Grenada	14,600	13,100	10,895	8,444
Guyana	108,500	67,500	59,790	46,276
Jamaica	271,300	228,600	236,597	145,654
Montserrat	4,000	4,000	1,983	765
St Kitts–Nevis	16,300	11,600	9,035	4,229
St Lucia	13,800	17,300	15,144	10,414
St Vincent	13,800	12,100	9,954	6,073
Trinidad & Tobago	70,700	58,800	55,265	36,120

1. includes hunting forestry and fishing
2. employed labour force.

Sources: Same as Table 6

data on Belize for the early post-war years, the figures indicate an increase in the agricultural labour force between 1960 and 1970. It is possible that given Belize's high dependence on agriculture, these figures may have increased further. I do not have up-to-date statistics on the number of people engaged in agriculture, or the sugar industry for all the territories. In St Kitts the sugar industry still provides employment for about a third of the labour force. In Jamaica, out of an employed labour force of 761,400 in October 1981, 269,200 or 35% were engaged in agriculture, forestry and fishing, as compared to 8,800 (1.1%) in mining, quarrying and refining, 84,800 (11.1%) in manufacture, 103,600 (13.6%) in commerce, and 106,300 (14.0%) in public administration. It is not possible to say what proportion of the agricultural labour was in sugar. In Barbados the in-crop employment by the sugar industry in 1980 was about 10,000 as compared to about 25,000 in 1946.[16] In Trinidad and Tobago the employed labour force (1980) was estimated to be in the region of 387,000, of which about 40,000 (10.3%) were in agriculture (including forestry, hunting and fishing), as compared to 62,000 (16.0%) in mining, quarrying and manufacturing and 81,000 (20.9%) in construction (including electricity and gas). It is estimated that in 1979 the sugar industry directly employed about 11,000 people. If we add to this registered cane farmers, we obtain a figure of about 18,000 directly dependent on sugar. If dependents are taken into account the industry would have far greater significance than the direct employment figures suggest.

The inability of the new activities to create the required number of jobs has had a critical influence on the governments of the region in their approach to the sugar industry in the post-independence period. When political independence was achieved, it was realised that given the uncompetitiveness of the industry, its existence would continue to depend on certain special traditional marketing arrangements which were not likely to continue forever. It was, therefore, necessary to rationalise the industry as quickly as possible in order to avoid the catastrophe which undoubtedly would have resulted from its sudden abandonment or closure. Rationalisation, however, has been slow in coming. The need to take control of the 'commanding heights of the economy' led to nationalisation during the 1970s where foreign ownership still prevailed. Sugar occupied the best lands in the territories, and it was thought necessary to regain control of this resource in the interest of national development (Table 8 gives some indications of the amount of land under cane cultivation in the post-war period). To the extent, however, that rationalisation meant a significant reduction in the labour force employed in sugar, this could not easily be tolerated in a situation where unemployment was already at unacceptably high levels.

As indicated earlier, the sugar industry in the Caribbean has been associated with the lowest wages and worst working conditions in the various territories. With nationalisation the pressures to improve these have been considerable. This has had further effects on costs which now tend to exceed prices received in foreign markets. It is worth pointing out here, however, that despite the gains in wages and working conditions made by sugar workers, they still tend to be at the lowest rung of the ladder in the national scale. The point is that high costs are not so much the result of these gains, as a failure to improve productivity to any extent and to put the industry on a more dynamic footing capable of adapting to a changing local and international environment. It is also noteworthy that the high level of research

TABLE 8

Acreage Under Cane-Cultivation, 1950–77

Territory	1950	1955	1958	1963	1972	1977
Antigua	10,200	10,550	12,450	n.a.	–	–
Barbados	41,241	46,083	47,241	60,000	60,000	46,000
Guyana	72,403	80,594	90,907	103,535	133,884	148,245
Grenada	n.a.	n.a.	1,400	–	–	–
Jamaica	104,885	150,377	153,123	148,252	163,000	138,746
St Kitts	12,514	14,214	13,007	13,656	10,809	12,000
St Lucia	3,007	3,898	3,767	–	–	–
St Vincent	n.a.	n.a.	1,774	–	–	–
Trinidad	83,717	86,846	90,257	94,849	99,704	98,740

n.a. not available
– none or very small

Source: West Indies Sugar Association (Inc.), *Annual Reports*, Various Issues

traditionally associated with the sugar industry with respect to finding better cane varieties, exploring conditions to improve yield, and finding new ways to counter the pests and diseases which afflict the growing of cane, has been on the wane for some time and in most cases has virtually been abandoned.

The question of productivity in the sugar industry is a very controversial one, since it is affected by a wide range of factors which are not always easy to single out in terms of their particular contribution. Certainly, technological improvements in the production of sugar have been lacking. Much of the machinery in use is worn out or outdated. With respect to the cultivation of the cane, there are several issues involved. One of the most important of these revolve around the quality of the soil and its effects on per acre yields, and the quality of the cane. In the absence of proper methods of cultivation, both are likely to be affected. A glance at Table 9 shows that in the case of Barbados, tons of cane per acre dropped from an average of 32.28 in 1955–60 to 23.30 in the 1972–77 period. It also took more cane to produce a ton of sugar in the 1970s than in the late 1950s. The same trend can be observed with respect to the other territories. Of some significance, and despite the peculiar problems associated with the growing of cane in Guyana, this country continues to obtain the highest cane yield per acre. In the period 1972–77 this averaged 29.07 tons as compared to

TABLE 9

Tons Cane Per Acre Reaped (a) and Tons Cane Per Ton Sugar (b)

Period	Barbados		Guyana		Jamaica		Trinidad & Tobago		St Kitts	
	(a)	(b)	(a)	(b)	(c)	(b)	(a)	(b)	(a)	(b)
1955–60	32.38	9.00	37.21	10.77	29.54	9.56	28.17	9.96	30.73	8.60
1972–77	23.30	10.82	29.07	12.06	27.36	10.46	26.27	10.95	26.84	8.86

Source: Calculated from West Indies Sugar Association (Inc.) *Annual Reports*, Various Issues.

23.30 for Barbados, 27.36 for Jamaica, 26.27 for Trinidad and 26.84 for St Kitts. In terms of the number of tons of cane required to produce a ton of sugar, it should be pointed out that St Kitts seems to get the highest yield: 8.86 in the 1971–77 period as compared to 10.82 for Barbados, 12.06 for Guyana, 10.46 for Jamaica and 10.95 for Trinidad. The difference in yield pointed out above may not only reflect cultivation practices, but the differences in the quality of the soil as well as the effects of weather conditions.

One measure often proposed to counter rising costs is increased mechanisation of the industry in the areas of cultivation and harvesting. The arguments here are not always clear. The main contention appears to be that a reduction in the labour force would not only directly reduce costs, but that this would also result in an increase of productivity per person. The implication here, of course, is that the main factor in the rapidly increasing costs of producing cane resides in the labour situation. This is a view not uncritically shared by everyone. While accepting the role of international sugar prices, some observers take the position that the losses experienced by the sugar companies in certain cases are to some extent the result of their own inefficiency, plus governmental policies with respect to the pricing of sugar in the domestic market and the inclusion of expenses which tend to have very little to do with the direct costs of producing sugar. Specifically, the argument is that if sugar is deliberately priced below the cost of production in the local market, and expenses relating to community services (which the government should provide) are going to be included in costs as is done, for example, in Trinidad, then the industry cannot be examined in terms of pure private profitability.[17]

The above argument takes on particular strength when seen against the inertia associated with the industry in terms of organisational changes required to streamline costs over the years and to make more rational use of resources at the disposal of the sugar companies. As Table 10 shows, attempts are being made to centralise production by eliminating marginal or inefficient factories. This can only be one step in a larger package required to reduce costs and to put the industry on an efficient basis. Other issues revolve around the division of cane growing between the farmers and the estates, and the kind of organisational framework in which the objectives of efficiency and employment maximisation can best be met.

TABLE 10

Number of Sugar Factories in Operation, 1955–77

	1955	1960	1970	1977
Antigua	1	1	–	–
Barbados	21	17	17[a]	9[a]
Guyana	14	11	11	11
Jamaica	20	20	15	12
St Kitts	1	1	1	1
Trinidad	7	6	6	5
Total	64	56	50	38

a. including fancy molasses factories.
Source: *Annual Reports* of the West Indies Sugar Association (Inc.)

One of the broader concerns overshadowing the future of the industry in the Caribbean is on what scale should it be re-organised. Traditionally, the bulk of the sugar produced has been exported (see Table 11). Given the widening gap between costs of production and prices received in international markets, the question has arisen as to whether the industry should cease as an export activity, since it appears that exporting countries are subsidising foreign consumers. The question has also been posed in terms of whether the industry should not be abandoned altogether since it may be cheaper to import sugar.

TABLE 11

Production, Consumption and Export of Sugar, 1950–81

'000 tonnes (raw value)

Years	Trinidad and Tobago			Barbados			Guyana			Jamaica		
	Production	Consumption	Exports	Production	Consumption	Exports	Production	Consumption	Exports	Production	Consumption	Exports
1950	149	22	117[a]	161	9	n.a.	199	15	183[b]	276	50	226
1960	221	30	211	156	12	132	340	20	314	431	62	359
1975	158	53	110	95	n.a.	118	300	30	295	349	105	265
1976	204	46	158	104	n.a.	85	343	37	306	368	104	250
1977	176	36	140	118	n.a.	108	253	36	218	297	113	222
1978	147	50	103	101	n.a.	88	342	36	295	306	115	203
1979	143	60	88	115	n.a.	101	316	33	280	291	101	194
1980	109	68	64	135	n.a.	120	270	34	263	223	117	135
1981	79	n.a.	n.a.	95	n.a.	63	320	37	282	204	995	125

a. 1952   b. 1951

n.a. not available

Source: Federal Ministry of Trade and Industry, *Sugar Statistics*, 1962;
Official Publications; GLC, *The Case for Cane*, London, 1983;
ISO, *The World Sugar Economy*, Vol. I, 1982.

The sugar industry, as we indicated earlier, does not lend itself to simple analysis. We have already alluded to the dilemma in terms of increasing productivity through greater mechanisation and the need to provide employment in a situation of high unemployment levels. In this case the state (as owner of the industry) picks up the financial loss which has to be measured against the 'social benefit' stemming from the employment provided. Where industry is privately owned (as, for example, the car assembly activity in Trinidad), the higher costs which consumers pay (as against the price of the imported product) are rationalised in terms of the jobs created by the protected enterprises. This policy it is often argued makes some sense since the problem 'is one of reducing employment rather than raising the level of income'.[18] The subsidy provided to the sugar industry in order to create jobs and generate income, the argument continues, is equivalent to the tariff and quota protection given to the manufacturing sector towards the same objectives. In fact, in the latter case, the cost to the economy may even be greater given the high import content of manufacturing activities in relation to the sugar industry. The net foreign exchange earnings or saving capacity of the sugar industry is far greater than that of many of the new activities whose costs to the economy may be more difficult to discern.[19]

THE EFFECTS OF THE INTERNATIONAL SUGAR MARKET

As indicated earlier, the present condition of the sugar industry in the Commonwealth Caribbean and its future have to be seen against the nature and the structure of the international sugar market over which Caribbean countries are unable to exercise any influence. They are essentially price takers. Left to the whims of the market the industry might have collapsed long ago. It is only the assistance and protection afforded by Britain which have kept it in existence as an export oriented activity.

The sugar market is one of the most unstable of all commodities markets. Prices can fluctuate widely from year to year in response to a wide range of factors. Like other crops, sugar cane is susceptible to weather conditions. It also has to contend with the problem of substitutes. One of the most outstanding peculiarities of sugar is that it can be produced both in tropical, sub-tropical and temperate climates. The rivalry between sugar produced from beet and sugar produced from cane goes back a long way. The problems faced by the sugar cane industry following the end of apprenticeship in 1838 and certain technological developments around this time served to encourage beet sugar production, which experienced a tremendous surge from about the middle of the last century. By 1890, beet sugar production accounted for a little more than half the world's centrifugal production of sugar. Despite this challenge, cane sugar production at the turn of the century was almost equal to beet sugar production, and this remained so until shortly before the First World War. As one observer noted, 'The reasoning lay in the improvement and cheapening of cane sugar production in overseas countries owing to better methods of seed selection and cultivation, the rationalisation of manufacture and improvements in selling methods.'[20]

The First World War devastated the beet sugar industry to the point where in the period 1915–25, beet sugar production averaged only about 36% of world centrifugal sugar production. After this period beet sugar production continued to increase, but was again disrupted by the Second World War. In the period 1945–46, beet sugar production amounted to about 30% of world centrifugal sugar production. In recent years the proportion has climbed back to about 35 to 40%, as a result of substantial increases in productivity resulting from technological advances, increased acreage under cultivation, improved methods of cultivation, the urge to satisfy requirements from domestic production, etc.

Since the early 1950s, the international sugar trade has been governed by a number of agreements which affect output, market prices and exports. One of these agreements is the International Sugar Agreement, the original text for which was adopted by the U.N. Sugar Conference in London on 24 August 1953. This agreement, which has been reviewed several times since, aims at regulating the export of sugar from exporting countries and areas by a system of quotas and by the placing of limits on stocks on hand. Member countries agree to adjust sugar production by regulating its manufacture, or the acreage, or the planting, as may be required. The purpose of this agreement is to avoid severe fluctuations in the price of sugar and the earnings of exporting countries.[21] The world free market in sugar, it should be pointed out, tends to be a residual market catering for sugar not traded under one of the special arrangements. Since its exclusion from the U.S. market in the early 1960s, Cuba (one of the world's largest producers) has been selling its sugar to the Soviet Union and other Eastern European countries on the basis of bilateral agreements. The import of sugar into the U.S. is governed by the U.S. Sugar Act of 1948 (and subsequent amendments). The volume of imports in any period depends on the differences between requirements and domestic production (including supplies from Hawaii and Puerto Rico). Under the Generalised System of Preference, beneficiary countries are eligible to ship a specified dollar value of sugar duty free each year. The new quota system announced by President Reagan in May 1982 is likely to affect this arrangement. As far as Caribbean countries are concerned, it is likely that sugar would either be exempted from the Caribbean Basin Initiative or be subject to strict import controls in order to protect domestic sugar producers, including cane growers in Hawaii and Puerto Rico. Indications point to an increasing policy of protection and self sufficiency in the U.S., which in recent years has been buying some of the Commonwealth Caribbean surplus sugar exports at prices above the world free market price.

Another important agreement associated with the international sugar trade in the post-war period has been the Commonwealth Sugar Agreement (CSA) which became operative in 1951. The purpose of this Agreement was both to ensure adequate sugar supplies for the U.K. and to provide Commonwealth producers with an assured market at prices 'reasonably remunerative to efficient producers'. Before the Second World War, sugar exported within the Commonwealth area enjoyed only a preferential tariff treatment. Apart from the effect of this tariff concession, the price at which this sugar was traded was that of the free market. Under the CSA there were two sets of export quotas for Commonwealth Sugar Exporters. The 'overall agreement quotas' (OAQ) limited total exports to preferential markets (U.K., Canada and New Zealand) in any one calendar year. The purpose of this arrangement was to reserve part of the preferential markets for domestic and other producers. The other set of quotas, termed the negotiated price quotas (NPQs), specified the quantities that the U.K. agreed to buy and the Commonwealth sugar exporters agreed to sell at 'negotiated prices which would be reasonably remunerative to efficient producers'. The difference between the OAQ and the NPQ was sold at world market prices plus the value of the duty. Toward the end of the 1960s and in the early 1970s the Caribbean obtained a negotiated price for some 60 to 70% of their total sugar exports. With the British accession to the EEC in 1973 the CSA gave way to the Sugar Protocol associated with the various Lomé Conventions. Under the Protocol provision is made for the EEC to purchase and import 1,225,000 tonnes per annum of raw and white cane sugar at guaranteed prices from ACP (African, Pacific and the Caribbean) countries. In addition, it committed itself to buying 39,000 tonnes from Belize and 14,000 tonnes from St Kitts–Nevis (two countries which were at the time not yet independent) and 25,000 tonnes from India. The guaranteed price is negotiated annually and is set within the price range obtaining in the community.

The guaranteed prices received by Caribbean sugar producers, first under the CSA and currently under Lomé, have generally been above the world free market price which tends to fluctuate widely, occasionally exceeding guaranteed prices. While the latter have not always been satisfactory, and are often arrived at after protracted negotiations, they nevertheless have enabled the sugar industry to survive in the Commonwealth Caribbean where it still makes a significant economic contribution. The industry, however, is now perhaps in a more serious crisis situation than it has ever been. With beet sugar increasing within the EEC, there has been a reluctance to increase guaranteed prices in line with production and transport costs, part of which are attributed to inefficiency. For most of the countries, the costs of production now exceed the price being received for a ton of sugar. For example, the Trinidad and Tobago government claims that while it costs Trinidad TT$3,700 to produce a ton of sugar, the guaranteed EEC price for sugar is less than TT$850 (the world price is even lower).[22] A glance back at Table 3 will show that in some years (e.g. 1972, 1976 and 1982) the costs of producing a ton of sugar in Barbados were higher than the average export price. In Guyana, too, the average earnings on a ton of sugar have in recent years been below the costs of production.

The widening gap between costs of production and the price being received for a ton of sugar is one aspect of the larger problem facing Caribbean producers. Another is the significant drop in production in recent years, the probable causes for which we have discussed earlier and which has led to difficulties in fulfilling agreed quotas under the Protocol. Until 1980 Jamaica appears to have met its quota requirements quite comfortably, even though there was a declining trend in production. It even had some surplus exports which were disposed of in the Canadian and U.S. markets. In 1980, for example, the latter accounted for 32% of Jamaica's sugar exports as compared to 68% for the EEC. In 1981, however, this country barely had enough to meet its EEC supply obligations. In recent years, Trinidad and Tobago has also had problems meeting its EEC quota. In fact, it has found itself in the position of importing increasing quantities of sugar to meet local consumption requirements, after exporting most of what it has produced to meet its quota obligations under the Lomé Agreement. Production in Guyana has been maintained at fairly high levels in recent years despite the many problems faced by the industry. Between 1975 and 1981, sugar exports to the EEC averaged 63% of Guyana's total sugar exports as compared to 19% to the U.S. and 11% to Canada. With falling or stagnating production levels in St Kitts and increasing domestic consumption, this country is also under pressure to meet its quota requirements.

CONCLUDING OBSERVATIONS

The prospects facing the sugar industry in the Caribbean, as presently organised, are not very encouraging. The evidence that sugar is associated with low income and price elasticities and even with falling elasticities once a certain level of income is reached, implies that the growth in demand for sugar in the importing industrial countries is likely to slow up. The move towards greater self-sufficiency and protectionism in major importing countries is a factor that is also likely to affect demand. The number of countries producing sugar has also been increasing over the years. Virgin or rested soil tends to give better yields in terms of tonnes per acreage and sucrose content.

The framework within which the international sugar industry functions has always overshadowed sugar activities in the Caribbean. With the nationalisation of the sugar enterprises, the various governments could not pursue the same exploitative policies with respect to wages and working conditions (at least not to the same extent) that the foreign owners did. In the absence of measures designed to increase productivity, costs were bound to increase at undesirable rates. Having taken control of the industry no serious attempts have been made to re-organise it in a form which could have maintained a high level of employment, while being more insulated from developments abroad. Sugar continues to be exported largely in raw form for refining abroad, and then re-imported back. Local refinery operations have been limited. Besides the production of rum and molasses little headway has been made in the development of further by-products capable of generating income, employment and even foreign exchange.

The production of sugar in the Caribbean has tied up some of the best agricultural lands in the Caribbean, leaving the marginal land for domestic agriculture whose performance has been far from satisfactory. The region finds itself importing a wide range of commodities and foodstuffs which might easily be produced locally. It should be pointed out, however, that this situation is not the result solely of the unavailability of suitable agricultural land. In the absence of proper land zoning policies a great deal of good agricultural land (including sugar lands) has been alienated to other uses, such as housing developments, warehouses, industrial estates, office building and even horse-racing tracks. Marketing problems, land tenure, absence of access roads, unavailability of sufficient credit, and lack of incentives are factors which have also had an adverse effect on agricultural production. Perhaps one of the most crucial problems bearing on the decline of agriculture, however, has been the unavailability of labour when it is most needed. Governments' policies to create employment by paying wages above what the agricultural sector could bear (sometimes for very unproductive work) tend to attract labour away from agriculture to which few return once they have left. There is no doubt that public policy has been a crucial factor in the decline of both domestic and traditional export agriculture.

One of the results of poor planning and badly conceived agricultural policies is a rapidly increasing food import bill which is now estimated to be well over US$600 million for the CARICOM region as a whole. This, in itself, indicates that there is a market for agricultural produce the increased production of which can lead to a saving of foreign exchange resources. Saving foreign exchange is as good as earning it. It has long been recognised that the region has ample resources to meet a substantial part of its food requirements, particularly if production is planned within a regional framework. Towards this end the Caribbean Food Corporation was set up some time ago, but it has been extremely slow in getting off the ground. With the expansion of the domestic agricultural sector, traditional export agriculture could have been more easily rationalised without fear of adverse economic and social consequences stemming from the displacement of workers and even loss of foreign exchange.

NOTES

1. In St Vincent the sugar industry was almost extinct by the end of the 19th century. By the time of the First World War exports had virtually disappeared. Towards the end of the 1920s, however, attempts were once more being made to revive it.
2. See *Report of the West Indian Sugar Commission*, London, H.M.S.O., 1930, p. 40.
3. See Cleviston Haynes, 'Sugar and the Barbadian Economy' in D. Worrell (ed.), *The Economy of Barbados*, Central Bank of Barbados, Bridgetown, Barbados, 1982.
4. *Ibid.*
5. *Ibid.*
6. See the Persaud Report, *Report of a Commission of Inquiry into the Sugar Industry in Guyana*, Georgetown, Guyana, 1968.
7. See O. Jefferson, *The Post-War Economic Development of Jamaica*, I.S.E.R., 1962, p. 75.
8. *Ibid.*
9. International Sugar Council, *The World Sugar Economy, Structure and Policies*, Vol. II, 1963, p. 9.
10. See Trinidad and Tobago Government, *Review of the Economy*, 1982, p. 19.
11. *The Spence Report* (Report of Committee to consider the Rationalisation of the Sugar Industry, 1978), p. 15.
12. International Sugar Council, *The World Sugar Economy*, pp. 8–9.

13. See L. J. Ragatz, *The Fall of the Planter Class in the British Caribbean 1763– 1833* (New York: 1971), p. 3.
14. *Ibid.*
15. With the settlement of the expatriate plantation owners in Barbados, the sugar industry in this country was among the earliest to be 'localised'. It was not until the 1970s that the governments in Jamaica, Trinidad, Guyana and St Kitts made serious moves to nationalise or localise the resources tied-up in the industry. In Belize, while the factories are owned by Tate & Lyle of England, most of the sugar lands are owned by the farmers.
16. Haynes, 'Sugar and the Barbadian Economy'.
17. For example, see Winston Dookeran, 'Sugar — Its Profitability and the Social Order in Trinidad and Tobago'. Paper presented at the International Sugar Workers' Conference held in San Fernando, Trinidad, 23–28 July, 1977.
18. See *The Spence Report*, p. 15.
19. *Ibid.*
20. 'Memorandum on Sugar prepared by Dr H. C. Geerligs et al.' for the *Economic Committee of the League of Nations*, 1929, p. 18.
21. The current International Sugar Agreement was established on 1 Jan. 1978 and was scheduled to end at the end of 1982. It was, however, extended for a further period of two years (i.e. it now ends at the end of 1984). Because the Agreement has not been operating satisfactorily, there have been strong demands for its termination and for a new agreement to be drawn up to include the EEC. The Agreement's goal is to maintain world surplus sugar prices in a price range of US$0.13 to US$0.23 per pound. From 1980 through 1982, however, prices have been below that range almost three quarters of the time. One reason for this has been the dumping by the EEC (which is not a member of the ISA) of large amounts of highly subsidised sugar on the world market (see *Sugar Y Azucar*, Jan. 1983).
22. Feature address by the Minister of State Enterprises, Mr Ronald Williams, at the Fifteenth Year Service Certificate function of Caroni Limited in Nov. 1982.

Sugar in Barbados and Martinique:
A Socio-economic Comparison

MICHAEL SLEEMAN

In this chapter I will be examining the role of the sugar industry in the economies of Barbados and Martinique from the post-war period up to the present. In both cases the sugar industry has suffered a decline in absolute and relative terms over the past two decades. Although I will be focussing upon the anatomy of this decline, I have attempted something more than just an overview of the period and the documentation of a process. In keeping with the general theme of this work, it is my intention rather to attempt to underline ways in which the sugar economies of two Caribbean territories continue to serve as legacies of the past. Historical continuity in these cases has been maintained by virtue of the fact that land and productive resources have remained to date in the hands of a restricted, white economic elite.

The cases examined here can be viewed as 'deviant cases' from the more general historical process which took place in all other sugar islands of the Caribbean in the nineteenth century, in which the sugar industry passed out of the hands of an independent planter class to a number of metropolitan British, French and American mercantile houses. The uniqueness of these cases invests them with special interest, not only because the maintenance of economic power ensured the survival of indigenous plantocracies during a period which witnessed the 'fall' of planter elites elsewhere, but also because the alternative strategies for economic development in each island today in the face of sugar's decline, are very much a function of the choices made by this minority. The continuing economic mastery of these traditional elites, therefore, still casts a long shadow over the future of these post-plantation societies.

In order to get a clearer perspective of some of the issues dealt with here, I have prefaced my analysis with an account of changes in the organizational structure of the Barbadian and Martiniquan plantation systems in the latter half of the nineteenth and early part of the twentieth century. Comparative data on organizational and structural change in other parts of the Caribbean is also included, together with an attempt to explain how Barbados and Martinique prevented the incursion of metropolitan monopoly finance capital.

ORGANIZATIONAL AND STRUCTURAL CHANGE IN THE NINETEENTH AND TWENTIETH CENTURY

Before proceeding to a discussion of changes in the Barbadian and Martiniquan plantation systems, I wish to deal briefly with the process of change which took place in other parts of the Caribbean during the same period. From the presentation of this comparative material, it will be evident that a minimum amount of change to accomplish a revolution in the sugar industry was introduced into Barbados and Martinique. The fact that this was undertaken by local elites had far-reaching consequences for the social organization of the plantation system in the twentieth century, and the economic base of each island.

By the 1890s control of the sugar industry in Jamaica, British Guiana, Trinidad and the smaller Windward and Leeward islands had passed into the hands of a corporate sector based upon West Indian mercantile houses located in the metropolis. The plantation system in Barbados in the last decade of the nineteenth century was by contrast still supported by a resident and absentee planter class, privately owning and separately managing over 420 sugar estates.[1] In the other British West Indian sugar islands, the passage of the West Indies Encumbered Estates Act of 1854 to facilitate the sale and transfer of land held by heavily mortgaged and insolvent proprietors, played a central role in reducing the numbers of estates and amalgamating them into larger units. West India houses had an advantage over local buyers with the setting up of a Central Court in London, since it enabled them to buy up plantations often below their market value in the face of very little competition.[2]

From the data contained in Royal Commission Reports between 1842 and 1897, the evidence indicates that there was an overall reduction in the number of sugar estates in the British West Indies from about 2,200 at the time of Emancipation to about 800 at the beginning of the twentieth century.[3] For the most part the motor force in this process of estate amalgamation was provided by the metropolitan merchant houses, aided by the speedy and efficient working of the Encumbered Estates Court in London in the conveyancing of property rights. However, the adoption of the Act was not a necessary and sufficient pre-requisite for the formation of corporate plantation structures in all these colonies. Where this trend was most marked, in British Guiana and to a lesser extent in Trinidad and St Lucia, the Act was not adopted, the local assemblies of these colonies considering a sufficient remedy to lie in the laws already prevailing, based on Dutch, Spanish and French legal systems.

The case of Guadeloupe is an interesting one when compared with the direction taken by its sister colony Martinique. Like Martinique it had a well-established local planter class of similar size at the time of Emancipation, comparative systems of credit and the same access to finance capital. However, the situation of the Grands Blancs was radically different from that of the Békés[4] in Martinique in 1848. Whereas during the French Revolution Martinique was occupied by the English, who supported the *ancien régime* and the interests of the plantocracy, the Victor Hughes Convention established in Guadeloupe forced those planters who escaped the guillotine into exile. In spite of the boom of the restoration period, the returning planters were unable to compete with the well-financed corporations of metropolitan France, which were already investing in the new central factories. During the 1860s and 1870s, the modernization of the sugar industry was therefore undertaken by metropolitan corporations rather than by groups of local planters. During this period the Grands Blancs' share of the colony's sugar output declined dramatically. By 1883 ninety-seven *habitations sucreries* owned by local interests produced only one-fifth of the colony's sugar. The remainder was produced by twenty *usines centrales* controlled for the most part by metropolitan interests.[5] By the early 1900s two-thirds of Guadeloupe's sugar production was controlled by three metropolitan joint stock companies: La Société Industrielle et Agricole de Pointe-à-Pitre, La Société Anonyme des Usines de Beauport and La Société Marseillaise des Sucreries Coloniales. Having created a number of vast *domaines*, these three companies between them controlled a total of 30,000 hectares in Basse-Terre and Grande-Terre.[6]

From the comparative data presented above, it is evident that metropolitan finance capital played a dynamic role in all the other areas of the British and French Caribbean in the second half of the nineteenth century. This was a general pattern which was duplicated in Cuba and Puerto Rico, with the difference that structural change was initially attempted by indigenous plantocracies in Cuba from the 1840s onwards,[7] and in Puerto Rico in the 1880s.[8] However, in both these islands no real impetus was attained until the early twentieth century, when the United States forged an imperialist role for itself which resulted in the penetration of American monopoly finance capital. It was during the years leading up to the First World War that really large central factories were established in Cuba. By 1913 United States sugar investments in Cuba totalled 200 million dollars, which represented 18 per cent of that country's investments in Latin America. Extensive American involvement in the sugar industry is reflected in a doubling of annual production between the late 1890s and 1918: from one million to two million tons of sugar.[9] In Puerto Rico during the same period sugar production increased eight-fold from 57,000 tons to 489,000 tons per annum.[10] By 1920 the several hundred small family mills owned by *hacendados* at the end of the nineteenth century were reduced to seventy-five, and 60 per cent of the sugar industry was controlled by American interests, with four corporations owning 46 per cent of Puerto Rico's sugar lands.

In the British Caribbean monopoly corporate power was achieved by two companies in the twentieth century. Tate and Lyle and its subsidiaries came to monopolize the sugar production of Jamaica, Trinidad and British Honduras. Booker McConnell became the successor to the seven merchant houses which monopolized the sugar industry in British Guiana in the late 1850s, and within a space of seventy years came to account for 90 per cent of that colony's total output of sugar.[11] By the early 1970s in Puerto Rico, as well as in the Dominican Republic and Haiti, most of the sugar exported was produced by five American corporations. In Guadeloupe the monopoly exerted by overseas interests increased in the twentieth century. The three major French corporations maintained their share of output, but a new factor entered the market: the creation of *latifundia* and factories capitalized by the Martiniquan elite in a process of 'secondary colonization'. Today 85 per cent of Guadeloupe's sugar production is accounted for by eight corporations of metropolitan and Martiniquan origin, or 80 per cent of the total area under sugar.[12]

Barbados and Martinique can be regarded as variants of this general process, insofar as they avoided 'outside capitalist exploitation'. The reasons as to how they managed to prevent the incursion of metropolitan monopoly corporate power are two-fold. First, in both islands the sugar industry was tradition-ally financed by local capital, unlike the situation elsewhere where credit to plantations was obtained via the 'consignee system'.[13] In Barbados land was considered a first rate secur-ity, and since mortgages were one of the few avenues for investment, it was the established practice for most Barbadian planters to obtain credit locally rather than from English merchants. Referring to the financial independence of the Barbadian planter community in the second half of the eight-eenth century, Richard Pares[14] noted that 'Barbadians had owed money not so much to Englishmen as to other Barbadians'. Trollope's observations[15] upon the financial independence of Barbados, as an island that 'owes no man anything' and 'pays its own way', reinforces the impression that the financing of the sugar industry was primarily a local affair. An analysis of Chancery Court records accords this impression the status of fact, since they clearly indicate that the plaintiffs represented in bills of complaint in a majority of cases were other planters and local merchants.[16]

Martiniquan planters were similarly used to obtaining credit locally, and were not dependent upon advances from merchant houses in Bordeaux, Nantes and Le Havre, as was the case with planters in Sainte-Domingue and Guadeloupe. The Martiniquan plantocracy was dependent for credit not so much upon other planters, but upon the *commissionnaires* of Saint-Pierre who operated as factors, handling sugar, slaves and plantation supplies for local planters as well as planters from other French islands. The commission earned on sugar and slaves throughout the French Caribbean made for rapid capital accumulation, which in turn was invested as loans to planters. Thus it can be argued, as Crusol does,[17] that the pierrotine *commissionnaires* played an active role in preventing the transfer of estates into the hands of metropolitan mercantile interests.

A second reason why the sugar industry remained in local hands is related to the question of political power. The existence of a relatively large resident planter class and the retention of the Old Representative System, which in almost all other British West Indian islands gave way to direct home rule by Crown Colony Government, gave the white oligarchy in Barbados a power of internal control which was unrivalled elsewhere in the Caribbean. Vested with the power to make its own laws, a number of measures were adopted by the Barbadian planter class in the second half of the nineteenth century which had the effect of retaining estate ownership in local hands, though these measures did not have the long-term effect of keeping estates in the same hands. Most important of these measures was the refusal of the local legislature to accept the Encumbered Estates Act. Barbados by contrast adopted its own version of the English Chancery Court system,[18] which ensured that indebted estates were re-sold to local buyers. Another important measure adopted by the local legislature at the height of the depression in 1887 was the enactment of the Agricultural Aids Act, which helped to prop up an ailing sugar industry and thereby prevent its total collapse.[19]

In Martinique the plantocracy's power of internal control was qualitatively different from that of their Barbadian counterparts. A high degree of centralization in French colonial affairs meant that all financial, administrative and legislative decisions were never located in the hands of local assemblies. Thus unlike the Barbadian oligarchy, the Martiniquan plantocracy was never empowered to make its own laws or formulate its own budget. In the French islands legislation took the form of decrees emanating from metropolitan France, which were presented to the *conseils généraux* for ratification, and all financial and administrative matters were in the hands of a metropolitan official. Lacking control over the central political mechanisms of power, the plantocracy, however, enjoyed well-established covert forms of wielding influence, through the formation of strategic alliances with the political, commercial and industrial elites of France.

When change came it took quite different forms, and was initiated by different forces. In the French Antilles it was initiated by the active intervention of the State, which resulted in a rapid economic transformation of the colony in the 1860s. In the case of Barbados an avowedly non-interventionist policy was adopted by the colonial office of the day,[20] and organizational and structural change was initiated by private investors with a minimal amount of support from the colonial government.[21] These different responses by the French and British were to have repercussions upon the respective organizational structures of the two sugar economies in the twentieth century.

In 1861 the passing of legislation to found the Crédit Colonial was of momentous importance to the future of the sugar industry in the French Antilles. The objective of this legislation was

to lend ... either to sugar proprietors individually or to syndicates of proprietors, the necessary sums to construct sugar factories in the French colonies or to renew and to improve the equipment of factories in existence at the present time.[22]

The importance of this legislation was two-fold. First, it made provisions for long-term credit which made the undertaking of capital projects possible, resulting in the construction of a central factory system in the French Antilles half a century before its introduction in Barbados. Second, it enabled the Martiniquan plantocracy to maximize the capital resources available for such an undertaking, since the shareholders of the Crédit Colonial represented an alliance of both Béké planters and French commercial and industrial interests. By 1884 at the onset of the depression, seventeen central factories had been erected at a cost of twenty-eight million francs: 80 per cent of this sum had been advanced by the Crédit Foncier Colonial.[23]

In the 1880s sugar production in Barbados continued to be organized along traditional lines. During the preceding twenty-five year period in which a revolution had occurred in the French Antillean sugar industry, technological innovations in Barbados had been limited. This was evident in the practice at the end of the nineteenth century for individual sugar estates to still grind their own cane. A total of 463 mills continued to operate on 448 plantations: 373 were still powered by wind and only 90 had been transformed by steam. The most important technological advance in the sugar industry, the vacuum pan, was to be found in only nine mills in the island, representing a very small quantity of sugar produced by the new method from less than 3,000 arable acres.[24]

When change occurred it was not initiated by the plantocracy, but by a new mercantile elite formed out of a dynamic trading sector in nineteenth century Bridgetown, which had risen to prominence during the Free Trade era. Throughout the successive sugar crises of 1884, 1892, 1905 and 1921/22, the Bridgetown mercantile elite proved to be the only group powerful enough to keep the ailing sugar industry afloat and to capitalize its modernization, and to displace the older planter class with its new found financial coercive power.

SOCIOLOGICAL BACKGROUND

Unlike the more general pattern documented for other territories in the region, the sugar industry in these two atypical cases remained in local hands. However, it must be said that it did not remain in the same hands. In both cases the maintenance of economic power by local white elites was linked with the emergence of new social classes in the second half of the nineteenth century, in a process which was coterminous with the birth of monopoly capitalism which was local rather than international. In Barbados the nucleus of this class was a locally based commercial and trading elite, which formed financial and familial alliances with the remnants of an older, established planter class. In Martinique, although the sugar industry remained in the hands of local planters, economic power in the twentieth century passed into the hands of a restricted minority of *usiniers* – the Grands Békés.

As a consequence of the limited extent to which structural change took place, local white hegemony survived in a modified form in the modern world. In each island the concentration of mercantile and planter interests in the twentieth century has produced a social hybrid, which I have designated an 'agri-business bourgeoisie'. By the early twentieth century this new economic elite had usurped the traditional commercial and productive functions of metropolitan merchant house and indigenous plantocracy, and came to extend a virtual monopoly over all sectors of the economy. In charting the new elite's consolidation of its economic power in the twentieth century, we are witness to a process in which merchants became planters in one island and planters became merchants in the other. The records of the Barbados Chancery Court are a rich mine of information attesting to a swift and dramatic shift in estate ownership. They clearly indicate that the Bridgetown merchants in a great number of cases had liens on sugar estates, and that many of the plaintiffs who filed bills of complaint against proprietors were merchants. Moreover, many of the purchases of estates out of Chancery were made by merchants, who in the early years of this century acquired groups of contiguous estates which formed the holdings of the first central sugar factories.[25]

When commercial life was re-established in Martinique after the volcanic destruction of Saint-Pierre in 1902, it was the returns from sugar realized by the *usiniers* in the last quarter of the nineteenth century which capitalized the new commercial houses in Fort-de-France, giving the Grands Békés a virtual monopoly in the tertiary sector as commission agents, wholesalers and produce exporters. Like their counterparts in Barbados, a restricted group of about ten families came to exert a tight control over every aspect of the colonial economy. By the early 1920s the Grands Békés had established an 85 per cent share of the export trade and held a similar percentage of shares in the town's business houses. In Guadeloupe they also became the owners of between one-fifth and one-quarter of the island's land resources, as well as setting up commission houses, sugar factories and distilleries.

Of paramount importance in this process was the control which the agri-business bourgeoisie exerted over access to credit, through insurance companies, banks and institutions designed specifically to finance the sugar industry. In Barbados this control was maintained through the Colonial Bank, the local branches of several Canadian banks, the Barbados Mutual Life Assurance Society, the Barbados Savings Bank and the Sugar Industry Agricultural Bank. In Martinique the Banque Coloniale de la Martinique, the Banque de France and the Crédit Foncier Colonial similarly served to maintain control over access to credit. Since the agri-business bourgeoisie held extensive shareholdings and directorships in these institutions, it had the power to decide who could raise the necessary capital to purchase land, construct sugar factories and open commercial houses. In Barbados where a system of patronage and sponsorship existed,[26] the agri-business bourgeoisie was able to control the entry of personnel into its ranks. In Martinique where the ranks of the Grands Békés were closed to outsiders, credit was usually only granted to other Grands Békés. In Barbados professional and trading associations also played an important role. For example, the all powerful Commission Merchants Association dominated by the 'Big Six'[27] operated a credit system which controlled the necessary supplies of credit to the Bridgetown traders for purchasing goods wholesale. Thus a combine of the major commercial houses was able to decide whom they would advance credit to at their own discretion.

Although in terms of function the agri-business bourgeoisie can be regarded as a modernizing elite, the very nature of its composition endows it with a traditional aspect, the survival of white economic supremacy representing an unbroken continuity with the past. Alongside strategic measures to maintain its supremacy, a number of social mechanisms exist which serve to maintain the *status quo*. The operation of these mechanisms gives each group a 'caste-like' appearance, all social behaviour — forms of associational life, inter-ethnic group relations and marital patterns — having the ultimate aim of maintaining the status boundaries of ethnicity in which a number of structural determinants are decisive for its operation rather than ethnicity *per se*.[28] To generalize further, one effect of the continuing salience of ethnicity in the social structure of each island is the existence of dual occupational structures, avenues of social mobility in the white sector still being confined to landownership and business, and in the non-white sector to politics, administration and the professions.[29]

Another consequence of the survival of local interests has been the maintenance of a certain continuity of form in the two plantation systems. Until fairly recently Martiniquan and Barbadian sugar plantations have continued to be clothed in archaic social forms redolent of manorial tradition. The retention of local ownership in the second half of the twentieth century meant that plantations as a type remained family plantations. This was a factor of momentous importance for the development of social relations of a highly personalized nature, since the organizational structure of the family plantation is a relatively simple one. Owner contact with the workforce is more or less direct, the execution of orders being personally supervised by the owner with the assistance of overseers. The degree of contact and control engendered by this kind of organizational structure makes for pervasive, highly personalized relations of a paternalistic kind, which represents an effective mechanism of social control. The development and growth of local monopoly capitalism, which resulted in a rationalization of the means of production on the plantation, did not alter the form of social relationships, since individual plantations continued to be managed as separate units deriving their labour supply from located sources.

THE SUGAR INDUSTRY SINCE 1945

Combined production figures for the period 1963–1977 for the six sugar exporting countries which are members of the Sugar Association of the Caribbean,[30] emphasizing the position of Barbados within them, are to be found in Table 1. Compared with an earlier dramatic increase in production during the 1950s, these figures indicate a continuing but slower upward trend during the period 1963–67. Thereafter production overall and in Barbados has steadily declined. The table also indicates a parallel decline in field efficiency. This is indicated by a decline in tons of cane per acre reaped, which naturally has consequences for the tons of sugar per acre reaped.

The main factors which affect production are: (a) climate, (b) acreage under cane cultivation, (c) varieties of cane, (d) labour, (e) field efficiency (cultivation, harvesting, cane delivery to the factory and control of cane fires), and (f) factory efficiency

TABLE 1

The West Indian Sugar Industry, 1963–1977

	Sugar Production (long tons)			Tons of cane per acre reaped			Tons of sugar per acre reaped	
	West Indies and Guyana	Barbados		West Indies and Guyana	Barbados		West Indies and Guyana	Barbados
1963/67*	1,253,373	184,138	1966	30.14	30.29		2.90	3.34
1964/68	1,239,063	177,814	1967	29.29	35.00		2.90	3.85
1965/69	1,223,170	173,406	1968	28.70	27.03		2.88	3.14
1966/70	1,190,401	164,931	1969	28.78	25.04		2.68	2.74
1967/71	1,160,972	157,736	1970	29.54	28.79		2.60	3.09
1968/72	1,127,172	139,882	1971	27.43	24.91		2.57	2.76
1969/73	1,071,194	131,339	1972	27.03	23.76		2.49	2.52
1970/74	1,045,015	125,159	1973	24.91	23.14		2.28	2.51
1971/75	1,016,811	113,541	1974	26.15	22.71		2.45	2.62
1972/76	995,126	107,064	1975	25.48	20.89		2.45	2.43
1973/77	974,011	108,395						

* Five year moving averages

Source: The Sugar Association of the Caribbean, *Monthly and Annual Returns* by Member Associations. *Abstract of Production and Commercial Statistics* appended to the Chairman's Annual Report, December 1975.

(tons cane/tons sugar ratios and methods of sugar extraction). At any given time all of these factors play a role in determining output. However, it is difficult to make an exact assessment of the relative weight to be given to each factor. Instead I will discuss those factors which have played a major role over the last three decades.

A major climatic factor, rainfall, is important over any period. A plentiful supply of rain, particularly during the growing season, is of prime importance since there is no surface water in Barbados, the greater part of the island being covered by a mantle of porous coral limestone some 200 feet thick. Holding all other factors constant, some positive correlation is provided by the example of 1948's disastrously low output of 78,000 tons, a result of the lowest rainfall recorded for twenty-five years. By contrast during the 'good years' of the 1950s and early 1960s average rainfall was high. During a cycle of drought which Barbados has been experiencing for over a decade, the drier parts of the island, such as the parishes of Christ Church and St Phillip, suffer most from rainfall deficits. It is true to say that low rainfall has played a significant role in declining production, and it is noteworthy that the greatest proportion of estate land which has gone out of production in the last decade is in the drier parts of the island. The evidence also suggests that drought may be a contributory factor accounting for the high incidence of 'uncontrolled' cane fires in recent years.

Technological advances have played a more central role in the past than over the last thirty or so years. The introduction of steam plants in the nineteenth century and vacuum pan technology in the new central factories in the twentieth century, played a vital role in increasing output six-fold between Abolition and the outbreak of the Second World War. Paralleled by these improvements in factory efficiency, and of equal importance, were the gains made by greater field efficiency in controlling pests and diseases and improving soil conditions, and the introduction of better, disease resistant cane varieties.[31] More recent technological advances at the factory level have sought to utilize the by-products of sugar cane, producing Comfith as a cattle feed and Comrind in the production of laminated timber, hardboard and paper. Attempts to fully mechanize field operations through the introduction of loading and cutting machinery have only been partially successful, estates having been subject to demands from the labour market to provide work during a period of increasing unemployment.

One feature of the Barbadian sugar industry in the contemporary period is the diversity of landownership, and the essentially private as opposed to public corporate nature of estate holdings. This situation, together with the relatively large number of factories for an island the size of Barbados, was described in 1957 in the following terms:

The industry of the island does not follow the pattern found in the other sugar producing territories of the West Indies ... It is probably unique in that no large companies, financed from outside the island, tend to dominate the industry. It is built up on a large number of small estates owned in the main by residents of Barbados, and managed by owners or local agents who themselves are Barbadians.[32]

The development of a fully centralized factory system has been a very slow and gradual process. In the mid-1970s Barbados had as many as ten sugar factories and plans were projected to reduce this number to six. Even in the late 1930s archaic remnants of the nineteenth century system of production persisted. Alongside a number of large-scale enterprises with extensive landholdings developed by the agri-business bourgeoisie, there were a number of much smaller vacuum pan factories, representing no more than modernized wind powered mills. According to the findings of the West India Royal Commission in 1939, 20 per cent of the island's sugar was still being produced by an additional thirty-five ordinary steam plants and thirty-seven mills powered by wind. Wide variability in size of the central factories of the period was another feature of the process system, average manufacturing capacity varying between 1,500 and 8,000 tons of sugar.[33]

In spite of the continuing predominance of sugar in the primary sector, its role in the economy of the island in terms of its export earnings has greatly diminished. In 1960 sugar and molasses accounted for roughly two-thirds of Barbados's export earnings. By the early 1970s sugar's contribution to export earnings had dropped to 8 per cent, its traditional pre-eminence having been superseded by tourism. Annual reports of Barbados Shipping and Trading indicate this decline in the relative importance of sugar in a parallel fashion.[34] In 1964 sugar products accounted for 35.8 per cent of company profits. This had dropped to 21.1 per cent by 1969, and had dropped even further in 1970 to 7.1 per cent. In spite of the gloomy picture revealed by this situation of both relative and absolute decline, agriculture in Barbados is still primarily tied to sugar. Indicative of the crisis in the sugar industry is the extent to which loans from the Sugar Industry Agricultural Bank increased in the 1970s: from 3,400,000 dollars in 1970 to 46,000,000 dollars in 1977.[35] Increasing overheads and decreasing revenues during the period of decline have resulted in financial loss for many estate owners, with the result that loans contracted in one year are not paid off the next, but are added on to the debt incurred in the following year.

The annual production of sugar has continued to show a downward trend as the following figures[36] indicate (tonnes): 1977 – 117,911; 1978 – 99,256; 1979 – 112,244; 1980 – 135,107; 1981 – 96,462; 1982 – 87,834; 1983 – 85,000. There has been a reduction of the acreage under cane and acreage reaped in recent years, factors which account for the continuing decline in production. No recent data has been published documenting this decrease in the area given over to cane cultivation for the plantation sector. However, one indication of the smaller acreages reaped can be seen in the fact that small-holdings (less than ten acres) in 1983 produced 32 per cent less cane than in 1982. A 'green cane incentive bonus' scheme was started in 1983 and resulted in an increase in the volume of green, unburnt cane delivered to the factories, and also in a significant reduction in the incidence of cane fires.[37] The field and factory sides of the industry have been amalgamated into one company, Barbados Sugar Industry Ltd., in the hope that this measure to promote greater efficiency will bring about a revival of the industry. A new factory was built in 1982 called Port Vale, and two older factories, Porters and Vaucluse, were closed. Today there are only six sugar factories operating. During the last few years mechanical harvesting (utilizing smaller machines developed locally) has increased and now accounts for one-fifth to one-quarter of the total cane harvested.

In response to this continuing decline, the Government of Barbados now takes a greater interest in the sugar industry and has projected an annual average target of 150,000 tonnes. However, given the extent to which cane land has gone out of production in recent years, it will be some time before this target can be achieved. In the meantime Barbados, in common with other CARICOM countries, has to cope with depressed world prices for sugar and rising production costs. Low world prices, however, should not affect Barbados seriously, since very little sugar is shipped on the world market, its secured outlets in the form of quotas in the EEC and USA acounting for nearly all the export sugar availability.

In Martinique during the post-war years other export crops, notably pineapples and bananas, have competed with sugar for land, capital, labour and management resources. During the 1950s sugar's share of total exports declined from 37 per cent to 30 per cent. During this period the share accredited to bananas increased from 26 per cent to 40 per cent, and that of pineapples from 7 per cent to 11 per cent. Including the value of rum exports, the percentage of sugar and rum together declined from 55 per cent to 44 per cent.[38] The decline of sugar in relative terms continued throughout the 1960s and into the 1970s as Table 2 indicates.

In a report compiled in 1960,[39] the authors highlighted a number of structural weaknesses in the sugar industry which underlined a serious imbalance in the agricultural sector. In terms of land, capital and labour, sugar in 1960 was still more

TABLE 2

Percentage Breakdown of Major Exports in Terms of their Export Values, Selected Years between 1961–1975

	1961	'70	'72	'74	'75
Bananas	44	50	53	42.6	47.8
Sugar and Rum	42	24	17	11.0	14.2
Pineapples	11	13	6	5.0	6.4
Refined petroleum	–	–	12	28.0	20.2
Miscellaneous	3	13	12	13.4	11.4
Totals	100	100	100	100	100

Source: Préfecture de la Martinique, Direction Générale des Douanes, *Le Commerce Extérieur de la Martinique*, 1975.

important than bananas and pineapples. Cane occupied 61 per cent of the total area given over to these three crops. Of total wages and salaries the sugar industry distributed 66 per cent. A structural imbalance in the resources allocated to these crops is indicated by the fact that the sugar industry only accounted for 44 per cent of export earnings, whereas land and labour accounted for roughly two-thirds of the resources allocated. Cane occupied twice the area given over to banana cultivation and the sugar industry distributed more than twice the percentage of salaries and wages: 66 per cent against 30 per cent. Additionally, since sugar involves an industrial process as well as an agricultural one, the amount of capital tied up in sugar is considerably greater than that employed in banana cultivation.

It is evident that these structural weaknesses in the sugar industry, as exemplified by the relatively low returns set against increasing overheads and high capital costs, have resulted in a progressive diversification by a number of Békés out of sugar into more valuable export crops. In analysing the crisis in the sugar industry in the 1960s, these structural aspects of the problem must be considered as being prior to other factors responsible for sugar's decline (which were operative in Barbados), namely, declining field efficiency and adverse weather conditions.

A progressively declining production throughout the period inevitably resulted in the closure of certain factories. Unlike Barbados where closure took place on the grounds of rationalization, closure in Martinique was the outcome of increasing indebtedness among factory owners. The financial situation of the six remaining *usines* in the mid-1960s indicates that all the survivors except Petit Bourg were operating at a loss (see Table 3).

In spite of the relatively healthy financial state of Petit Bourg in 1966, its situation by 1970 had appreciably worsened and the administrator of the factory was constrained to make the following announcement to the shareholders:

In order to prevent ourselves from getting deeper in debt I ask you to accept the closure of the factory, and the re-investment of part of our assets from the sale of capital equipment in France ...

TABLE 3

Financial Situation of the Usines Centrales, 1965/66

Usines	Debt/Liquidity at end of 1965 (francs)	Losses estimated for 1966 (francs)	Forecast of financial situation up to the end of 1966 (francs)
Galion-Bassignac	− 1,502,787	− 755,900	− 2,258,688
Lareinty-Lamentin	− 5,116,050	− 2,483,061	− 7,599,111
Marin	− 865,705	− 514,568	− 1,380,273
Petit Bourg	+ 1,385,906	− 721,216	+ 664,691
Rivière Salée	− 1,382,874	− 957,106	− 2,339,981
Sainte-Marie	− 2,430,636	− 1,410,421	− 3,841,057
Total debt	− 9,912,147	− 6,842,272	− 16,754,419

Source: Syndicat Général des Planteurs et Manipulateurs de Canne

It is evident that the financial situation of the factories deteriorated progressively as the total area under cane declined, since they were operating far below their capacity. Table 4 indicates the extent to which factories were operating below capacity in the early 1970s.

In an attempt to save the industry the French Government pumped a total of 157 million francs into sugar in the form of aid and cheap loans,[40] with the aim of stabilizing declining production at around 70,000 tonnes per year. By 1969 production

TABLE 4

Optimum Versus Actual Sugar Production in Martinique, 1972–74

Usines	Optimum Production (tonnes)	Actual Production (i) in tonnes and (ii) as a percentage of the optimum		
		1972	1973	1974
Sainte-Marie	16,800	668 3.9%	ceased production	
Galion	12,600	7,328 58.1%	9,358 74.2%	4,895 38%
Lareinty	16,800	6,422 38.2%	8,128 48.3%	9,512 56%
Rivière Salée	12,600	7,372 58.5%	5,457 43.3%	ceased production
All Martinique	58,800	21,790 37.0%	22,940 39.0%	14,407 24%

Source: Direction Départementale de l'Agriculture, Service Départementale de Statistique Agricole

was half what it had been a decade earlier, and the total area under cane had declined from 13,000 to 7,000 hectares. After a seven year programme of aid to revive the flagging sugar industry, production was further reduced to 14,000 tonnes in 1974. Today the surviving area under cane is utilized primarily in the rum industry, and Martinique has become an importer of refined beet sugar from metropolitan France.

ALTERNATIVE STRATEGIES FOR ECONOMIC DEVELOPMENT

The crisis in the sugar industry has not resulted in the demise of the economic elite in either island; rather it has led them to seek a wide range of alternative strategies to maintain their traditional economic mastery. Generally speaking, these strategies (of economic power maintenance) have involved the fragmentation of sugar estates and real estate speculation, crop diversification and diversification of capital into other sectors of the economy, such as tourism, commerce and agri-business. Structurally and ideologically the transition has been relatively easy, since as I have already argued, the economic elite in both cases is no longer a traditional planter class but an agri-business bourgeoisie, with long established, diverse business and planting interests.

In comparing the solutions adopted in each territory to the crisis, an important variable has been that of the structural situation of each island's elite. Unlike the Barbadian elite, the Békés have been successful in promoting bananas as an alternative crop of high export value comparable to that of sugar.[41] The Békés have been equally successful at commercializing the production of other crops, notably pineapples, avocadoes, aubergines and citrus, showing great flexibility in crop diversification by switching rapidly from one crop to another as market conditions change. Their response to crop diversification has had an inimical effect upon the Martiniquan economy, since it is essentially short-term and opportunistic, being limited to quick returns in a fluctuating market.[42]

One vitally important aspect of their success has been the strategic role they play in determining economic policy, through the Five Year Development Plan Commissions for overseas departments. As members of the Commission for Agriculture, Forestry and Fisheries, they are in effect responsible for deciding their own agricultural policies.[43] It might appear to be an over-simplification to view the decline of the sugar economy in the late 1960s as the outcome of a conscious attempt by the Békés systematically to run down the sugar industry, notwithstanding official French policy to revive flagging production. Their strategic role in the formulation of economic policy, however, seems to have given them the opportunity to maximize their returns in other areas, particularly where foreknowledge of subsidies and aid for other export crops was concerned. Arising out of the aid programme to increase and stabilize sugar production, an official commission was ordered to look into the administration of the loans and subsidies advanced by the French Government. An official report was never published. However, it was revealed by a leak in official sources that factories, distilleries and planters had been involved in a gross misuse of public funds, utilizing cheap loans to finance their commercial activities and to develop the production of other crops. In spite of the embarrassment caused by this disclosure, or perhaps even because of it, no action was taken by the authorities.

From the late 1960s onwards attempts by the Barbadian elite at crop diversification have been less successful, and in agriculture sugar still predominates. Lacking the influence of the Békés and the strategically powerful position they occupy in the administration, their success in other areas of agricultural production has been limited. Continuing dependence in agriculture upon an industry which has progressively declined into the 1980s does not appear to be a good strategy for economic survival. Recent production figures indicate a continuing decline well below 100,000 tonnes. This progressive downward trend means that production is now less than half of what it was during the peak years of the mid-1960s.

Paralleled by this decline in production is a decline in the area under cane and the acreage reaped, a process which has continued into the 1980s. This process (which I have already referred to above) highlights a serious problem in a country of scarce land resources, since it is irreversible. It also highlights that the Barbadian elite in different ways have also practised a similar policy of contraction in the sugar industry. Elsewhere,[44] I have described a process of land speculation in the 1960s and 1970s in which whole estates were sub-divided into two, four, six and eight acre lots, and others were much reduced in size by partial fragmentation.[45] In some respects the sale of land for either smallholdings or house spots can be regarded partly as an attempt to rationalize the sugar industry during a cycle of drought, rising production costs and imminent mechanization. In many cases unproductive land and terrain not susceptible to mechanical reaping had been portioned off into house spots. However, large tracts of prime agricultural land were also fragmented for building purposes, which indicates an uncertainty about the future of sugar and a need to channel capital into other areas of investment.

Another consequence of the decline of sugar has been the transfer of capital tied up in the industry into the commercial sector. The substantial diversification of the holdings of the 'Big Six's' parent company, Barbados Shipping and Trading, in the 1960s and 1970s, which was faciliated by the sale of its sugar interests, has given the agri-business bourgeoisie the opportunity to diversify its assets to an even greater extent than ever before. Indicative of the extent to which it divested itself of its sugar interests, is the wide range of new businesses acquired by Barbados Shipping and Trading in the retail grocery trade, clothing and manufacturing, automobile sales, property invest-ment, agricultural machinery and the recording industry. With the expansion of the airport it has also acquired considerable investments in an air freight company, Seawell Air Service Ltd. As a measure of its growth during this critical period, a reflection of the economic growth and diversification of Barbados away from a 'pure plantation economy', the authorized share capital of the corporation has increased fourfold: from three million dollars in 1960 to twelve million dollars in the mid-1970s.[46]

Of comparable importance to the switch to banana culti-vation in Martinique has been the commercialization of the tourist industry. A statistical analysis reveals a strong correlation between the decline of the sugar industry in the 1960s and the rapid growth of tourism in the latter half of the decade. Barbados Shipping and Trading's entry into the retail distributive trade sector and property investment coincided with the growth of tourism. Both these sectors can be considered tourist related, since their larger investments are to be found in major areas of tourist development in Christ Church and St James. Now with an annual average tourist intake larger than the population size itself, tourism has long since superseded sugar as the island's major source of export earnings, and sugar now accounts for less than 8 per cent of the annual average.

During the 1960s the Békés sunk a total of thirty million francs into the tourist industry, and channelled further assets into the retail distributive trade sector. During the first half of the 1970s the value of imports into Martinique more than doubled.[47] Related to a progressive increase in imports during this period, is the effect of the French Government's delay in putting into effect the full measures of equality of Martinique with the metropolis, as laid down by the Law of Assimilation of 19 March 1946.[48] Forms of economic discrimination which have persisted for a long time after assimilation should have taken effect from January 1948, such as the guaranteeing of minimum salaries and wages and the granting of full welfare rights, have only recently been removed. In response to the increased purchasing power that these measures represent, the Békés in the 1970s have established large retail outlets in the central shopping area of Fort-de-France, and in the new commercial complexes of the *cités* on the periphery of the capital.

Another effect of the decline of the sugar economy has been the 'flight' of capital overseas, a process which paralleled the closure of sugar factories in the late 1960s and early 1970s. Data exists on the transfer of funds to metropolitan France,[49] but it is far from comprehensive, since there are also large outflows of capital entering Latin America and other European countries. For example, Békés have invested in the manufacturing sector in Venezuela and Colombia, and investments in property have been made in Switzerland and the South of France. Reliable informants in commerce and banking have indicated that some seven or eight Grand Béké families also have large cash deposits banked in other Caribbean islands, such as Puerto Rico, Bermuda and the Bahamas.

CONCLUSION

From the cases examined above, it can be seen that local elites played a decisive role in producing a unique variant of the more general direction taken by the West Indian sugar industry in modern times. In acting as a bulwark against the incursion of metropolitan monopoly finance capital, the heirs of the slave owning plantocracy provided an element of historical continuity in these islands, since their continuing control over the sugar economy ensured the survival of white economic supremacy. Thus the history of the sugar industry in nineteenth and twentieth century Barbados and Martinique has been inextricably bound up with the struggle of a social group to survive, the ownership of land and productive resources being prerequisites for maintaining intact traditional social and economic structures. In the contemporary period from the 1960s onwards, the decline of the sugar economy has illustrated in a similar fashion the way in which the future of the industry has been closely bound up with the fact of survival, through each group's pursuit of purely sectoral interests.

Although survival and continuity are key themes throughout the period, it is evident that the composition of the white economic elite is not immutable. Firstly, during a critical period in the late nineteenth century, the planter class was transformed, and only a sector of this class survived to occupy an economically dominant position in the twentieth century. Secondly, the composition of the elite has undergone more recent further change. In Martinique the switch from sugar to bananas has resulted in the elevation of a number of Békés Moyens, who, having seized the opportunities afforded by the commercialization of banana production over the past twenty-five years, have now been incorporated into the dominant planter/mercantile class. In Barbados a similar process of social mobility has taken place within the white creole social structure, in which numbers of white plantation supervisory staff have risen in the social hierarchy to form a new entrepreneurial class: operating construction and plant hire companies and garages, owning tourist properties, speculating in real estate and manufacturing cement, paint and agro-chemicals.

Three events are of crucial importance in the Barbadian context when considering the recent history of the agri-business bourgeoisie: the granting of universal suffrage in 1951, the abolition of the Vestry System in 1959 (the planters' power base in local government) and independence in 1966. Refusal to accept the consequences of political change led to the departure from the island of a number of prominent families between the early 1950s and early 1970s, and the sale in many cases of estate land to members of the upwardly mobile new entrepreneurial class, less ideologically committed to the cultivation of sugar. In Martinique the collapse of the sugar industry and the subsequent re-investment of capital overseas have resulted in the departure of members of the Grand Béké elite. Under the present quota system providing a secure market through the EEC, it is not feasible to increase banana production, and this has tended to further increase the numbers of Békés leaving the island to invest their capital elsewhere. Additionally another process is under way which is serving to decrease even further these minorities, and that is the tendency for the younger generation increasingly to seek vocational and professional training overseas and to settle permanently away from home.

NOTES

1. 'List of sugar plantations' in *The Barbados Almanac and Diary for the Year 1888.*
2. The Act was initially adopted by St Vincent and Tobago in 1854, and over a period of thirteen years the local assemblies of eight other territories had voted in favour of adopting it: the Virgin Islands and St Kitts (1860), Jamaica (1861), Antigua (1864), Montserrat (1865), Grenada (1866), and Dominica and Nevis (1867). See R. W. Beachey, *The British West Indies Sugar Industry in the Nineteenth Century* (Oxford, 1957), Ch. 1.
3. *Ibid.* p. 127.
4. The creole term 'Béké' can be employed in two different senses according to the context in which it is used: (a) in a strict sense whereby persons are not defined exclusively by a racial co-ordinate. Here it applies only to white Martiniquans belonging to the dominant landowning/mercantile class (i.e. Grands Békés). (b) In a more general sense which does refer to race. In this second sense 'Béké' is synonymous with being white, and a complex terminology is evoked which points to the existence of a highly differentiated white social substructure.
5. Alain Buffon, *Monnaie et Crédit en Economie Coloniale: Contribution à l'Histoire Economique de la Guadeloupe, 1635–1919* (Basse Terre, 1979), p. 267.
6. E. Légier, *La Martinique et la Guadeloupe. Considérations Economiques sur l'Avenir et la Culture de la Canne, la Production de Sucre et du Rhum et les Cultures Secondaires dans les Antilles Françaises* (Paris, 1905), p. 147.
7. Repeated attempts by the plantocracy to modernize sugar mills in the nineteenth century by the introduction of equipment manufactured by the French firm Derosne et Cail, foundered upon insufficient capital and the lack of suitable labour, see Manuel Moreno Fraginals, *The Sugarmill: The Socio-Economic Complex of Sugar in Cuba* (New York, 1976), pp. 81–127.

8. Puerto Rican *hacendados* made repeated attempts to establish central sugar factories between 1876 and 1899, but most of these attempts failed due to lack of capital. In his study of Hacienda Vieja, Sidney Mintz describes how land in Cañamelar was sold or rented to American corporations in the early twentieth century, planters moving to urban centres to live on rents and interest from re-invested capital. See his *Caribbean Transformations* (Chicago, 1974), pp. 95–130.

9. Hugh Thomas, *Cuba or the Pursuit of Freedom* (London, 1971), pp. 536–56.

10. Truman Clark, *Puerto Rico and the United States, 1917–1933* (Pittsburgh, 1975), p. 107.

11. A. Adamson, *Sugar Without Slaves: The Political Economy of British Guiana, 1838–1904* (New Haven, 1972), Ch. 5.

12. Jean Benoist, 'Types de Plantations et Groupes Sociaux à la Martinique', *Cahiers des Amériques Latines*, Vol. 2, 1968, pp. 130–59.

13. Under this system, sugar proprietors acquired plantation supplies on credit from an English merchant. A planter's crop would then be automatically consigned to the same merchant who would arrange for its sale on the English market. After the sale of the crop, the consignee made deductions on the planter's account for supplies shipped to the estate on credit and duly charged his commission.

14. Richard Pares, 'A London West Indian Merchant House, 1740–1769' in R. Pares and A. J. P. Taylor (eds.), *Essays Presented to Sir Lewis Namier* (London, 1956), p. 100.

15. Anthony Trollope, *The West Indies and the Spanish Main* (London, 1859; reprinted Frank Cass, 1968), p. 121.

16. Between 1840 and 1920, out of a sample of 600 cases of debt foreclosure, in only 18 cases was the plaintiff an English merchant. See Barbados Archives, *Index of Estates in Chancery*.

17. Jean Crusol, 'La Martinique, économie de plantation: survol historique', *Les Cahiers du Cerag* No. 28, 1973, p. 9.

18. Unlike the English system mortagees did not have the power to bring an encumbered estate to sale in the open market. Property under Barbadian law could only be disposed of by the Chancery Court. An encumbered sugar estate had to be given the chance to work off its debts before outright disposal was reverted to. Theoretically an estate in chancery which paid off all its debts during a twelve month period reverted back to its original owner.

19. By 1897 roughly one-third of the sugar estates in Barbados were supported in this way. *West India Royal Commission, 1897 Appendix C. Volume II, C. 8657.*

20. It is noteworthy to compare the speed with which the French government acted, in 1860, to the need for some kind of measure to meet the threat of competition from sugar beet after the enactment of Free Trade legislation, with Chamberlain's attitude to the request in 1896 for a loan to construct central factories in Barbados: 'As at present advised ... I am opposed to any loan of government money except upon absolute security, and do not consider either land, machinery or buildings absolute security in a colony where all values depend upon the sugar industry ...'. Extract of a despatch for the Secretary of State to the Governor of Barbados, dated 29/12/1896 in *Official Gazette*, 18/2/1897.

21. Barbados was granted £80,000 for modernizing the sugar industry under the Plantations-In-Aid Acts. This sum was subsequently used to capitalize the Sugar Industry Agricultural Bank in 1907, from which loans were made to planters and merchants at an interest.

22. *Letter dated September 8th 1860, sent by the Minister of Colonial Affairs to the Minister of Agriculture, Commerce and Public Works* (Archives D'Outre-Mer, Général C32 D265).

23. The Crédit Colonial was renamed the Crédit Foncier Colonial in 1863 and its capital increased from three to twelve million francs.

24. 'List of sugar plantations' in *The Barbados Almanac and Diary for the Year 1888*.

25. Barbados Archives, Barbados Chancery Court, *Chancery Sales Ledgers: 1879–1885, 1885–1893, 1894–1901, 1901–1904, 1900–1956*.

26. An interesting facet of the white elite's economic power consolidation was the existence of a system of sponsored social mobility for poor whites, which effectively squeezed out both black and Jewish businessmen from the Bridgetown commercial world. By the early twentieth century no black or coloured merchants of any prominence were to be found in Bridgetown, nor were there any of the older Portuguese Jewish names featured among those of the elite. On the other hand many 'redleg' merchants prospered considerably during the 1920s and 1930s, and gained admission to the ranks of the agri-business bourgeoisie.

27. The six largest commercial houses in Bridgetown: Manning's, Gardiner Austin, Da Costa's, Musson's, Challenor's and Wilkinson and Haynes. In 1920 this powerful combine of commercial and trading interests was consolidated under the umbrella of a parent company, Barbados Shipping and Trading.

28. From fieldwork data the evidence suggests that the 'closure' of both groups is not related directly to ethnocentrism, but to the fact of institutionalized power. I would therefore argue that closure is based more upon the historical fact of the white creole elite's superordinate position in the structural distribution of wealth, power and esteem, which has nothing to do with notions of cultural and biological superiority.

29. An exception to this is to be found in the case of non-white groups of 'Grands Mulâtres' in Martinique, who in terms of wealth and financial interests can be ranked alongside the Béké agri-business bourgeoisie. However, compared with the Grands Békés, their share of business interests is quite small, probably less than 10 per cent.

30. Namely Antigua, Barbados, St Kitts, Guyana, Jamaica and Trinidad.

31. The earliest of these achievements is connected with the work of Professor D'Albuquerque, who carried out manurial trials in the 1860s which led to the importation of guano, and to experimentation with sulphate of ammonia and nitrate of soda in the 1880s. In the late 1920s Sir John Saint successfully carried out mulch and fertilizer trials, in an attempt to find an alternative to pen manure. Allied to these advances was the important contribution made by the intro-duction of disease-resistant varieties of cane in the 1920s, 1930s and 1940s, by Bovell, McIntosh and Harrison.

32. Government of Barbados, *Report of an Inquiry into the Sugar Industry of Barbados*, compiled by R. F. McKenzie (October 1958), p. 1.

33. Public Records Office, *West India Royal Commission, 1938–39*. C.O. 950/938.

34. Barbados Shipping and Trading Co. Ltd., *Reports and Accounts: 1964–1970*.

35. Barbados Statistical Service, *Financial Statistics: 1964–1974*; and Central Bank of Barbados, *Annual Reports: 1975–1977*.

36. These more recent production figures, gleaned from a variety of sources, were supplied by Raymond Norris, former Secretary of the Sugar Association of the Caribbean.

37. In order to counteract the incidence of malicious 'uncontrolled' cane fires which became an increasing problem in the late 1960s, the Barbados Sugar Producers'

Association introduced 'controlled' burning in 1970. 'Controlled' burning was abandoned in 1975, since it reduced the fertility of the fields and caused a diminution of the sucrose content of the cane reaped.

38. J. F. Ferré, *La Canne à Sucre. Les Industries de Sucre et du Rhum à la Martinique: Evolution contemporaine (1950–1974)* (Bordeaux, 1976), p. 36.

39. Syndicat des Planteurs et Manipulateurs de la Canne de la Martinique, *Note Succinte Sur L'Economie Sucrière et Rhumière de la Martinique en 1960*.

40. Direction Départementale de l'Agriculture, *Files on Agricultural Policy*; and Préfecture de la Martinique, *Fonds d'Investissement pour les Départements D'Outre-Mer*.

41. In the north of the island from the inland communes of Saint-Joseph and Gros-Morne to the communes on the Atlantic coast of Marigot, Lorrain, Sainte-Marie, Trinité and Robert, 1,000 hectares were converted from sugar to banana production between 1960 and 1970. In the coastal communes the area under cane halved between 1963 and 1971, 700 hectares being converted into banana estates.

42. This kind of response by the Békés has been analysed and criticized in the following document: *Livre Vert de l'Agriculture Martiniquaise* (Fort-de-France, Chambre Départementale d'Agriculture, 1977).

43. When subsidies were made available in 1975 for aubergine and citrus cultivation, many Békés had already ploughed up cane land and abandoned pineapple cultivation in response to the new opportunities offered by such measures.

44. Michal Allen, 'Sugar and Survival: The Retention of Economic Power by White Elites in Barbados and Martinique' in M. Cross and A. Marks (eds.), *Peasants, Plantations and Rural Communities in the Caribbean* (Leiden, 1979), pp. 220–62.

45. As a result since 1960 120 estates went completely out of production, representing an estimated 19,500 acres.

46. Barbados Shipping and Trading Co. Ltd., *Reports and Accounts: 1960–1977*.

47. Institut D'Emission des Départements D'Outre-Mer, *Rapports D'Activités, 1971–76*.

48. Under the Law of Assimilation the former colonies of Martinique, Guadeloupe, French Guiana and Réunion were accorded the new status of *départements*. After 1 Jan. 1948, all laws and decrees operative in metropolitan France were applied to those overseas *départements*, thus putting them (theoretically at least) upon an equal footing with the metropolitan *départements*.

49. See Institut D'Emission des Départements D'Outre-Mer, *Rapports D'Activités, 1971–76*.

The Sugar Protocol of the Lomé Conventions and the Caribbean*

PAUL SUTTON

When the first Lomé Convention was signed on February 28, 1975, between the 46 states of Africa, the Caribbean and the Pacific (ACP) on the one hand and the nine member states of the European Economic Community (EEC) on the other, there was concluded alongside it, and intimately related to it, a Sugar Protocol granting named countries access to the EEC for specified quantities of sugar for an indefinite period at a guaranteed price. The chief concern of this chapter is with the operation of this Protocol in the interests of the sugar producing countries of the Caribbean. In the nature of things this largely concerns the Commonwealth Caribbean (and within this specifically Jamaica, Trinidad and Tobago, Guyana, Barbados, Belize and St Kitts – Nevis), although it also necessarily considers at the margin the effects of the Protocol on Suriname and the French Antilles. Conversely, in its European focus it is the attitude of Britain which is all important and is considered at greatest length, with just the occasional foray into other European dimensions.

BACKGROUND: THE OFFER OF ASSOCIATION AND THE SAFEGUARD FOR SUGAR

In his opening statement on the negotiations for British entry into the EEC made on June 30, 1970, Anthony Barber, the then British minister chiefly concerned, emphasised there were a number of issues for which satisfactory solutions would have to be found: 'our main problem', he said, 'concerns certain matters of agricultural policy; our contribution to the community budgetary expenditure; Commonwealth sugar exports;

New Zealand's special problems; and certain other Common-wealth questions'.[1] From the beginning sugar was thus an element conditioning British attitudes to the EEC as well as one of direct and crucial interest in the Commonwealth sugar producing countries themselves.

The 'crucial interest' arose from notice given by Britain at the end of 1968 that should it enter the EEC it could not be held to its contractual obligations under the Commonwealth Sugar Agreement (CSA) beyond 31 December, 1974. This spelt potential disaster for the high cost Commonwealth Caribbean sugar producers who viewed the CSA as the foundation of their sugar industry. This arose from a commitment by Britain under the agreement to import annually 1,750,000 tons of sugar (745,500 of which were from the Commonwealth Caribbean) at prices 'reasonably remunerative to efficient producers' (which in the case of the Commonwealth Caribbean permitted premium payments of £4 sterling per ton). Against this was set the prospect of a sugar regime in the EEC which regularly produced large surpluses derived from beet sugar and in which the only cane sugar allowed privileged entry was from the Départements d'Outre-Mer (DOM) of France who occupied, by virtue of their département status, a unique position within the EEC, and from Suriname, then classed as a dependent territory of the Netherlands.[2]

The British and Commonwealth Caribbean dimension of this problem was quickly clarified by a meeting of ministers of some Commonwealth Caribbean states with Geoffrey Rippon (Britain's new chief negotiator) in September 1970, and con-firmed for Britain by a visit made to the Caribbean by Rippon in February 1971. This saw the future of the region as best secured in the case of the Associated States and other dependent territories by association under Part IV of the Treaty of Rome and in the case of the independent Commonwealth Caribbean by seeking a form of associate status not unlike that available under the Yaoundé Convention.[3] However, while the EEC could have no quarrel with the first proposition their attitude on the second was, to say the least, ambiguous. Although they continued to offer associate status to the Commonwealth African states in line with the Declaration of Intent issued in July 1963, they were not now prepared to extend it to the

Commonwealth Caribbean as well. The reason given was sugar, which was seen as complicating the issue and requiring a solution in its own right prior to any offer of association with the EEC. The difference finally came to a head in the EEC ministerial meeting of March 15/16, 1971 when Rippon, drawing on his recent visit to the Caribbean, argued strongly that it would be a 'gigantic blunder' if British entry into the EEC produced economic and political chaos in these countries as a direct consequence of any failure to ensure access to Europe for their sugar.[4] Although this argument was to persuade several, especially Malfatti, then president of the EEC, the French significantly remained unmoved. It thus required a Franco-British summit between Heath and Pompidou on May 8, and a French proposal a few days later offering to the Caribbean and Pacific an association equivalent to the African countries, for any forward momentum to be recorded. Finally, on May 12, Rippon extracted from the EEC a commitment 'to have at heart the interests of those countries whose economies depend to a considerable degree on exports of primary products, notably sugar'.[5] This was then retailed to the House of Commons on May 17 and approved at a subsequent ministerial meeting of Commonwealth sugar producing countries on June 2/3. The communiqué issued at the end of these discussions summarized the 'achievements' to date:

The governments represented (United Kingdom, Antigua, Barbados, Fiji, Guyana, India, Jamaica, Kenya, Mauritius, Swaziland, Trinidad and Tobago, Uganda, St Kitts–Nevis–Anguilla and British Honduras) expressed their satisfaction at the Community's readiness to offer the governments concerned a choice of forms of association or a trading agreement; and also at the readiness to recognise the United Kingdom's contractual commitments to all the CSA member countries up to the end of 1974.

They noted that, in negotiations with the enlarged Community on association or trading agreements, it would be open to the governments concerned to act individually or collectively. They further noted the negotiations were due to be concluded by 1975, and that pending conclusion their existing patterns of trade with the United Kingdom would be maintained.

There was a full discussion of the Community's offer on sugar after 1974. The British delegation assured other delegations that the Community's proposals constituted a specific and moral commitment by the enlarged Community, of which the United Kingdom would be a part. The

British Government and other Commonwealth Governments participating regarded this offer as a firm assurance of a secure and continuing market in the enlarged Community on fair terms for the quantities of sugar covered by the Commonwealth Sugar Agreement in respect of all its existing developing member countries. The developing Commonwealth countries will continue to plan their future on this basis.[6]

The 'guarantee' of this 'understanding' and the starting point for subsequent negotiation was Protocol 22 annexed to the Treaty of Accession signed on 22 January, 1972. It not only offered three forms of association – (a) association under a new 'convention of association' on the expiry of Yaoundé II'; (b) some other form of association on the basis of article 238 of the Treaty of Rome; or (c) a commercial agreement – but, of direct relevance to sugar, stated in its final paragraph:

The Community will have as its firm purpose the safeguarding of the interests of all countries referred to in this Protocol whose economies depend to a considerable extent on the export of primary products, and particularly of sugar. The question of sugar will be settled within this framework, bearing in mind, with regard to exports of sugar, the importance of the product for the economies of several of these countries, and of the Commonwealth countries in particular.[7]

THE NEGOTIATION OF THE PROTOCOL

The negotiation of the Protocol was an exceedingly tortuous and complex affair involving, as one authoritative study has noted, no less than four distinct, though interrelated, levels of policy-making: 'the sectoral level of the EC's internal sugar regime, the broader political level arising from the commitment of principle made during the British accession negotiations, the added complication of British renegotiation which partly explained the particular response to the British sugar shortage of 1974, and the international negotiations to include a sugar protocol in the EC-ACP trade and talks'.[8] As the story is well known, in this section only the main points of interest are summarized.

Negotiation of the EEC Sugar Regime

The common organisation of the EEC sugar market was introduced in July 1968. This sought to establish by means of quotas for which markets and prices were guaranteed, a degree of protection for EEC beet growers and a measure of self-sufficiency for sugar in the Europe of the six. In the case of the former protection meant an intervention price in 1971/72 of £95.72 per ton (well above both the world price and that paid to the CSA producers) for 6,480,000 tonnes of sugar, plus a further guarantee of a market at a reduced price for an additional 2,050,000 tonnes. As this total was above production in that year of 8,071,000 tonnes and well above total consumption of 6,325,000 tonnes, it meant, in effect, that the EEC was a net exporter of 1.7 million tonnes of sugar. It was this situation which the EEC Commission sought to remedy with its Memorandum of July 12, 1973.[9] Three measures were envisaged: (i) in the spirit of Protocol 22 to import 1.4 million tonnes of cane sugar into the EEC; (ii) to participate in a new International Sugar Agreement (ISA) with an export quota of 800,000 tonnes; (iii) to limit basic quota beet production to 8.4 million tonnes in a Europe of the nine, this being equivalent to the difference between expected consumption in 1975/1976 of 9.8 million tonnes less the 1.4 million tonnes import commitment. This final provision immediately encountered hostile reaction from the Conféderation Internationale des Betteraviers Européens (CIBE) representing the national beet producers' associations, backed by France and to a lesser degree West Germany, Belgium and Italy. Such opposition meant revised proposals would be needed and these were brought forward in July 1974. They were tabled in a new context of instability and incipient shortage in the world sugar market and followed a meeting of the CIBE and the Commonwealth Sugar Exporters Association (CSEA) in June 1974 where the 'war of two sugars' was temporarily set aside in an agreement in which:

the European sugar beet growers agreed that in return for support from the EEC sugar lobby for guaranteed access to the Community and for the sugar negotiations being kept separate from the ACP talks on re-negotiating the Yaoundé Convention (a philosophy not always shared by the European Commission), the Commonwealth exporters would not object to EEC producers being allowed to export unlimited quantities on to the world market. Should the world situation make restrictions necessary, these would only be envisaged as part of an international agreement.[10]

Accordingly, the Commission now recommended marginal increases in quotas and total abandonment of any physical limitation on production, alongside a commitment to import 1.4 million tonnes of cane sugar.[11] The matter then passed to ministers meeting in the Agricultural Council in October, 1974, where the new sugar regime was to all intents and purposes finally decided. This envisaged a further increase in basic quotas to reach 9.136 million tonnes, with a generous provision in the first instance for a market guarantee of additional sugar to total in 1975/1976 some 13.25 million tonnes.[12] A significant increase in EEC beet sugar production was therefore encouraged. The price system as applied under the 1968 regulation was to remain with its built-in 'insurance' element for beet growers should prices on the world market fall dramatically.

British Re-negotiation and World Sugar Shortage

In December 1971 agreement was reached under the CSA for a negotiated price for the years 1972, 1973 and 1974 of £61 sterling per ton f.o.b. for sugar from the West Indies and Guyana. This price appeared to confirm yet again for the Commonwealth sugar producers the advantage of the CSA over the ISA given the London 'free market' daily price prevailing throughout 1971 of around £40 sterling per ton. This advantage was not, however, to continue as a variety of factors – poor harvests in sugar producing countries, unanticipated increases in consumption in Europe, and the onset of world inflation – pushed world prices upward in 1973, thereby turning a benefit into a liability and leading to calls from the Commonwealth Caribbean sugar producers (the Caribbean Cane Farmers Association and the West Indian Sugar Association) for new negotiations and a new price with Britain. In February 1974 this was conceded and a price of £83 sterling per ton agreed for the remainder of the CSA. In the event it turned out to be no more than a holding operation. To put pressure on the British government for the February increase several Caribbean sugar producers had already banned exports or stopped shipments to Britain[13] and trade diversion to the United States and non-traditional buyers gathered momentum as sugar prices escalated. For an incoming Labour government, and especially one pledged to re-negotiate terms of entry into the EEC, this proved an acute embarrassment at home and in Brussels. In the case of the former, security of supply and optimum use of existing refinery facilities dictated large quotas and high prices for cane sugar producers whilst, in the case of the latter, guaranteed access to a protected and now potentially financially rewarding beet sugar market required the exact opposite. The screw was turned still further in August 1974 when Guyana refused to complete shipments of sugar until another increase in price was agreed, this time to £140 sterling per ton. Even this price, however, was still below world market prices which were to reach an all time high in November 1974 of £650 sterling per ton. By then, however, the price was largely academic to the British government, for in the meantime it had secured an agreement from the EEC to buy sugar to meet Britain's immediate needs at world market prices and subsidize it for sale on the British market at internal EEC prices. Undoubtedly a successful and expedient short term measure as far as all parties were concerned, its longer-term effects were somewhat more negative, especially for the cane sugar producers, since it heralded the destruction of the 'gentleman's club' atmostphere which was held to be so conspicuous a feature of the workings of the CSA.

Negotiation of Lomé I and the Protocol

When the Seventh Heads of Commonwealth Caribbean Governments Conference met in Trinidad in October 1972 they considered among their deliberations a memorandum containing the unanimous views of everyone connected with the Commonwealth Caribbean sugar industry – cane farmers, sugar manufacturers and workers. In the memorandum reasons were advanced to separate the sugar negotiations from other negotiations with the EEC and to support the developing view that there should be a Commonwealth Caribbean approach to the wider negotiations within an even broader Commonwealth approach.[14] This was substantially accepted and further confirmed in March 1973 when a second meeting was held at Lancaster House between Britain and the Commonwealth countries seeking 'association' with the EEC. At this Britain once again confirmed its commitment to the Commonwealth sugar producers and machinery was set in motion to formulate a position on sugar in the negotiations. It was eventually to take

the form of an *aide-mémoire* of 24 April 1973 which was
subsequently presented to the EEC and 'in which the position
of the developing Commonwealth countries was made abundantly clear'.[15] For its part the EEC Commission, in its Memorandum of July 12, as already noted, referred to a purchase
guarantee of 1.4 million tonnes and proposed that a 'reference
price' should be discussed on the basis of the price being
negotiated at the time for the CSA. Thereafter matters appear
to have stalled until mid-1974. That they did so is not a reflection
on the sugar negotiations *per se* but arose from the fact that
while the Commonwealth sugar producers might have wished
that their negotiations be parallel to those for association, in
practice it was not possible to separate them, largely because
the same set of protagonists were involved in both and because
several Commonwealth Caribbean political figures were taking
a leading part in the discussions. It was not, then, until a 'break-
through' was achieved in the wider discussions in July 1974 that
any progress could be recorded – and by then, of course, it
was in the favourable context for the Commonwealth sugar
producers of the world sugar market in turmoil. This latter
aspect was incorporated, in part, in the new Commission
proposals of July 1974 which have already been considered. It
meant, in effect, little disagreement over the size of the quota
from the developing Commonwealth sugar exporting states and
the figure, of 1.345 million tonnes for white sugar (equivalent
to 1.4 million tonnes for raw sugar), was agreed at the meeting
of Foreign Ministers of the EEC in November 1974. The EEC
also agreed, without too much difficulty, a guarantee of access
for at least seven years in recognition of the extended production
cycle for sugar cane growers.

The problem lay with price. The proposals put forward by
the Commission in the revised Memorandum suggested taking
two reference points: on the one hand, prices then in force under
the CSA and, on the other, the lowest intervention price
applicable inside the EEC. In October 1974 there was initially
no difference between these prices – the CSA price at £140 per
ton and the EC threshold price at £140 per tonne – the real
difference existing between these prices and a world price of
£385 per tonne.[16] Such a price was, however, far above the
price the EEC would give to its own producers and on the

principle of no price discrimination in favour of third country producers the EEC was virtually united. It thus became clear that any guaranteed price which would emerge would be negotiated within the prices applied in the EEC. At the same time, and in recognition of the extraordinary circumstances then prevailing, the EEC accepted that prices paid for sugar in the market could be higher, subject to free negotiations between buyer and seller; and that Britain, in order to secure supplies, could extend a national subsidy.[17] On this basis prices were finally settled in the early part of 1975 though not until the very last moment. At this juncture the Commonwealth Caribbean countries, by virtue of their delivery periods being in the first half of the year, had a particular advantage and exploited it to the full. From the EEC they were able to extract a guaranteed price of £150 sterling per tonne (as against what was being asked at £180 per tonne) and from Britain, where negotiations almost broke down being rescued at the last minute only by the dispatch to London of the Chairman of the Sugar group, Sir Ratu Mara, a 'final' offer of £260 sterling per ton for twelve months (as against what was being asked at £283 per ton for eighteen months).[18] With the addition of special quotas for the period to July 1975 (of which the Commonwealth Caribbean secured 62%) the Protocol was finally agreed twelve hours after the Lomé Convention itself was settled. The linkage was explicit, summed up in a comment accredited to an African diplomat: 'If sugar did not exist, or if certain ACP countries did not produce it, perhaps there would have been no Lomé Convention'.[19]

THE TERMS OF THE PROTOCOL

The specific provisions concerning sugar are in Title II, Chapter II, of the Lomé Conventions. Under the terms of Article 15 the implementing arrangements of this article are laid down in Protocol No. 3 annexed to the First Convention (and repeated unchanged as Protocol No. 7 in the Second). The agreement is based on three elements:[20]

(a) *The principle of a mutual purchasing/supply commitment for an indefinite period.* Unlike the Lomé Convention itself which was concluded for a period of five years only, the Sugar Protocol was concluded for an indefinite period, subject to denunciation after five years but then only after giving two years' notice of intention to do so. Security of supply for the EEC and of purchase for the ACP was thus guaranteed for seven years. At the same time, however, provision was made for review before the end of the seventh year of application. A further unique feature of the Protocol as against the Convention proper is that the safeguard clause set out in Article 10 of the Convention for all other products does not apply to sugar. The EEC therefore cannot plead disruption within its own sugar sector as grounds for reducing access as guaranteed under the Protocol.

(b) *Agreed quantities.* Article 3 lays down the 'agreed quantities', that is the quantities which have to be supplied in each 'delivery period' (from July 1 to June 30 of the following year) for the ACP countries of the Commonwealth Caribbean as follows: (expressed in tonnes of white sugar) Barbados — 49,300; Guyana — 157,700; Jamaica — 118,300; Trinidad and Tobago — 69,000. For the relevant Overseas Countries and Territories (OCT), i.e. the then dependent territories, the quotas were as follows: St Kitts—Nevis — 14,800; Belize — 39,400; Suriname — 4,000. The Commonwealth Caribbean was thus to secure a guaranteed quota of 448,500 tonnes — only just over half that permitted under the CSA.[21] This, however, was deliberate, the general strategy at the time being to maximise sugar earnings in a buoyant market by selling a greater proportion of sugar on the world market than heretofore. In return for access of 'agreed quantities' the sugar producers had to concede a penalty in the event of non-delivery. That is, for default other than for *force majeure* a state is liable to have its guaranteed quota reduced for each subsequent delivery period by the undelivered quantity. The Commission then has the option of redistributing the shortfall among the other suppliers after consultation with the states concerned (Article 7).

(c) *A guaranteed price.* The Protocol provides for a minimum price guarantee to be negotiated annually within the range of prices operative in the EEC. It must be at least equivalent to the EEC intervention price and should be decided at the latest by May 1 immediately preceding the delivery period to which it will apply. As laid out in the Protocol two prices are quoted — for raw sugar and for white sugar — and refer to sugar of standard quality, c.i.f., unpacked at European ports.

Much has been made of the fact that the price is a guarantee only and that the Protocol specifies that sugar shall be marketed at prices freely negotiated between buyers and sellers. In practice this means a price determined in negotiations with Tate and Lyle, the sole British cane sugar refiner. An example of this is that whereas the Protocol laid down a price for the period February 1, 1975 to June 30, 1976 of 255.3 units of account (EUA) per tonne the reality was that the entire quota had already been bought by Britain at a price of £260 sterling per ton (corresponding to 500 EUA per tonne), i.e. almost double the price guaranteed.

THE OPERATION OF THE PROTOCOL

An EEC view of the Protocol in 1983 was that it constituted 'an excellent scheme, in terms of both the volumes involved and as the condition for guaranteeing prices'.[22] This generous interpretation was also confirmed by the foremost expert on sugar in the Commission's Development Division, Albert Te Pass, in his comment that the Protocol 'has functioned well, by and large'[23] and so may be taken as the prevailing view within Europe at this time. It is not one shared by the ACP and particularly by the Commonwealth Caribbean figures who have had to deal directly with the issue. Thus while Oliver Jackman, Ambassador of Barbados to the EEC and until recently chairman of the ACP Committee of Ambassadors, concedes that 'in a number of respects the protocol has worked relatively well', the tone of his comment is generally critical.[24] So also have been those of S.R. Insanally, until recently Ambassador of Guyana to the EEC, and Dr James O'Neil Lewis, Ambassador of Trinidad and Tobago to the EEC from June 1973 to December 1982. Given the latter's length of service his comments deserve particular consideration:

The ACP states had hoped that the better features of the Commonwealth Sugar Agreement, including its provisions for real negotiations on prices, would have been incorporated into the ACP–EEC Sugar Protocol. This was not done; and the Protocol and its application have become an annual source of contention and conflict between the ACP and the EEC.

Apart from the first year of the Convention, the application of the Sugar Protocol has never been undertaken by the Community with any degree of enthusiasm. If obstacles are not deliberately put in the way of the effective application of the Protocol, the Community has tended so to interpret its provisions as to limit as much as possible the benefits accruing to the ACP producers.

The spirit of Protocol 2 to the Treaty of Accession has evidently dissolved into thin air; and the letter of Protocol 3 of the Lomé Convention has been nullified by unilateral action on the part of the Community.[25]

On the one side, then, there is clearly satisfaction; and on the other dissatisfaction. As far as the Commonwealth Caribbean countries are concerned their discontent arises, above all, from two issues which are at the heart of the Protocol: continuing access and negotiated prices. An examination of both reveals the depth of disappointment and the levels of frustration engendered by the operation of the Protocol.

CONTINUING ACCESS

There are three main dimensions to this problem: the question of *force majeure*; the internal sugar regime of the EEC, and the relationship to the British multinational company, Tate and Lyle.

1. The Question of 'Force Majeure'

The corollary in the Protocol to guaranteed access to the EEC is guaranteed delivery by the ACP. Non-delivery for reasons other than *force majeure* is liable to result in a penalty up to and including the entire loss of quotas. It therefore follows that an acceptable definition of *force majeure* is of importance to the ACP in securing continuing access. Such a definition, plus a conciliation procedure for applying it, was, in fact, agreed in December 1977 and reported to the Second ACP–EEC Council of Ministers in 1978. It has not, however, prevented disputes arising, one of which has proved virtually intractable. It concerns the reduction of the quotas of the People's Republic of Congo, Kenya, Suriname and Uganda, to the extent of quantities not delivered in 1977/1978 and for which pleas of *force majeure* had been entered.[26] The Commission found these unacceptable and in the case of Suriname reduced its quota to 2,667 tonnes, i.e. the difference between the original quota and the amount undelivered.[27] This was then contested at the ACP–EEC Council of Ministers in 1980 and it was decided to resort to the good offices procedure and, if this failed, to the arbitration procedure. The two conciliators appointed were Mr Francis, Permanent Secretary, Ministry of Foreign Affairs, Jamaica and Mr Krohn, former Director-General of the EEC Commission. Their report was submitted to the Commission in September 1980. This found that *force majeure* was indeed admissible but since it did not believe Suriname would be able to meet its delivery commitments in the future it recommended the quota be reduced to a realistic level of 2,000 tonnes.[28] In March 1981 the EEC informed the ACP that they were unable to accept the report of the conciliators and that in their view there were no grounds for setting aside the Commission's original decision in the four cases. At the request of the ACP states the matter was therefore placed before the ACP–EEC Council of Ministers in April 1981. The Council ruled both ways. While it regarded the Commission decision in the cases of the four states as still valid, it also noted that these states remained eligible for re-allocations under Article 7(4) of the Protocol.[29] An option to market sugar in the EEC at the guaranteed price thus remained open to them. The offer was subsequently taken up by Kenya and the Congo who, after considerable delay, were granted new allocations of 80% of original quota with effect from 1 July 1982 and 1 July 1983 respectively. Meanwhile Suriname's quota was further reduced to 1634 tonnes (1980/81) and then to 200 (1981/82). In the short run this may be an advantage for the country given that the cost of sugar production was so high that, in the words of a recent report, 'its participation in the protocol was in fact a burden'.[30] In the long run, however, it could have repercussions if Suriname once more sought a quota under the Protocol following any successful rehabilitation of the sugar industry as a consequence of a change of government policy – by no means an impossibility given the fluidity of the political situation in the country. As for the Commonwealth Caribbean they have, with the exception of Trinidad and Tobago in 1981, when only 60,300 tonnes were delivered (88% of its quota), and in 1982, when there was a shortfall of around 12,000 tonnes, always met the quota in full.[31] This has sometimes led to inconsistencies, as in the case of Jamaica where to meet its quota (not always achieved on time) it began in 1981 to import sugar for its domestic needs. That it has resorted to such practice, however, only serves to underline the significance of the Protocol as a guarantee of foreign exchange in times of depressed world sugar prices — a view which the rest of the Commonwealth Caribbean undoubtedly shares.

2. The EEC Sugar Regime

As noted earlier, the sugar regime of the EEC for the period 1975/76 to 1980/81 saw an increase in basic quotas for beet sugar aimed at redressing the 'shortage' in sugar experienced in 1974. In 1980/81 a new five year regime was established which further increased the basic quota to a level equal to average EEC sugar consumption and which by means of infrastructural and institutional support stimulated production well beyond this point.[32] The consequence has been such a massive expansion of sugar beet production that the EEC is now by far the world's biggest sugar producer (15.5 million tonnes in 1982) and is second in the table of sugar exporters (5.6 million tonnes in 1982).[33] Given this, the position of ACP sugar in the EEC market is, to say the least, precarious. It rests, ultimately, on only one factor — the continuing commitment of the British government to meet its need for sugar through cane imports (since virtually all ACP sugar is marketed in Britain which alone possesses sufficient refining capacity) and explains the close watching brief the ACP maintain on the British sugar industry. Two cases illustrate this particularly well. The first concerns the British reaction to the EEC Commission proposals for the current sugar regime which were presented in November 1979 and were the subject of a thorough study by the Select Committee on the European Communities of the House of Lords in early 1980.[34] They found the Commission proposals, which envisaged a modest cut in beet sugar production, as realistic and fair. This view was not shared by the British government which claimed the proposals discriminated against Britain and threatened the viability of the sugar beet industry in the country. The uneasy truce of the 'war of two sugars' in Britain, which rested on an 'understanding' of 50% of the market for beet and 50% for cane, appeared in jeopardy.[35] Accordingly, the ACP countries pressed for a meeting with the British Minister of Agriculture, Peter Walker, to express their concern.

The press statement issued at the end of this is worth reproducing at length since it has remarkable similarities in style and tone to that issued at Lancaster House nine years earlier, thereby showing how little had actually been achieved:

The British Minister assured the ACP Ministers that the British Government fully recognized the need to reduce the European sugar surplus and the desirability of the EEC acceding to the International Sugar Agreement as soon as possible. He had himself pressed for an early decision to cut the total of the EEC quotas substantially and had made clear his willingness to accept a cut in the present UK quota but he was opposed to the imposition of a disproportionate and damaging cut in the quota of the UK which he considered had not contributed to the EEC surplus. He reaffirmed that Her Majesty's Government remained fully committed to the sugar Protocol and accepted the importance for the ACP countries of their traditional outlets in the UK market. He confirmed that the UK government was not seeking to pursue policies which in any way ran counter to preserving those outlets and this intention was reflected in his negotiating position in Brussels.

The ACP Ministers stressed that their quotas under the sugar Protocol had remained fixed so that ACP sugar could not be responsible for any part of any surplus in Britain. Accordingly they considered that any sugar exported from Britain should be beet sugar and not cane sugar. The British Minister agreed that ACP supplies to the Community had not increased and that the growth of the Community's exports had come from beet production. He undertook to have further consultations with the ACP Ministers should a situation arise in the UK market which was harmful to their interests and to keep the ACP Ministers generally informed of developments in the current EEC negotiations.[36]

The other case concerns Tate and Lyle. In presenting their evidence to the House of Lords committee Tate and Lyle noted that should the Commission proposals not be accepted and British sugar beet production be allowed to expand by a planned 25% then it would be 'very hard to see how it would be possible for us in Tate and Lyle to avoid the closure of yet another refinery, and that in an area of intolerably high unemployment'.[37] The following year, and following the revision of Britain's sugar beet quota upward from the Commission's proposed 936,000 tonnes to 1,040,000 tonnes, Tate and Lyle announced the closure of their refinery in Liverpool with a loss of capacity of 300,000 tonnes and of 1,570 jobs. All that now remained was a capacity to refine 1.12 million tonnes a year in Britain — just about half the capacity which had existed but eight years before.[38] Faced with this prospect one saw an unusual alliance forged between the Commonwealth Caribbean diplomatic community in London and trade unionists in Liverpool as each fought to retain the refinery in being. These attempts failed, but they left in their wake a tangible legacy for the Commonwealth Caribbean in a reactivated *ad hoc* informal committee who consult in London from time to time on sugar matters and co-ordinate their representations accordingly, both to the British Government and the EEC.

3. *Tate and Lyle*

The link with Tate and Lyle is not only that its refining capacity should be maintained but that its operations should be profitable and hence its commitment to sugar refining be unquestioned. Neither, however, is certain. Taking the latter first, it must be remembered that Tate and Lyle is a large multinational company with 20 subsidiaries based in the UK and 47 others in 25 countries. Its interests are diverse, with divisions of the Company being involved in agribusiness, storage of chemical and petroleum products, production of sweeteners and starch, commodity trading, warehousing and packaging, production of malted barley, distribution, shipbuilding and production of construction and packaging materials. Profits for the year to September 1982 showed £67 million from Tate and Lyle PLC with the same again for subsidiaries and related companies. While traditionally these have been centred around the production, refining and trading of cane sugar, in respect of production and refining this has been a diminishing share which in the case of refining has been further reduced proportionately between Tate and Lyle's British and North American interests in favour of North America.[39] Assurances by Tate and Lyle management that it has 'confidence in the future' and that it has given effect to this by 'a very substantial capital expenditure programme to modernize its refineries'[40] need, against this background, to be treated with caution. Further undermining this is the measure of its profitability vis-à-vis its beet sugar rival, the British Sugar Corporation (BSC). As the House of Lords committee reported:

there is already a lack of price competition in the United Kingdom market, as the Community's institutional pricing structure means that Tate and Lyle gets too small a margin to enable it to continue refining and selling cane sugar in the United Kingdom unless there is a substantial market premium above intervention, whereas the same pricing structure allows the BSC a very handsome margin (£13 per tonne on the 1978/79 crop, as against £2 per tonne for Tate and Lyle). This means that BSC can afford to cut the premium to make Continental sugar less competitive – a danger which the sugar users recognised when they said of the present United Kingdom market situation that if it continued 'the ACP will wither on the vine because it is not competitive within the United Kingdom'.[41]

NEGOTIATED PRICES

Article 5(4) of the Protocol states in part that the guaranteed price 'shall be negotiated annually within the price range obtaining in the Community, taking into account all relevant economic factors'. Apparently a fairly straightforward form of words, its interpretation in practice has proved to be among the most contentious issues in the operation of the Protocol leading to charges by the ACP that because of it the spirit, if not the letter, of Lomé has been seriously compromised. The substance of these charges generally have two elements: that negotiations do not take place and that all relevant economic factors are not considered. In the investigation of this two other issues are raised – the extent to which prices are 'artificial' and whether in their determination the Protocol acts as a form of 'disguised' aid.

1. Negotiated v. Unilateral Pricing

In the formal record of the discussions leading to the conclusion of the Protocol the following is to be found: 'The Community undertakes that the Commission, in connection with Article 5 of the Protocol No. 3, will consult the sugar exporting ACP states each year before making its proposals to the Council of the European Communities for the determination of sugar prices within the Community for the following campaign'.[42] Subsequent practice shows this undertaking to have been consistently violated from the beginning. That is, whilst negotiations of a sort can be discerned for the price determined for the year 1976/77 the ACP even then registered their dissatisfaction with the interpretation of Article 5(4) by the EEC.[43] The following year they did so again in respect of the redefinition of the intervention price by the EEC whereby it was automatically equated with the lowest intervention price for EEC raw beet sugar. 'The ACP cannot accept', they said, 'that the Protocol empowers the Community to unilaterally change the structure of the price range, redefine its intervention price, deduct whatever charges it deems fit and then place the resulting figure before the ACP as its firm and final guaranteed price offer to the ACP. This is not by any interpretation honouring the letter of the Protocol that there should be annual negotiations to determine the ACP guaranteed price.'[44]

The pattern fixed, the process and protests thereafter became routine until the determination of price for the year 1981/82. At this juncture the Commission departed from the letter as well as the spirit of the Protocol offering the ACP only a 7.5% increase for raw sugar, 1% less than that proposed for white sugar. This immediately provoked an angry reaction from the ACP and an adjournment of the price negotiations, following which the ACP submitted an *aide-mémoire* to the EEC on the price issue. In this they noted that the raw intervention price had been increased by less than the white intervention price, not so much for reasons concerned with the structure of prices for EEC producers as in order to improve the margin of the British cane refiners. It also pointed out that with only a 7.5% increase in the ACP price, the take-home price for ACP sugar net of Monetary Compensation Amount (MCA) would actually be less in July 1981 than it was on 1st July 1980.[45] The EEC were unmoved and in July replied they were unable to increase the offer, whereupon Hugh Shearer, deputy Prime Minister of Jamaica and President of the ACP Council of Ministers, proposed that an extraordinary meeting of the ACP–EEC Council be held to deal with this and related problems associated with Stabex.[46] In the event this proved unnecessary, as the Council of the EEC in its January 1982 meeting agreed to an 8.5% increase in the guaranteed price and on this basis negotiations resumed in February 1982 resulting in an eventual agreement. Indeed, for a brief period thereafter it almost appeared as if a measure of mutual understanding might prevail. The negotiations for prices for 1982/83 which took place in June 1982 were relatively untroubled, with the EEC even agreeing that the problem of maritime freight costs for sugar should be examined 'as a matter of urgency'.[47] However, with the negotiations for a price for 1983/84 conflict re-emerged. The EEC offer of a 4% increase over the previous year's price was flatly rejected as falling short of the 9.5% increase claimed by the ACP as necessary. It also saw once more the intervention of a senior ACP figure with the Chairman of the ACP Council of Ministers, Mosese Qionibaravi of Fiji, writing to his EEC counterpart emphasising that 'inadequate proceeds from the sale of sugar resulting from the absence of remunerative levels of price will have serious consequences for the local sugar industries and affect the process of development of the ACP states'.[48] Be that as it may, toward the end of 1983 the ACP had got nowhere and reluctantly agreed to 4%, not least because for several months, and due to failure to fix a price, they had been receiving only the price for the previous year.

2. Relevant Economic Factors

The determination of price by the EEC with only scant regard to ACP submissions means that as far as the ACP are concerned the EEC are reneging on their commitment to take into account 'all relevant economic factors'. This issue has come to a head over freight though it had an earlier important aspect for the Commonwealth Caribbean in retroactive pricing. This arose from the simple fact that the 'sugar year' for the EEC is not coincident with that of the Caribbean. Most Commonwealth Caribbean sugar is produced and shipped in the first six months of the calendar year whereas the EEC 'sugar year' begins on 1 July and runs to 30 June following, so giving a price advantage, in terms of costs in times of high inflation, to those who produce in the second half of the calendar year. All this might not have been of much moment if the trend for the guaranteed price had not been invariably upward and were it not for the fact that most Commonwealth Caribbean sugar is produced at costs close to prices received. Hence any relief is welcome. The principle of retroactivity was conceded to 1 April for the 1976/77 year and 1 May for 1977/78, but not thereafter. In the light of this its status is now that of a lost cause.

The same cannot as yet be said of the issue of maritime freight, though it too is proving difficult. The Protocol states that the guaranteed price refers to unpacked sugar, c.i.f. European ports of the Community, i.e. the ACP bear a maritime

freight charge which in recent years has been escalating considerably. The matter first became urgent in the 1980/81 price
negotiations when it was noted that freight charges had almost
doubled over the previous two years and now constituted not
an inconsiderable amount of the costs of sugar produced.[49]
This was followed up in November 1980 by the preparation of
a memorandum which showed that since 1979 the average costs
of ACP ocean freight had increased by 43% alongside an
increase in prices entering into ACP sugar production costs over
the previous twelve months of some 15%.[50] What was implied
was not only a significant increase in the guaranteed price to
meet this (which was not granted) but a change in the basis for
calculating the ACP price to include shipping, recognising, of
course, that most sugar is shipped and insured by EEC-based
companies. As noted above, the issue has been recognised by
the EEC as a 'problem' and is now under study. Whether
anything will come of it, however, is another question, the view
within the EEC being that the marketing of ACP sugar is first
of all a purely commercial matter between private buyers and
sellers, with the corollary that any relief on freight cost is a
matter of aid not trade. The Commission has thus so far
restricted itself (as in the 1981 price negotiations) solely to an
offer to determine for each ACP state member of the Protocol
'the transport costs from the factory to the port of destination'.
As a result of that study, 'individual or regional projects could
be envisaged within the framework of the Lomé II Convention
under the provisions for financial and technical co-operation
as and when appropriate requests are received from the ACP
states'.[51]

3. Theoretical price

The intervention (guaranteed) price for ACP sugar is negotiated
annually between the Commission and the ACP exporters. It is
derived by subtracting an estimated processing margin between
the production for white and raw sugar from beet and is then
applied to all ACP raw cane sugar imports. The price as set out
in the negotiations for 1975–1984 is as follows (European Currency Unit, tonne): 1975/76 – 255.3; 1976/77 – 267; 1977–78
– 272.5; 1978–79 – 278.1; 1979/80 – 341.3; 1980/81 –
358.9; 1981/82 – 389.4; 1982/83 – 426.3; 1983/84 – 443.4.

It appears to show an upward movement in price but it has not been one deemed sufficient by the ACP to offset the combined effects of the agromonetary system and of the increases in maritime freight. The latter has been considered. The operation of the former demonstrates how the price is in a sense 'artificial'. It is so since no ACP sugar has been sold into intervention (i.e. at 'the guaranteed price'); nearly all of it has been bought by Tate and Lyle at a price above intervention. As such, it is the sterling price which is important. The problem to which this then gives rise is shown by the example of the 1980/81 figures. These purport to show a rise in intervention price over 1979/80 of 5.16%. However, if expressed in sterling the rise was negligible at 0.4%. The reason for this difference was the strength of sterling on the foreign exchange markets which had led to the virtual removal of ACP sugar from the EEC system of levies or subsidies applied to inter-EEC agricultural trade to offset exchange rate fluctuations. Indeed, it is possible to go further and argue that the price for 1980 had actually fallen over that of 1979 by some 13% and that effectively the sterling price had not increased for three years.[52] On this reading the ACP clearly had cause for complaint. Against this, however, and very important for the Commonwealth Caribbean given its trading pattern, is that strength in sterling implies weakness in dollars and *vice versa*. For example, translated into dollars via sterling the guaranteed price rose by 10% in 1980 as against 1979,[53] thereby arguably enhancing the real purchasing power of the region. At the end of the day this is probably a case of 'swings and roundabouts', although one trend is crystal clear and can be demonstrated by the example of Jamaica:

In 1965, 20.84 tonnes of sugar sold by Jamaica at the average price bought one Ford 5000 tractor. By the first half of 1979, 57.87 tonnes of Jamaican sugar were needed to buy a Ford 66000 tractor which replaced the earlier 5000 model. That is, it took nearly three times as much Jamaican sugar to buy the tractor − a slightly more powerful one than the previous model but used for the same purposes − as it did in 1965. Comparing the increase of the unit export value of manufactured goods with the price of sugar, by the second half of 1979 it took Jamaica 2.7 times as much sugar as in 1970 to buy exactly the same amount of manufactured goods.[54]

4. Disguised Aid

The determination of the exact revenue earned by the ACP from the Protocol has given rise to a number of controversies in respect of its calculation leading in one study to a figure varying from 887 million ECU to 1077 million ECU.[55] The obvious and unambiguous method is to calculate the difference between the guaranteed price for ACP sugar and the world free market price and on this basis the yield to the Commonwealth Caribbean from 1975 to 1983 is £201.15 million sterling (see table).

	A London Daily Price, £/tonne	B Average Price paid EEC quota	B-A per tonne	x 448.5 (000) t = £ million
1975/76	216.47	210.44	(6.03)	(2.70)
1976/77	153.44	182.65	29.21	13.10
1977/78	114.88	210.76	95.88	43.00
1978/79	101.21	220.14	118.93	53.34
1979/80	114.7	211.2	96.5	43.28
1980/81	291.5	222.0	(69.5)	(31.17)
1981/82	202.2	240.9	38.7	17.36
1982/83	118.9	263.7	144.8	64.94

Source: Calculated from GLC *The Case for Cane*, p. 40.

Even this is not absolutely correct for to arrive at the real figure it would be necessary to add the premium negotiated between the ACP and Tate and Lyle, plus or minus the MCA, to the EEC guaranteed price on the British market. A further difficulty arises from the fact that the addition of the above quantity of sugar on the world free market would have been most likely to depress prices by a marginal amount so raising the level of benefit (though equally it can be argued that over production of beet sugar by the EEC and its refusal to join the International Sugar Agreement has seriously depressed world market prices).[56]

Setting aside these difficulties it is nevertheless possible to conclude that the benefits of the Protocol have been tangible and substantial. This point was repeatedly made in interviews

I conducted with Commission officials in Brussels and in the Commonwealth Caribbean where every attempt was made to represent the Protocol as a form of 'disguised aid'. It first explicitly appears in connection with the Commission's proposals for the 1981/82 – 1985/86 sugar regime which were presented in such a way as to attribute to ACP sugar the costs of surplus disposal, which had arisen not from any increase in production on their part, but from the increased production and export of beet sugar, i.e. an attempt was made to detach ACP sugar from the 'common market' for sugar, to treat it as 'external' and as a 'concession', which meant that the cost of 're-exporting' 1.3 million tonnes of sugar from a sugar surplus market should properly be charged to the development sector and not the agricultural sector of the budget. Such an interpretation has been vigorously resisted by the ACP and the British Government, both of which have emphasised the historical commitment to cane sugar entered into when Britain joined the EEC. Ambassador Jackman of Barbados, when chairman of the ACP Subcommittee on Sugar, was particularly forceful on this point:

In this connection I must draw attention once again to the objections raised in the ACP countries by the Community practice, which could be described as 'idiosyncratic' of presenting its budget in such a way that, to the layman the Community appears to have entered into an obligation equivalent to providing aid for the export of 1.3 million tonnes of sugar, and of showing this fictitious expenditure to be attributable to imports of ACP sugar. The fact is, of course, that sugar imports into the Community have not increased since the entry into force of the protocol and that there is no calculation which indicates that the ACP countries can be held responsible for the sugar surpluses in the Community and hence for the cost of aid to export of these surpluses.[57]

Nevertheless, the view persists, and has now entered the thinking of the ACP's 'friend' within the Commission – the Development directorate (DG8), extending even to the senior desk officer concerned with Commonwealth Caribbean affairs within that body.[58] This is not, to say the least, a very hopeful sign for the future from the point of view of the ACP states.

THE FUTURE OF THE PROTOCOL

Under Article 2(2) of the Protocol the guarantee in Article 1 which defines the fundamental commitments of the contracting parties 'shall be re-examined before the end of the seventh year of their application'. The review was formally initiated on 19 February 1982 and at the time of writing is still proceeding, with all the wrangling usually attendant on anything to do with the Protocol. Thus when the ACP prepared a draft 'Joint ACP/ EEC Declaration on the Protocol' the EEC refused to accept that the ACP could determine what the EEC thought and accordingly prepared its own submission for transmission to the ACP. As of April 1984 this was being considered by the ACP in revised form.[59] Not surprisingly, the principal bone of contention is Article 5(4) with the EEC attaching considerable importance to the common organisation of the sugar market in Europe as expressed in the intervention price and the ACP claiming that no real negotiations on price take place and that the phrase 'all relevant economic factors' did not imply that any specific factor should have particular importance attached to it, i.e. the question of freight charges and revenue earned by ACP sugar producers are as relevant and admissible as the intervention price. Article 7(4) has also been disputed, with the ACP claiming that reallocation of shortfalls under the Protocol should be undertaken in consultation with the states concerned and the EEC maintaining that it must retain absolute discretion over this as implicit in the text of Article 7.[60]

Given that there is little will to bridge these differences the consensus that is emerging is to 'agree to disagree' and to 'roll over' the Protocol unchanged as was agreed in the negotiations for the second Lomé Convention.[61] Far from ideal, this course paradoxically recommends itself at present more to the ACP than the EEC on the simple grounds of expediency ('of not rocking the Lomé boat' by opening 'a Pandora's box of problems'). By contrast, the Commissioner for Development in the EEC, Edgar Pisani, has let it be known that he dislikes the denunciatory diplomacy of the Protocol, and at the ACP– EEC Joint Parliamentary Committee in Brazzaville in February 1984 intimated that if the ACP were unhappy with the Protocol they should seek to re-negotiate it.[62] Among the ACP sugar producers there are likely to be few, if any, takers for this particular scenario.

The immediate prospect is therefore to maintain the *status quo*. At the same time this does not mean that changes could not be made to the environment in which the Protocol operates. Two have been seriously canvassed. One, emanating from within the Commission, is to view the Protocol as aid, not trade. As recently expressed by Te Pass, it is that as a commercial pact between equal partners the Protocol cannot be maintained, logically implying its conversion 'into an aid convention in which, by definition, the forces are unequal'.[63] Totally opposed to this is the ACP view which, as set out by Jackman, asserts: 'Nowhere is the truism "trade, not aid" more apt ... ACP sugar producers want precisely what is set out in the Protocol, an opportunity to sell their produce at fair prices, with reasonable guarantees of access to the markets of the developed countries ...'.[64] As a difference of opinion it is understandable, and has an origin going back more than ten years in the 'trade-off' engineered by Jean Deniau (Commissioner for Development 1969–1973) whereby special privileges to sugar exporting countries (primarily in the Caribbean, Pacific and Indian Ocean and of direct interest to Britain) would be counterbalanced by special privileges attaching to the production of a specific number of basic commodities (principally of interest to the African countries and especially those enjoying strong links with France).[65] The former gave rise to the Protocol and the latter to Stabex. The linkage between the two is not officially acknowledged but it is there, nonetheless, not least in the mention of both under Title II of the Lomé Conventions. Stabex is, as often argued, a 'hybrid' of trade and aid, financed from the aid section of the EEC budget. It has been beset, in its operations, by as many problems as sugar though this, in itself, given the internal workings of the EEC, does not automatically disqualify it from consideration. Indeed, quite the reverse, for what is so apparent about the sugar issue in the EEC over the past fifteen years is its overall irrationality fed largely by the power of lobbies.[66] Foremost among these is CIBE which has, since 1978, sought to stop all ACP exports of sugar into the EEC and to redirect the same to sugar importing ACP countries to be labelled as 'aid' i.e. to sever the connection of ACP sugar with Community agricultural policy.[67] Diametrically opposed to this are the interests of Tate and Lyle, where capital invested requires continuing cane sugar imports into the United Kingdom.[68] As yet, the battle is not lost by either side, although, in the long term, it appears the odds will be increasingly stacked against cane.

The other proposal for change has emerged from the Committee on Development and Cooperation in the European Parliament. The fundamental premises governing its recommendations are twofold: (1) 'the irrevocable nature of the commitment undertaken by the Community in signing the sugar protocol'; and (2) a belief that 'In spite of its weaknesses and deficiencies, the sugar protocol continues to be necessary in its present form'.[69] Accordingly, the Committee do not recommend changes to the Protocol but specify a number of 'auxiliary measures' which, if implemented, would improve the position both within the EEC and for the ACP states concerned. First and foremost, it calls on the EEC to accede to the new international sugar agreement currently being negotiated. In making this recommendation the Committee notes that the debility of the present international sugar agreement stems in part from the failure of the EEC to be party to the agreement; and points out that, if it accedes, the Community will need to set an example by imposing a ceiling on beet production, and consequently on sugar exports.[70] Secondly, the Committee ask for Community aid for the economic diversification of ACP countries which export cane sugar. In proposing this the Committee point out that it is not simply a question of efforts made within ACP states but is also a matter of EEC policy as a whole. For example, it notes that when Mauritius sought to diversify its economy by establishing a textiles industry, it was forced to accept a voluntary agreement in respect of its exports to the Community. Hence future measures for effective diversification may in some instances require waiving of the EEC safeguard clause.[71] Third, the Committee supports the idea of a market-sharing scheme guaranteeing the sugar exporting developing countries a share in the markets of developing countries which are sugar importers. If necessary, financial assistance to effect this could involve an investment to establish sugar refineries at a regional level.[72] And finally, the Committee call on the Community to provide technical and financial assistance to developing countries which export cane sugar to improve yields and develop substitute crops; to modernise the appropriate infrastructure; and to train staff.[73]

All of these measures have much to recommend them even if they, in their turn, can be the subject of specific criticism, the most telling of which, perhaps, is the failure of the report to deal adequately with the major problem: the EEC's internal sugar policy. As one critic notes:

> The report argues that the Sugar Protocol does not make economic sense. Yet the Community's system of subsidising the production of huge beet sugar surpluses makes even less sense. Beet accounts for less than 3% of the value of EEC agriculture yet the subsidies attached to it account for between 10% and 20% of EEC spending on agriculture ... Moreover, it would be far easier for the Community to replace its sugar beet crop with other crops than it would be for ACP exporters, constrained as they are by climatic, economic and social factors.[74]

But to call for this, or indeed any reform of the Common Agricultural Policy is, on past record, to ask for the impossible. The Sugar Protocol (for the immediate future) is thus likely to remain a tail being chased by a European mongrel of established parentage but of uncertain temper and given to wagging it and biting it by turns.

CONCLUSION

Elsewhere I have concluded 'for the Commonwealth Caribbean ... Lomé is very much a second best ... the product of an historical relationship with Britain that has been multilateralised by British entry into the EEC but not changed in essence by that fact'.[75] In respect of the Sugar Protocol it is difficult not to reach a similar judgement. Within the Commonwealth Caribbean this is widely understood and everywhere unfavourable parallels are drawn between the operation of the old CSA and the Protocol. If the clock could be put back in this instance it would be universally welcomed. Yet this is not going to happen and nor is the Protocol likely to be changed. The Commonwealth Caribbean is therefore going to have to live with it and with the damaging war of attrition between the 'two sugars' which seems its inevitable accompaniment. A temporary ally may be found in British governments but such relief will be conditional on circumstances well beyond Commonwealth Caribbean influence, let alone control. Ultimately the Commonwealth Caribbean are therefore on their own in this matter, albeit alongside other ACP sugar exporting countries. It has become unfashionable of late to look favourably on international commodity cartels resting on what is acknowledged as a limited and weak base. Yet, in the last instance, and in the international arena, moves in this direction by the Commonwealth Caribbean and other cane sugar exporting countries appear an ineluctable choice if they are to remain in the production of cane sugar for export to traditional markets.

NOTES

*   The author gratefully acknowledges the assistance of a grant from the Nuffield Foundation for fieldwork in the Commonwealth Caribbean and in Brussels, 1981–1982.

1. Cited in Haruko Fukuda, *Britain in Europe: Impact on the Third World* (London, 1973), p. 18.
2. The totals were fixed at 465,000 tons (basic production quota) and 4,000 tons (duty free import) respectively, *ibid.*, pp. 75, 130.
3. For a topical account see, in particular, Anthony Kershaw MP, 'The Developing Countries in the Official Negotiations' in Overseas Development Institute, *Britain, the EEC and the Third World* (London, 1971), pp. 22–27.
4. Informations Méditerranéenes, *The New Sugar Policy of the European Community* (Brussels, July 1975), p. 38.
5. *Ibid.*, p. 40.
6. Reproduced in Central Office of Information, *British Membership of the European Community* (London, 1973), pp. 29–30.
7. *Treaty Concerning the Accession of the Kingdom of Denmark, Ireland, the Kingdom of Norway and the United Kingdom of Great Britain and Northern Ireland to the European Economic Community and the European Atomic Energy Community* (London, Command 4862, 1 Jan. 1972).
8. See Carole Webb, 'Mr Cube versus Monsieur Beet: The Politics of Sugar in the European Communities' in H. Wallace, W. Wallace and C. Webb (eds.), *Policy Making in the European Community* (Chichester, 1978), p. 198.
9. Commission of the European Communities, *Memorandum on the future sugar policy of the Community*, COM (73) 1177, 12 July 1973.
10. Informations Méditerranéenes, *The New Sugar Policy of the European Community*, p. 46.
11. *The Community's Future Sugar Policy*, SEC (74) 2784 Strasbourg, 9 July 1974.
12. Within the French quota of 3,480,000 tonnes some 676,000 tonnes was reserved for the DOM.
13. See the *Financial Times*, 30/1/1974, 9/2/1974, 16/2/1974.

14. See West Indies Sugar Association (Inc.), *Annual Report 1972* (32nd Barbados), pp. 13–14.
15. West Indies Sugar Association (Inc.), *Annual Report 1973* (33rd Barbados), p. 9.
16. Figures from European News Agency, *Sugar: Europe's New Policy* (Brussels, 1980), pp. 131–2.
17. A useful account of the interests involved in reaching this is contained in Webb, 'Mr Cube versus Monsieur Beet', pp. 211–22.
18. Figures from Informations Méditerranéenes, *The New Sugar Policy of the European Community*, pp. 48–50.
19. Cited in European News Agency, *The Lomé Convention: Renegotiation and Renewal* (Brussels, 1978), p. 121.
20. The complete text of the Lomé Conventions and the Sugar Protocol is carried in *The Courier* (Special Issue) No. 31, March 1975; and *The Courier* (Special Issue) No. 58, November 1979.
21. Reductions on CSA quotas were for Barbados – 60%; Guyana – 13%; Jamaica and Trinidad – 44%; St Kitts–Nevis – 55%. By contrast, the quota for Belize was practically doubled.
22. Europe Information, *Sugar, the European Community and the Lomé Convention* (Commission of the European Communities, Brussels, DE19. Feb. 1983).
23. *The Courier* No. 75, Sept./Oct. 1982, p. 56.
24. *Ibid.*, p. 58.
25. 'The Road to Lomé: Some Thoughts on the Development of ACP–EEC Relations', Memorandum prepared by J. O'Neil Lewis (Brussels, 9/9/81), paragraphs 140, 134, 132.
26. This was not the first instance of default by these states. In the year 1976/1977 the P. R. of Congo, Kenya and Suriname were deprived of their export entitlement (10,000 tonnes, 5,000 tonnes and 4,000 tonnes respectively) while Uganda saw its quota reduced from 5,000 to approximately 3,000 tonnes, all for nondelivery in the year 1975/1976. The ACP questioned this and asked for *force majeure* to be applied. At the ACP–EEC Council of Ministers in 1977 the EEC relented and agreed, essentially for political reasons of 'goodwill', to reinstate for these countries their original export entitlement. In so doing 'The community indicated that it was taking this action as an autonomous political gesture which would not be retroactive and which would not call into question the validity of the Commission's original decision'. ACP–EEC Convention of Lomé, *Second Annual Report of the ACP–EEC Council of Ministers* (Brussels, 14 March 1978), p. 42.
27. ACP–EEC Convention of Lomé, *Report of the ACP–EEC Council of Ministers: ACP–EEC Co-operation – Analysis – Applications* (Brussels, 25 July 1980), p. 86.
28. ACP–EEC Convention of Lomé, *Annual Report of the ACP–EEC Council of Ministers* (1 March 1980 – 28 February 1981), pp. 46–47.
29. ACP–EEC Convention of Lomé, *Draft Annual Report of the ACP–EEC Council of Ministers* (1 March 1981–31 Dec. 1981), p. 40.
30. *The Courier*, No. 70, Nov.–Dec. 1981, p. 47.
31. In the case of Trinidad and Tobago in 1981 a plea of *force majeure* was accepted. *The Courier* No. 73, May–June 1982, p. 19.
32. For details see European Community Commission, 'A New Common Organization of the Markets in Sugar as from 1 July 1981', *Green Europe 180* (Luxembourg: Office for Official Publications of the European Communities, 1981).
33. Figures from International Sugar Organization, *Statistical Bulletin* Vol. 43, No. 3 (March 1984) and include an element of cane sugar production from the

DOM. In 1981/82 the total for this was approximately 320,000 tonnes of which less than one quarter was derived from the Caribbean.

34. See House of Lords, Select Committee on the European Communities, Session 1979–80, *EEC Sugar Policy* (London, 19 March 1980).
35. *Ibid.*
36. Reproduced in Barbados Sugar Producers Association (Inc.), *Barbados Sugar Review* No. 43, March 1980 (memeo), pp. 7–8.
37. House of Lords, *EEC Sugar Policy*, p. 10.
38. Greater London Council, Industry and Employment Committee, *The Case for Cane – a study of the cane sugar refining industry in London* (London 27/4/1983), p. 31.
39. *Ibid.*, Appendix D.
40. *The Courier* No. 75, p. 61.
41. House of Lords, *EEC Sugar Policy*, paragraph 41, p. xiii.
42. ACP Group, *Transmissions Note* ACP/948/80, Sect. Sugar (Brussels, 9 Dec. 1980).
43. ACP–EEC Convention of Lomé, *Annual Report of the ACP–EEC Council of Ministers* (1 April 1976 – 31 March 1977), (Suva 14 April 1977), pp. 34–9.
44. ACP–EEC Convention of Lomé, *Second Annual Report of the ACP–EEC Council of Ministers* (1978), p. 40.
45. ACP–EEC Consultative Assembly, Working Documents 1981–1982, *Report Drawn up on behalf of the Joint Committee on the Fifth Annual Report of the ACP–EEC Council of Ministers – Rapporteur: Mr S. R. Insanally* (Document ACP–EEC 29/81/B, 25 Sept. 1981), paragraph 77.
46. *Ibid.*, paragraphs 78–9.
47. ACP–EEC Convention of Lomé, *Draft Annual Report of the ACP–EEC Council of Ministers for 1982*, p. 32.
48. *The Courier* No. 81, Sept.–Oct. 1983, p. x.
49. In July 1980 transport costs as a percentage of guaranteed prices stood at 9.3%; in July 1978 at 5%. Figures from Commision of the European Communities, *Communication: ACP Sugar: the problem of ocean freight cost* COM (83) 242/final (Brussels, 28 April 1983).
50. ACP–EEC Consultative Assembly, Working Documents, *Report on the Fifth Annual Report of the ACP–EEC Council of Ministers*, paragraph 74.
51. E.C. Commission, *Communication: ACP Sugar: the problem of ocean freight cost* (28 April 1983).
52. ACP–EEC Consultative Assembly, Working Documents, *Report on the Fifth Annual Report of the ACP–EEC Council of Ministers*, paragraph 74; European News Agency, *Sugar: Europe's New Policy*, pp. 137–8.
53. *Ibid.*
54. World Development Movement, *Sugar: Crisis in the Third World* (London, 1980), pp. 8–9.
55. European News Agency, *Sugar: Europe's New Policy*, pp. 139–40. The figure of 887 million ECU's is derived from calculating the difference between the world price and the EEC price for raw sugar; that of 1077 millions on the theoretical cost of re-exporting 1,250,000 tonnes of white sugar.
56. See on this House of Lords, *EEC Sugar Policy* and GLC, *The Case for Cane*, Chapter 5.
57. Statement of 18 Sept. 1981 cited in European Parliament, Working Documents 1983–1984, *Report Drawn up on behalf of the committee on Development and Cooperation on the medium and long-term problems of the Community's sugar policy in relation to the ACP–EEC sugar protocol of 30 September 1981 – Rapporteur: Mr V. Sable*, P.E. 80, 196/fin. (20 June 1983), p. 19.

58. See, for example, the internal report of policy toward the region prepared by Yves Roland Gosselin (Acting Desk Officer — Caribbean and Pacific), *La CEE et la région des Caraibes Lomé I et Lomé II* (CEE/DGD. Direction B. Caraibes) (Brussels, 15 Feb. 1982).

59. African, Caribbean and Pacific Group of States, *Draft: Joint Declaration by the Contracting Parties to Protocol No. 7 on ACP Sugar for incorporation in the minutes of the ACP—EEC Subcommittee on Sugar* (ACP/63/020/84, Brussels, 26 March 1984).

60. *Ibid.*

61. The Protocol was specifically excluded from negotiations. However, some Commonwealth Caribbean countries were not adverse to having it considered but were firmly overruled by Fiji and Mauritius.

62. Source: Interview in Brussels, April 1984.

63. *The Courier* No. 75, p. 57.

64. *Ibid.*, p. 59.

65. For an elaboration of this see European News Agency, *The Lomé Convention: Renegotiation and Renewal*, p. 80. Deniau put the case very forcefully at a lunch in the House of Commons in July 1972 when he stated that a system of compensation was needed, which would guarantee developing countries exports at minimum prices and in minimum quantities, particularly for those countries dependent mainly on one product.

66. See, especially, the excellent article by Chris Stevens and Carole Webb, 'The Political Economy of Sugar: A Window on the CAP' in H. Wallace, W. Wallace and C. Webb (eds.), *Policy Making in the European Community* (Chichester 1983, 2nd edition), pp. 321—47.

67. *The Economist*, 10 June 1978 reporting a conference of representatives of 450,000 beet growers in Copenhagen.

68. In the furtherance of these interests Tate and Lyle have recently purchased a controlling interest in one of the Portuguese refining companies, Alcântara, to enable it to influence the Portuguese refining industry as a whole on its policy line in connection with what happens to sugar in Portugal after entry into the EEC. Portugal imports annually around 300,000 tonnes of cane sugar of which some 30% comes from non-Protocol ACP sources i.e. Portugal is a sugar deficit country.

69. European Parliament, Working Documents, *Report drawn up on behalf of the committee on Development and Cooperation on the medium and long-term problems of the Community's sugar policy in relation to the ACP—EEC sugar protocol*, pp. 31, 36.

70. *Ibid.*, pp. 36—7.

71. *Ibid.*, pp. 37—9.

72. *Ibid.*, p. 39.

73. *Ibid.*, pp. 39—40.

74. Ken Laidlaw, 'The Sugar Protocol: Room for Improvement', *Lomé Briefing No. 12, 1983* (Liaison Committee of Development NGOs to the European Community, Brussels).

75. 'From Neo-colonialism to Neo-colonialism: Britain and the EEC in the Commonwealth Caribbean' in A. J. Payne and P. K. Sutton (eds.), *Dependency under Challenge: The Political Economy of the Commonwealth Caribbean* (Manchester, 1984), p. 231.

Citizenship and Parliamentary Politics in the English-Speaking Caribbean

ANTHONY MAINGOT

There are only two countries in the world which do not have written constitutions: Great Britain and New Zealand. Written documents are universally regarded as necessary complements to the system of customs and conventions which provide a framework for formal political actions and institutional relationships. The expectation is that the written document will give authority, by making explicit and concrete, that which exists in abstract. Unfortunately, the expectation has not universally borne fruit. Constitutions have tended to be rewritten as often as regimes have been changed. It is not in jest that Peaslee's *Constitutions of Nations* is regarded as one of the most revised and revisable works in print anywhere and at any time. In this sense the United States constitution has been unique, especially when the background of post-World War II constitution-making is used for contrast and comparison. For one, it has endured. For another, its framers were not professional 'constitutional lawyers' or 'constitution-writers'; the age of this specialized 'expert' had not yet arrived. The idea of an expert sitting down to single-handedly write a constitutional document for a nation very often quite distant in culture and history from his own, was then unimaginable.[1] The United States constitution was written by men who had a social and economic stake in the country and consequently real political interests in its operation.

In contrast to the post-World War II trend in the West Indies of holding public discussions around proposed constitutional documents, the United States constitutional proceedings were private; no day-to-day journalistic 'scoops', not even official transcripts. Today's T.V., radio and daily press releases make constitution-making (or at least the discussions of prepared drafts) anything but the publicity-shy and shielded exercise of Philadelphia in 1787. Additionally, in contrast to the specific and legalistic 'terms of reference' associated with contemporary constitution-making, the drafters of 1787 were quite in the dark as to the scope of their authority. They were guided more by their class interests, civic and political instincts and recent political experiences, than by any 'non-political' mandate.[2] The self-interest of a landed gentry and mercantile ruling class was unmistakably present, yet one marvels even today at the sheer genius of their product. Aware that the ratification of their ideas would generate wide and heated discussion, as it indeed did, they watered down their objectives, 'and they settled, like the good politicians they were, for half a loaf'.[3] The relevance and profundity of the constitutional – political debates surrounding that ratification rightfully continue to serve as lessons in democratic discourse to social scientists and interested laymen alike.[4]

While clearly it is unrealistic to expect that constitution-making today will replicate that first republican experience, there are certainly lessons which can be learned from that case. One is that the legitimacy of the system was not established by the constitutional instrument itself but rather through the process of active (often violent, as in the Civil War) politics. In this sense their genius was to have devised a principle of 'rationally *calculating* how to marshal public support for national policy'.[5] In other words, a system that was both responsive and effective. Surely this case of effective constitutionalism contains a lesson for new nations quite beyond the realm of radically different cultures. There is a universal validity to tying effectiveness to principles but it carries special meaning to the new nations of the Third World. These nations face a special sociological problem of the post-World War II era: the need to reconcile nationally and democratically two potentially contradictory social trends. On the one hand there is the drive to assert national identities, to resist not just economic penetration but also cultural and intellectual imperialism, to push back what Kwame Nkrumah quite rightly termed 'neocolonialism'. This identity-preserving trend is there; its center of gravity is the relatively small, but no less important, intellectual and educated sectors which, in a way, both mirror and project more broadly based but latent feelings.

The other trend is in the world-wide drive towards modernization, which is a process involving not just the quest for higher levels of material comfort but also a concomitant secularization of values and customs. As different and uncomparable as these trends may appear, they are related and tend to create a sociological dilemma which translates readily into a political—intellectual dilemma. How they challenge today's constitution-makers is apparent from the following pair of questions that are invariably faced in 'new' nations:

1. Should a constitution be specifically tailored and trimmed to fit the national social body, disregarding 'foreign' elements in so far as possible? Constitution-making as part of the identity-building process.

2. Should a constitution adopt, from whatever source, those elements which best guarantee the fulfillment of the 'good' (i.e. modern) life? Constitution-making as a contributor to the modernization process.

There is a strong and constantly increasing call for constitutional documents which reflect, as faithfully as possible, the native configurations; that is, nationalist and autochthonous constitutions. But how is this to be reconciled with the equally strong desire to have a system of laws and conventions which facilitates, and indeed encourages, modernization or development as the governing elites interpret it?

This query is the classical one of political philosophy usually posed in terms of the following two propositions:

(*a*) 'John has an interest in X';
(*b*) 'X is to John's interest'.

While proposition (*a*) is a matter of empirical enquiry, proposition (*b*) involves both an empirical question and a value judgment.

It must not be assumed that only authoritarian systems resolve this dilemma by automatically opting for proposition (*b*); it is a dilemma central to all political philosophy systems. Even a liberal democrat such as Walter Lippman made a distinction between what people wanted and what was good for them: 'The politician says, "I'll give you what you want." The statesman says, "What you think you want is this. What it is possible for you to get is that. What you really want, therefore, is the following." [6]

Where, then, does this leave that proclamation which prefaces so many constitutions, 'We the people of ...'? While it is clear that the expectation is that a progressive and democratic regime will attempt to reconcile both proposition (*a*) and proposition (*b*), the reality is that such a reconciliation will be more a function of the political process than of any constitutional mandate. It is the recognition of this fact which has led numerous scholars to agree with S. A. de Smith that 'In developing countries, constitutional factors will seldom play a dominant role in the shaping of political history.'[7] S. A. de Smith additionally believes that this is a result of the erosion of the principles of constitutionalism which has taken place in the Third World. He cites several reasons why this has been so: (1) the colonial authoritarianism which preceded independence clearly demonstrated that a country could be governed without popular consent; (2) power held too many temptations for the nationalists who first secured independence; (3) long exclusions from power made 'loyal' oppositions very unlikely; (4) so many of these states are divided by communal conflicts (racial, linguistic, religious) just as the integrity of the state has become a prime goal of power.[8]

B. O. Nwabueze accepts most of de Smith's explanations but places special emphasis on corruption and the general abuses of privileges by those in public office. In an explanation which closely follows Gunnar Myrdal's description of a 'soft state',[9] Nwabueze refers pointedly to 'the ability to help one's friends and relatives with jobs and contracts', a privilege highly prized in countries where 'the government is the main employer of labour'[10] and where there are few political checks and balances on its power. Both de Smith and Nwabueze thus see the failure of constitutionalism and the Westminster system not in terms of defects within the system itself, but in terms of defects within the societies which have implemented and corrupted the system.

In the West Indies, however, the major thrust of the recent criticisms of parliamentary constitutionalism has not focused so much on particular facts of corruption or abuse of office as on the failings of the political–constitutional structure itself.

The main criticism is that the Westminster model is incapable not only of generating the decisions necessary to meet demands from the masses but also of creating democratic government. It fails the tests of both effectiveness and legitimacy to such a degree that it is seen as contributing to what one scholar calls 'an evolutionary process of system disorganization', unable to deal with the frustrated masses.[11] Given those popular pressures, the critics continue, revolutionary change and the single-party regimes, such as that which existed in 1979–83 in Grenada, are legitimate opinions:[12] a form of true democracy.

It is an attractive and tempting idea which the leaders of the New Jewel Movement themselves had propagated. They spoke of a 'radically different political framework' called 'participatory democracy'. 'Political power', they claimed, 'has been taken out of the hands of a few privileged people and turned over to thousands of men, women and youth ...'[13] It is an ideal epitomized by the French Revolution, the ideal of a plebiscitarian democracy: a system in which citizens participate directly with no (or at least minimal) intervening groups or organizations.

The case of revolutionary Grenada poses many questions to those interested in constitutionalism in the West Indies. An immediate one, of course, has to be: did it work? The dramatic and bloody events of October 1983 should in themselves answer that question. Sadly and tragically, the lessons of the failure of attempts at plebiscitarian democracy in post–1789 France appear to have been repeated in Grenada.[14] For the purposes here, however, the interest is in another aspect of the Grenadian case: was it, if not in its entirety at least in its inception, proof of the failure of the Westminster system, of its incapacity to handle the types of crises seen as structural in the West Indies? What does that tragedy tell us about constitutionalism in the West Indies? It should be evident that any meaningful answer has to be in two parts, an empirical–historical one and a theoretical one.

WEST INDIAN PARLIAMENTARIANISM

As Table 1 shows, free alternation in office has been a widely and repeatedly practiced event in the West Indies; certainly much

TABLE 1

The Alternation in Power of West Indian Political Parties

State	Party	No. of Terms (Periods)
Jamaica	PNP	4 (1955–1958; 1959–1962 (Fed.); 1972–1980)
	JLP	6 (1944–1955; 1958–1959; 1962–1972; 1980–)
Trinidad	PNM	6 (1956–)
St Kitts	SKLP	6 (1952–1980)
	PAM/NRP	1 (1980–)
Antigua	ALP	6 (1951–1971; 1976–)
	PLM	1 (1971–1976)
Montserrat	MLP	5 (1952–1970)
	PDP	2 (1970–1978)
	PLM	1 (1978–)
St Lucia	SLP	5 (1951–1964; 1979–)
	UWP	3 (1964–1979)
Dominica	INDS	3 (1951–1961)
	DLP	4 (1961–1979)
	DFP	1 (1980–)
Grenada	GULP	6 (1951–1957; 1961–1962; 1967–1979)
	GNP	2 (1957–1961; 1962–1967)
St Vincent	8th Army	1 (1951–1954)
	Inds.	1 (1954–1957)
	PPP	3 (1957–1967)
	SVLP	3 (1967–1972; 1974–)
	PPP/Mitchell	1 (1972–1974)
Barbados	BLP	3 (1951–1961; 1976–)
	DLP	3 (1961–1976)

Source: Patrick Emmanuel, 'Elections and Parties in the Eastern Caribbean', *Caribbean Review* (Spring, 1981), p. 16 (with additions)

more the rule than the exception. Indeed, so much are elections a part of West Indian political lives that scholars periodically compile fat volumes with quite precise statistics about them.[15] These electoral data in turn become the gist of rigorous and revealing studies on the operation of West Indian public opinion and political behavior.[16] In other words, there is wide recognition of the importance of political parties and the electoral process in the West Indies. And not without reason, for despite its many failings — including the major one to be outlined here — West Indian political systems have provided these societies with regular, usually honest, and basically reliable mechanisms for elite recruitment and circulation. Whatever the particular circumstances which led to the coup d'état in Grenada in 1979, the fact is that five years later there is not only a re-evaluation of the degree of success of that experience[17] but also what appears to be an increase in the credibility of the electoral approach. The recent journalist's theme of 'the Springtime of Election' appears well justified.[18] What is more, since 1979 West Indian political systems have handled many difficult transitions under conditions which, in other contexts, would have appeared ready-made for widespread abuse or even the rise of authoritarian rule. One can instance in this regard the case of Jamaica in 1980, when the system survived a period of enormous turmoil and stress to bring about a peaceful transfer of rulers; and the case of Trinidad and Tobago in 1981, which showed that the system can manage the transition following the sudden demise of a leader who had governed for 25 years. Similarly, we should add the survival of legality in Dominica and St Lucia after different, but equally difficult, circumstances.

The intrinisic legitimacy of such systems has allowed them then to survive some dramatic challenges. The purpose here is not to put that legitimacy in doubt but to point to one central feature of the system which might eventually contribute to the erosion: *the electoral method*. This distinction is essential because much of the criticism of the parliamentary system has been criticism of *the electoral system*. This was certainly the approach, for example, of the Constitutional Reform Commission of Trinidad and Tobago which reviewed the electoral system inherited from Britain in the context of a new constitution for the island and concluded that 'At the very centre of recent political agitation has been the demand for electoral reform.'[19]

Since none of the West Indies (except Guyana) have had experience with any other system than first-past-the-post, the analysis which follows necessarily takes place on a hypothetical plane. Within it the question of 'opportunity' or 'alternative' costs which is advanced is, admittedly, purely speculative. Nevertheless, the approach appears warranted on several grounds, not the least being that much political philosophy is in itself speculative and that in such speculation the issue identified earlier is obviously relevant: should the statesman merely ask whether 'John is interested in X' or does he have the responsibility of also asking: 'Is X to John's interest?'?

It is the central hypothesis of the chapter that much of the discontent with constitutionalism in the West Indies stems from deficiencies in the electoral system used, not in the nature of parliamentarianism or political pluralism proper.[20] The constitutional dilemmas discussed in the opening section, if they are to be faced effectively and sincerely, will require an electoral method which is not only fairer but also more representative of the social trends (including social conflicts) and aspirations (including ideological ones) of the society.

Three cases will explore our hypothesis.

JAMAICA

The electoral transition from 1944 to 1962 consolidated several features of the Jamaican system. While the issues were strictly bread-and-butter ones (except for the 1959 West Indies Federation elections and the 1961 Referendum on the Federation), a tradition of deep party loyalties by locality was established. The 'safe' constituencies were secured and in turn rewarded with ample patronage, especially housing and jobs.

But clearly political competition in the full democratic sense of the word had to await independence. This came in 1962 and an analysis of the election which ushered the nation into independence is revealing. With 78% of the electorate voting, the Jamaican Labour Party (JLP) won this crucial election with a margin of less than 10,000 votes of the 567,901 cast, yet that margin gave it 7 parliamentary seats more than the opposition Peoples National Party (PNP). Since the Senate was an appointed one, the winning JLP controlled that chamber also. The important point is that had the distribution of House seats been made on a strictly proportional basis (i.e. one man, one vote), seats in the first House in independent Jamaica would have been distributed 23 for the JLP and 22 for the PNP. Most importantly, this would in fact have reflected the popular sentiments at the time.

In 1967 the JLP again received a 5 seat advantage with only a 0.8% popular margin. The crucial first decade after independence, therefore, was dominated by a party with a majority in the House which was considerably greater than its popular support; additional to which, its majority in the appointed Senate provided an even greater 'sense' of supremacy in Parliament and in the nation.

The 1962 election was to establish — and that of 1967 was to reinforce — the JLP's populist anti-communist stance and the PNP's mild and rhetorical democratic socialism. By 1967 this issue, and other issues which would govern Jamaican politics for the next three elections, had also made their appearance: the JLP's Puerto Rican style import-substitution program and its incentives to the bauxite, tourism and manufacturing sectors; plus the PNP's critiques of the inequities resulting from these programs. But such considerations aside, and more fundamentally, that first decade confirmed the principle that to the victor go the spoils, distributed at the all crucial constituency level. The division of the country, and especially the Kingston area, into competing, and occasionally bellicose camps, was accordingly consolidated.

By 1972, the JLP had lost the support of the swing voters as accusations of widespread corruption and immoral class divisions, combined with growing Rastafarian and American style Black Power appeals, coalesced to create a revolt of righteous indignation against 'Babylon' and JLP sponsored 'materialistic capitalism'. In the first election without either of the original giants, Norman Manley and Alexander Bustamante, Michael Manley carefully cultivated the sentiments of moral indignation by introducing a new image: that of Joshua carrying the 'Rod of Correction' given to him by Haile Selassie.[21] The 'swing' to the PNP in 1972 was 7.27% giving Manley a considerable victory and thus a 'mandate'.

The margin of victory for Manley and the PNP was even greater in the general elections of 1976 and appeared to justify pushing the party and the government further to the left ideologically, at least as regards rhetoric. The conflict between parties, in terms of symbols and in terms of patronage, thus intensified and with it the level of violence.

In the 1980 elections the swing vote went towards JLP and its leader, Edward Seaga. At the rhetorical level of ideology the shift was cited as monumental, even transcendental, a fact further accentuated by the election that same year of the conservative U.S. President Ronald Reagan and by the fear of the Grenadian 'revolution'.

A close analysis of the 1972, 1976 and 1980 elections, however, raises serious questions about the nature of these 'mandates'. As Table No. 2 shows, the 'realistic–democratic' cost of a seat in 1972 was 9,086, the victorious PNP got their seats 2,000 votes cheaper than that while the losing JLP paid 4,500 over the realistic cost. We call this the 'democratic cost'.[22]

TABLE 2

The 'Democratic Costs' of Elections in Jamaica

	1972[1]		1976[1]		1980[2]	
	(Voting: 78%)		(Voting: 85.21%)		(Voting: 75.5%)	
	J.L.P.	P.N.P.	J.L.P.	P.N.P.	J.L.P.	P.N.P.
Votes Won	204,779	267,735	318,180	417,768	432,766	317,650
	(43.4%)	(56.36%)	(43.2%)	(56.8%)	(57.6%)	(42.3%)
Seats Won	15	37	13	47	51	9
	(28.8%)	(71.1%)	(21.6%)	(78.3%)	(85%)	(15%)
Cost of each Seat	13,651	7,236	24,475	8,888	8,485	35,294
Realistic Cost per Seat (1)	(9,086)		(12,265)		(12,506)	
Democratic 'Cost' (2)	− 4,565	+ 1,850	− 12,265	+ 3,377	+ 4,021	− 22,788
Seats on a P.R. basis	22.5	29.4	25.9	24.1	34.6	25.4

Calculations (1) The total vote cost divided by number of seats in House.

(2) The overplus (+) or deficit (−) of votes actually needed to get a seat relative to the Fair cost.

Source: (1) 'Election 1980', *A Special Gleaner Publication for Voters*, 18 Oct. 1980, pp. 11–13.

(2) *Sunday Gleaner Election Feature*, 2 Nov. 1980, P. v.

This distortion of the one-man, one vote principle became even more absurd in the 1976 election and by the 1980 election there was an incredible 26,809 vote difference between what the winning and the losing parties 'paid' for each seat.

The question of just how distorted the system has to become, to what level the 'democratic cost' may rise, before it is considered undemocratic is presently impossible to answer. It is not even clear that the Jamaicans themselves are concerned with the weaknesses in this aspect of the electoral process.[23] In part this might be due to the fact that at least at the level of the individual constituency the electoral system seems to reflect the will of the people. There develops an image of 'popular sweeps' and 'mandates', images which are not supported when seen from a national perspective. In 1976 Michael Manley carried his constituency of Kingston East Central with 77% of the vote while in 1980 Edward Seaga carried his stronghold of Kingston West with 94%. The corresponding percentage won nationally by each party was 57% and 58% respectively.

The central question remains, however, the extent to which these election results express national sentiments for fundamental change. Not only does it appear that they do not but that 'in their minds' both parties understand this. Carl Stone's analysis of continuities and differences in party policies over the 1962–1978 period leads him to conclude that his finding 'completely destroys any suggestion (so emphatic in inter-party propaganda) that the parties are so far apart that changes in party government mean fundamental new directions in public policy.'[24] For the fact is, as Stone has repeatedly demonstrated, that both parties are polyclass entities 'competing for votes in the same electoral marketplace.'[25] This explains why ideology – especially as it is expressed in foreign policy – is such an important rhetorical aspect of party competition: it is supposed to camouflage the lack of fundamental policy differences at home. But surely the fact that in 1980, for instance, Edward Seaga began his 'mandate' for free enterprise with a 50 to 9 seat majority in the House rather than the 35 to 25 margin that a one-man-one-vote proportional system would have given him, makes a difference politically and psychologically. It poses as relevant in turn the question as to whether such a lop-sided majority in the House did not encourage the view that the controversial snap election in November 1983 was constitutionally and politically proper, despite widespread objections to its being held.[26]

In sum, the case of Jamaica illustrates how the first-past-the-post or single member constituency system not only incurs a patently undemocratic 'democratic cost' but in the process distorts the reality of a two-party political system. It raises the issue of what is 'good' for Jamaica as distinct from what Jamaicans have become accustomed to believing is good for them.

TRINIDAD AND TOBAGO

The same issue is relevant to the case of Trinidad and Tobago where the effects of the electoral method introduced by Britain have been arguably even more detrimental. As distinct from Jamaica, where an essentially polyclass two-party system developed out of the trade union movement, Trinidad's major parties are ethnically based. Neither organized labor nor other sectoral groups have ever succeeded in establishing an independent political foothold. Table No. 3 provides a view of two crucial elections in the island's political history. The 1956 election represented the beginning of responsible (cabinet) government and the entry to the electoral scene of the first truly organized party (the People's National Movement).

TABLE 3

Elections in Trinidad and Tobago, 1956 and 1966

	1956 Election in Trinidad and Tobago				
Party	No. of Seats Contested	Total Votes Polled	% of Votes Cast	Seats	Democratic Cost per Seat
PNM	24	105,153	38.7	13	8,088
PDP	14	55,148	20.3	5	11,029
Butler P.	20	31,071	11	2	15,535
TLP–NDP	11	13,692	55	2	6,846
POPPG	9	14,019	5 +	0	–
Independents	39	40,523	15	2	20,261

Fair Cost per seat (Votes/Seats) = 11,314

	1966 Election in Trinidad and Tobago				
Party	No. of Seats Contested	Total Votes Polled	% of Votes Cast	Seats	Seats on a P.R. Basis
PNM	36	158,573	52.41	24	19
DLP	36	102,792	33.98	12	12
Liberal	36	26,870	8.88	0	3
Workers and Farmers	36	10,484	3.46	0	2

Source: Constitution Commission of Trinidad and Tobago, *Report of the Constitution Commission* (January 22, 1974), Table 3.

The significance of this election is that while most Blacks were in the PNM and most Indians in the Democratic Labour Party (DLP), there were at least two 'parties' which made ideological rather than ethnic appeals: the radical and labor oriented Trinidad Labour Party–New Democratic Party (TLP–NDP) and the conservative, business oriented Party of Progressive Popular Groups (POPPG). They both reflected a real attempt to compete on the basis of ideas and class interests rather than race. Their efforts were not rewarded or encouraged by the existing system. While the POPPG received more popular votes than the TLP–NDP it received no seats while the latter received two. The lesson from that election was evident to many: join forces with the two major ethnic groups,[27] Black and Indian, if any representation was to be had. The approach of independence made the message all the more compelling. In 1966, the first election after independence, the logic of this course was shown in the opportunity costs to the society as a whole: voting for the two major racially-based parties had risen from 59% of the total vote in 1956 to 86.5% in 1966. The 37,354 who voted for the class-based Liberals (conservative) and Farmers and Workers (radical) essentially wasted their vote. It is interesting to note that this was the margin by which in 1961 Jamaicans voted to leave the West Indies Federation,[28] and nearly four times the margin which allowed the JLP to form the first government in independent Jamaica (with a 6 seat majority in the House). In consequence, it is not mere idle speculation to wonder what Trinidadian politics would have been like in the years before the 1970 Black Power demonstrations if its House had been divided into a multi-racial and multi-ideological 19–12–3–2 rather than the straight 24–12 racial split.

GRENADA

The question has been raised as to whether the 'costs' of this system are high only in multi-racial societies such as Trinidad. The case of Jamaica should answer that, as does the example of Grenada where the operation of the system has been no less detrimental. This fact can be seen in terms of the two objections raised against the first-past-the-post system: the 'democratic costs' and the 'opportunity costs'. Table No. 4 illustrates the democratic

TABLE 4

Grenada's 1972 Election

Party	Total Votes	% of Vote	Seats	% of Seats	Votes for each Seat
Gairy's Grenada United Labor Party	20,005	58.56	13	86.67	1,539
Blaise's Grenada National Party	14,155	41.44	2	13.33	7,077

Source: Constitution Commission of Trinidad and Tobago, *Report of the Constitution Commission* (January 22, 1974), Table 3.

costs. It demonstrates that the opposition Grenada National Party (GNP) needed five times more votes than the victorious Grenada United Labour Party (GULP) to win each seat.

The issue of opportunity costs is more speculative but given the events of 1979 equally necessary of analysis. Had the parliamentary seats been allocated proportionately in 1972 the ruling GULP would have received nine and the opposition GNP six. Did the candidates of the GNP (people like Nyack, Simon, Strachan and Whiteman) who failed to secure seats, move towards the new, radical New Jewel Movement (NJM) because the system exerted too high a cost? In 1977 a coalition of convenience was formed by all groups opposed to Gairy's GULP. Competing as the People's Alliance they won 48.2% of the popular vote and 6 out of the 15 seats. Given the fact that the three elected members of the NJM effectively took control of the Opposition in Parliament it is an interesting question to ask just what was the level of their popularity as measured by the 1976 polls. Interestingly enough, this is a case where the single-member constituency allows some 'approximate' answer, bearing in mind that it is hard to tell the general impact of the party (or alliance) in the votes for individual members. Be that as it may, one notes that the major political leaders in 1976 won their seats by the following margins: Herbert A. Blaize, 76.7%; Maurice Bishop, 52.3%; Eric Gairy, 64.3%. The NJM candidates, who only three years later would ride a wave of moral indignation (and a barrage of bullets) to power, fared as follows: Bernard Coard (won, 56.1%), Lloyd

Noel (lost, 44.1%), Kenrick Radix (lost, 46.9%), Selwyn Strachan (lost, 35.7%), Unison Whiteman (won, 55.9%). A rough calculation tells us that a total of 48.5% of the Alliance votes went to the NJM candidates which is 9,530 votes or 23.4% of the total votes cast. Hardly a landslide or popular 'mandate' for seizing power. Did the NJM's leaders' success in three individual constituencies help distort their sense of the reality of Grenadian public opinion or was the *coup* to have occurred regardless of electoral outcome i.e. had the Leninist path already been decided upon?[29] It is hard to answer and even harder to figure out to what extent the polls before 1979 really matched parliamentary power to popular sentiment, let alone provided mandates.

It is not difficult to see, however, just how easily those already indifferent or hostile to what they consider to be the inefficiency and basic corruption of parliamentary politics can cite real cases to support that attitude. Pat Emmanuel is one who has been concerned with the inability of the first-past-the-post system to meet the tests of fairness and representativeness. The gist of his concerns should be an integral part of any discussion of the events leading up to 1979 and not just the oft-repeated brutality and corruption of Eric Gairy. Emmanuel cites this example from Grenada in 1954 and 1957: 'The GULP ... went on to take the largest single share of the poll, 44.0%, in 1957, yet it was not able to win more than the same number of seats (2) taken by the GNP with a 24.4% poll, PDM with 21.6% and Independents with 8.7%.'[30] That this is hardly a system which respects or responds to the individual voter or which gives an accurate picture of relative political strengths cannot be disputed. Whether equally it can be blamed for the cynicism about parliamentary politics which expressed itself in Grenada and elsewhere in the Commonwealth Caribbean remains, of course, a very relevant empirical question.

CONCLUSION

The above analysis has attempted to show that West Indian political systems have worked in the past. This, however, is a relative statement. The evidence thus far demonstrates that the mechanisms of a parliamentary system, including parliamentary supremacy and cabinet responsibility (with the systems of votes of no confidence and/or the forcing of new elections before the end of a full term), are preferable to the other two models currently available to sovereign Caribbean states: the U.S. and Latin American executive system or the U.S.S.R. – Cuban one-party state.[31] The point is, of course, that its operation requires an ideological acceptance of (or at least resignation to) the rules of the game, i.e. an acknowledgement of its legitimacy. Jamaica in 1980 was saved from a real crisis by the personal acceptance of those rules by the majority of the PNP and by Michael Manley. Past performance makes it highly likely that the JLP and Seaga will do the same.

And yet, within the broader soundness of this parliamentarianism, there is a fly in the ointment – the electoral system. While the effects of the first-past-the-post system have been different in each island, they appear to have been detrimental, especially if any 'opportunity costs' approach is taken. The impact of this system is not merely the distortions in the House and in the system generally which result from an ever-increasing 'democratic cost', for there are also sociological and, it could be hypothesized, psychological consequences.

The sociological cost stems from the fact that given the security provided by the combination of their appeal to race and the electoral mechanism itself, the leadership of these parties tends to be virtually immovable. The cases of Trinidad and Guyana and certain of the islands in the Eastern Caribbean come to mind.

The problem is that even if one were to accept theoretically the apparent inevitability of elite rule,[32] additional theory warns us about the built-in dangers to both democracy and progressive government of the perpetuity in power of entrenched leaders of political parties. The very demands of secular and systematically efficient administration tend to impose on these parties (especially if in power) specific configurations. In turn, these special configurations were precisely what Robert Michels theorized would tend to make a minority leadership dominant. He designated this the 'iron law of oligarchy' and posited what he termed the 'fundamental sociological law of political parties': 'who says organization, says oligarchy', and oligarchy (i.e. power) has always meant self-preservation.[33] It was the compelling nature of this theory that led Michels to enquire: 'Is it impossible for a democratic party to practise a democratic policy, for a revolutionary party to pursue revolutionary policy?'

While Michels's answer was clearly in the affirmative, it need not be so in fact. The general competition and conflict of society can be channeled into the political system where party competition becomes its reenactment. As Lipset has noted, elections and political parties are the 'democratic translation of the class struggle'.[34] This, fundamentally, should be what any electoral system should provide for: to channel the inevitable social conflicts into a decision-making body where the rules of the game are known and shared. However, such an opening up of the political system to different sectoral and ideological group representations is discouraged by the present first-past-the-post electoral system as the case of Trinidad (Table No. 3) demonstrates.

The system, it is hypothesized, also has a negative psychological impact: it inhibits the development of an individual's full identification with the nation by throwing him or her back to primordial identities such as race or locality group (Jamaica's 'political tribes'). Instead of building citizens, the dynamic tension creates purely partisan parochials evident in an ever-increasing 'micro-state nationalism' in the area which ranges from anti-CARICOM sentiments in places like Trinidad to threats of secession in places like Tobago.

While there is clearly a deep cultural dimension to the West Indian sense of locality,[35] in the past three decades the impact of race and ethnicity in Guyana and Trinidad and political 'tribalism' in Jamaica has been dramatic and has served to weaken the role of citizenship as a resource. The trend is stimulated by the fact that in such a context of ethnic and political polarization certain groups do make relative gains, at least in the short term. The question remains, however, whether these short-term achievements made during periods of political supremacy are sufficient to anchor the long-range rights of even that group, much less minority groups in the body politic. The rights of the European working class, for instance, resulted from a gradual process of citizenship-building, that is, integration and incorporation of this class into the political system, into full community membership. With this full membership in the community goes the sharing of the rights and also duties of securing and perfecting the basic human equality that such a membership promises. This is not to say that citizenship promises the abolition of social inequality; it only opens the way for the systematic and constructive challenging of those inequalities. In large part it does so by creating a legitimacy (consensus) around its requirements. As such, citizenship is not a natural law principle, it is a developing principle, that is, it requires the active promotion of the rights and duties that are its essence. Citizenship-building is like community-building in that they both require full membership and participation in the enterprise. T.H. Marshall is worth quoting here:

> There is no universal principle that determines what those rights and duties shall be, but societies in which citizenship is a developing institution create an image of an ideal citizenship against which achievement can be measured and towards which aspiration can be directed.[36]

If the functional idea of Trinidad and Tobago or Jamaican or Grenadian citizenship has tended to create the idea of people being mere citizens, then the hope is that an emphasis on the developmental idea will change that to the idea of fellow citizens. To the extent that the pursuit of ethnic grievances inhibits the growth of community, it also obstructs the development of the fellowship of citizens.

Any constitutional system has to be evaluated, therefore, in terms of how well it promotes citizenship. Since the right to elect one's representatives is a fundamental part of citizenship, how that election is carried out becomes, by definition, also fundamental. Here we have focused on the weakest aspect of the Westminster system as the West Indies inherited it, the first-past-the-post electoral system. A change is worth both study and serious consideration.

The specific dilemma of whether to adopt a constitution which reflects the national identity of a nation or adopt one which puts that nation on the path to modernization, is not much different from the universal question of political philosophy as to whether the function of government is to give John what he is interested in or what is good for him. Political pluralism – constitutional parliamentarianism – has thus far proven its capacity to handle these issues. In the West Indies it deserves a better electoral system.

NOTES

1. It must not be thought that the rewriting of constitutions, the emulation of foreign models, and the penmanship of a single or a few constitutional authors, is strictly a Third World phenomenon. The history of modern France proves it is not. Carl J. Friedrich notes that 'the prime drafter' of the Fifth Republic's constitution, Michel Debre, preferred the British parliamentary system while De Gaulle preferred the presidential. The end result was a curious mixture of both systems.

2. See John P. Roche: 'A small group of political leaders with a Continental vision and essentially a consciousness of the U.S. international impotence, provided the matrix of the movement'. 'The Founding Fathers: A Reform Caucus in action', *American Political Science Review* Vol. 60, 1961, p. 801.

3. *Ibid.* p. 816. Stanley Elkins and Eric McKitric also emphasize the political experience and therefore the respect for 'political realities' of the Founding Fathers. See their 'The Founding Fathers: Young Men of the Revolution', *Political Science Quarterly* Vol. 76, 1961, pp. 202 ff.

4. This is, of course, the case with the 85 letters to the public published under the pseudonym Publius during 1787–88, later to be called the Federalist Papers.

5. Seymour Martin Lipset, *The First New Nation* (New York, 1967), p. 36. Lipset's book first revealed some of the comparisons attempted here.

6. *Preface to Morals* (New York, 1929), p. 279. Equally the conservative Edmund Burke declared that 'Your representative owes you not his industry only, but his judgement; and betrays instead of serving you if he sacrifices it to your opinion'.

7. *The New Commonwealth and its Constitution* (London, 1964), p. 83.

8. 'Foreword' in B. O. Nwabueze, *Constitutionalism in the Emergent States* (London, 1973), p. ix.

9. 'The laxity and arbitrariness in a national community', says Myrdal, 'that can be characterized as a soft state can be, and are, exploited for *personal gain* by a people who have economic, social and political power'. *The Challenge of World Poverty* (New York, 1971), p. 209.

10. Nwabueze, *Constitutionalism in the Emergent States*, p. 301.

11. See Vaughan A. Lewis, 'Political Change and Crisis in the English-Speaking Caribbean' in Alan Adelman and Reid Reading (eds.), *Confrontation in the Caribbean Basin* (Pittsburgh, 1984), p. 93.

12. See Lewis, 'Political Change and Crisis'; also Tony Thorndike, 'Grenada: The New Jewel Revolution' in Anthony Payne and Paul Sutton (eds.), *Dependency Under Challenge: the political economy of the Commonwealth Caribbean* (Manchester, 1984), pp. 105–30.

13. *Is Freedom We Making! The New Democracy in Grenada* (People's Revolutionary Government, Grenada, 1982), p. 22.

14. It is a sad commentary that the best approach through which to analyse the Grenadian revolution is Crane Brinton's study written in the 1930s, *Anatomy of a Revolution* (New York, 1938). How applicable his conclusion that 'social systems are still almost as perversely unaffected by revolutionary good intentions as tides or rubber bands' (p. 214).

15. Patrick Emmanuel, *General Elections in the Eastern Caribbean: A Handbook* (Cave Hill, Barbados: I.S.E.R. Occasional Paper No. 11, 1979); Douglas Midgett, *Eastern Caribbean Elections 1950–1982* (University of Iowa, Development Series No. 13, n.d.). Midgett early on alludes to an increasing 'infusion of outside financing and direction of election campaigns' (p. 8) but never deals with the subject again.

16. The most outstanding of these are Carl Stone, *Electoral Behaviour and Public Opinion in Jamaica* (Mona, Jamaica: I.S.E.R., 1974); J.E. Greene, *Race and Politics in Guyana* (Mona, Jamaica: I.S.E.R., 1974); Selwyn Ryan, Eddie Greene, Jack Harewood, *The Confused Electorate – A Study of Political Attitudes and Opinions in Trinidad and Tobago* (St Augustine, Trinidad: I.S.E.R., 1979).

17. In a survey carried out in Grenada by Trinidad's St Augustine Research Associates in December 1983, 86% of Grenadians welcomed the United States' Eastern Caribbean invasion as a 'good' thing; only 38% of the sample felt that on balance the P.R.G. of Bishop had been 'good' for Grenada. See Selwyn Ryan, 'Grenada: Balance Sheet of the Revolution' (Paper presented to the Caribbean Studies Association Conference, St Kitts, 30 May 1984).

18. See Bernard Diederich, Don Bohning and Juan Tamayo, 'The Springtime of Election', *Caribbean Review* (Summer, 1982), p.5 ff.

19. Trinidad and Tobago, *Report of the Constitution Commission* (Port-of-Spain, 1974), p.47. The Report noted that 'we do not dispute that it is not enough to establish in the abstract that the disadvantages of the first-past-the-post system outweigh its advantages. The issue must be judged in the circumstances which exist in Trinidad and Tobago' (p.51).

20. It is important in this context to note that earlier on even the British colonial authorities had recognized the deficiencies of their system as it operated in British Guiana. Thus the Secretary of State for the Colonies concluded that proportional representation should be introduced to Guyana reasoning that 'it is absolutely fair' and that it would 'encourage inter-party coalitions and multi-racial groupings', *British Guiana Conference, 1963* (London: Command 2203, November 1963), pp.6–8. Furthermore, it is not our purpose here to analyse the contentious operation of the system of proportional representation in Guyana. The reader should refer to Edward Greene, 'The 1968 General Elections in Guyana and the Introduction of Proportional Representation' in Trevor Munroe and Rupert Lewis (eds.), *Readings in Government and Politics of the West Indies* (Mona, Jamaica, 1971), pp.134–6.

21. What Carl Stone called the 'mystique of Manley's Rod of Correction' was found to tap a number of symbolisms: 'pro-Rastafarianism, anti-corruption, old fashioned discipline'. See his *Electoral Behaviour and Public Opinion in Jamaica*, pp.25–7.

22. In the social sciences the concept of costs is taken from economics, i.e. that which is sacrificed in order to obtain anything. It may be calculated not only in monetary terms but in pain or disability. In other words, it implies either surrendering something of value or engaging in activities which are painful at the margin. See J. Viner, 'Cost' in E.R. Seligman (ed.), *Encyclopaedia of the Social Sciences* (New York, 1931), Vol. 4, pp. 466–7.

23. It is revealing that in none of Carl Stone's excellent treatises on Jamaican electoral politics is this issue of the 'democratic cost' raised.

24. Carl Stone, *Democracy and Clientelism in Jamaica* (New Brunswick, N.J., 1980), p.252.

25. *Ibid.* p.253.

26. Under the Westminster system it is the constitutional right of any government to call elections at its discretion. However, the P.N.P. opposition, which boycotted the election, did have a point in the issue of 'reasonableness', ably put by Carl Rattray when he posed it as 'the right of the people and the ability of the people to exercise their franchise when the election is called'. This was especially important, Rattray argued, under the single member constituency system. See *The Weekly Gleaner*, 13 Feb. 1984. At issue in November 1983

was the use of the 1980 Voter's List which had not been updated with new (especially young) eligible voters. As a result of the boycott 54 of the 60 seats in the House were declared elected unopposed. A similar situation occurred in Trinidad and Tobago in 1971.

27. As John La Guerre notes, 'Voters had returned to the tribe and anchored the relationship between politics and social structure' – *The Politics of Communalism* (Trinidad, 1982), p. 60.

28. The vote was 217,319 to remain in the West Indies Federation and 256,261 to leave.

29. Electoral support is, of course, not the only form of support in politics, but lacking other measures such as opinion polls it clearly has to be considered in any calculation of popularity. Pat Emmanuel, from whom these figures are taken, does make the important point that eighteen-year-olds voted for the first time in 1976 and that the Alliance was the principal beneficiary. *General Elections in the Eastern Caribbean*, p. 51.

30. *Ibid*. p. 55.

31. See, for instance, Carl Stone's discussion of Jamaica's comparative rankings on a series of scales by various international agencies in his *Democracy and Clientelism in Jamaica*, pp. 1–9.

32. It was Wilfredo Pareto who best stated the principle which is generally accepted today when he concluded that 'every people are governed by an elite, by a chosen element in the population'.

33. See Robert Michels, *Political Parties* (New York, 1912).

34. Seymour Martin Lipset, *Political Man, the Social Basis of Politics* (New York, 1963), p. 230.

35. In a recent paper Selwyn Ryan quotes J. D. Elder's view that in Tobago, for instance, village loyalty is akin to tribal loyalty. This author's critique of Ryan's paper was that both he and Elder had failed to analyse how an electoral system with geographically based constituencies had reinforced that parochialism. Ryan, 'Political Style in Tobago' (Paper presented to the Caribbean Studies Association Conference, St Kitts, 1 June 1984).

36. T. H. Marshall, *Class, Citizenship and Social Development* (New York, 1964), p. 92.

The Political Economy of Independence of the Former Associated States of the Commonwealth Caribbean

TONY THORNDIKE

On 19 September 1983 in Basseterre, St Kitts and Charlestown, Nevis, the final curtain fell on the last act of the British decolonisation production, 'Associated Statehood'. The actors had for long played to diminishing audiences, although a touch of drama persisted to the very end, with the Kittitian Labourite opposition boycotting the *dénouement*. But within a matter of weeks, the USA invaded Grenada and installed a government to its liking, with the official support of all the other Commonwealth Leeward and Windward Islands. The question of their political and economic viability and vulnerability as very small territories — the reason for their particular route to formal decolonisation — was by that act dramatically reinforced. The USA, and Grenada's neighbours, would not tolerate political or economic experiments designed to first circumvent and then rise above the twin constraints of small size and underdevelopment, which did not conform to rule as bequeathed by British colonialism.

THE PHENOMENON OF DEPENDENCY

The tragedy of Grenada was a violent manifestation of the deep-rooted problem of dependency which that island and its neighbours have experienced from the time of their original colonisation three centuries ago. A condition common to all Third World countries, its impact is specific to the structure and size of each economy and socio-historical environment. The story of the former Associated States of the Commonwealth

Caribbean – Antigua, Dominica, Grenada, St Kitts–Nevis, St Lucia and St Vincent – and the remaining colonies in the Leeward island group – Anguilla, British Virgin Islands (BVI) and Montserrat – is closely related to the four dimensions of dependency. In summary, these are the structural, the directed, the functional and the psychological. To most dependent economies, these are ranked in a rough order of impact: not so in these islands.

Normally the most pervasive is structural dependency, whereby the basic structure of the economy is substantially determined by external market pressures and sources of supply over which producers and consumers – or, more simply, society at large – have little or no control. It is complemented by directed dependency, whether through government economic policy such as the determination of import quotas and preferential price levels, or multinational company commercial practice, to ensure continuance of privileged positions. Functional dependency, on the other hand, is reflected in the goals and instruments of economic policy which not only perpetuate but reinforce imported life-styles without proper consideration of what the economy can bear. It is, therefore, closely allied to the psychological variant.[1] This is defined as a deep attachment to the values and preferences of the metropole – and its economic, social and political institutions. This is understandable in view of the history of slavery and the long exposure to colonialism. It meant the transplant of British political institutions and assumptions, regardless of their efficacy and relevance, and a resistance to new institutional forms. It follows that, for these islands, only by reformist action to undermine functional and psychological dependency can the effects of structural dependency be lessened and an effective challenge to the directed dimension be mounted.

In the Eastern Caribbean, therefore, psychological dependency is at least as important as structural, to the extent that it represents a deep-seated, and what has appeared for decades to be an intractable sense of inadequacy. Nobody, least of all the islanders themselves, felt that they could cope on their own: indeed, leaderships of the smallest islands – those of Anguilla, the BVI and Montserrat – perceived the problems to be too insoluble to permit independence, albeit from different

standpoints and for particularist reasons. Some of the difficulties which helped instil the feeling of inadequacy and helplessness were, and remain, directly related to geographical smallness
and topography; others were, in effect, societal and highly
characteristic of all Commonwealth Caribbean societies; while
yet others were common to all Third World communities, which
smallness aggravated. In short, their perception of their political
economy was to detemine directly their constitutional progress.
This perception was to critically condition the most important
constitutional decision of all, that of seeking independence.
Their historical experience provided an alternative culture to
those lost in the dehumanising conditions of the notorious
Middle Passage from Africa, but it was inherited and undermined the development of a sense of West Indian identity.
Independence was not sought to reverse this and inculcate a
sense of nationhood, whatever the public protestations to the
contrary. Independence was ultimately sought in order to gain
access to multilateral aid funds and to participate in international
fora primarily concerned with economic development: in short,
to help alleviate only one aspect of their dependency, the
economic, caused by years of neglect and underdevelopment.
The world, like the slave master of yore, was expected to look
after them; aid was their right. Thornton labelled this aspect
of the legacy of slavery an 'emotional logic'. 'They see nothing
amiss', he wrote, 'in calling upon other resources other than
their own (for) they owe it to us.'[2] Logically, this expression
of inadequacy also translated itself into a ready willingness to
accept anything which the pre-independence metropole was
prepared to offer, or, after independence, what others deigned
to give, whatever the conditions. Not for nothing did the London
Times call an Eastern Caribbean delegation 'a beggars opera'.

It was not until 13 March 1979 that dependency in all its forms
was to be challenged, by the *coup* of the Grenadian revolutionaries led by the New Jewel Movement (NJM), and the establishment of the Peoples Revolutionary Government (PRG). But
elsewhere, inadequacy persists. Antigua once hosted the Space
Research Corporation, a disguised South African company
which used Antigua as a staging point for weapons deliveries
to combat anti-apartheid forces. Once unkindly described as
'a nation of waiters and barkeepers',[3] the alleviation of its

severe financial problems caused by a bloated public sector and huge payments deficit is made all the more difficult by the aura of alleged corruption. Dominica suffered three attempts at armed coups in 1981 alone, by mercenaries with Ku Klux Klan and other sinister connections, who hoped to exploit a poverty-stricken and hurricane devastated island for their marginally legal activities. In St Lucia, a prolonged struggle for power resulted by 1982 in excessive political fragmentation and a severely weakened ability to plan and direct a battered economy.

What, then, are the roots of this sense of inadequacy which has dictated the pace of constitutional advancement and shaped the direction of economic development? Some are 'Caribbean' and so common to their larger neighbours. An example is the propensity to import, particularly food, in the manner of their former masters, paying for a preferred lifestyle through export crops. Inefficiently produced, their marketing depends largely on what Britain and later, the European Community, are prepared to offer. The islands certainly saw themselves as relatively poor as compared to their larger neighbours, the so-called More Developed Countries (MDCs), particularly as their economic expectations rose quickly with sustained exposure to North American lifestyles and tastes after the mid-fifties, via emigration, tourism and the media. Occasionally, the disparity between expectations and resources was admitted: as one Leewards Premier once remarked, 'we have bicycle societies with Cadillac tastes'.[4] Another Caribbean characteristic was a marked reluctance by each island leadership to cooperate with each other for mutually beneficial purposes and to help alleviate geographical handicaps. Cooperation was often feasible only if it meant that some form of political or economic gain would be wrung out of a parsimonious Britain or USA, potential aid givers. The Organisation of Eastern Caribbean States (OECS), formed after much argument in 1981 as the successor to the virtually moribund West Indies (Associated States) Council of Ministers, achieved little and was barely known outside the region. The eyes of the world suddenly focussed on it in October 1983 when, through its chairperson Prime Minister Eugenia Charles of Dominica, it appealed for assistance to rescue 'our kith and kin' in Grenada.[5] Article 8 of its Treaty was invoked: this called upon members to cooperate 'on arrangements for collective security against external aggression ... with or without the support of internal or national elements'.[6] With the help of a post-invasion appeal for military intervention by Grenada's Governor-General, it was liberally interpreted to justify the call for US action to expunge both the threat of radical change by what Reagan called 'leftist thugs'[7] who had murdered the PRG Prime Minister, Maurice Bishop and most of the NJM cabinet, and that of an alleged 'pro-Cuban and Soviet gnat' in their midst.[8]

Another set of problems shaping their political economy and attitudes was physical. Geographical fragmentation, reinforced by the tradition of individualistic administration, meant that just over half a million people live under nine separate administrations, none of which governs more than 120,000. Population growth is high; at nearly 900 per square mile, Grenada is one of the most densely populated agriculturally based countries in the world. These individually small markets are further disadvantaged by high transport costs and, notwithstanding the existence of the Caribbean Community (CARICOM), and within it, the Common Market, many erstwhile trading partners see difficulty in viewing them as a single entity. The diseconomies of scale considerably limit development options except, where circumstances permit, tourism.[9] That, however, creates social problems in the West Indian context.[10] Some, notably Anguilla and St Vincent, have developed flourishing offshore finance centres. Although they swell government revenue,[11] few are employed by them; they also have a reputation for handling dishonestly acquired funds for disreputable people, hardly an appealing image.

Small size also brings other, lesser known problems. The cost of administration, for instance, is inordinately large and leaves little revenue for development. It has been calculated that, for instance, 75 per cent of St Vincent's tax revenue is spent on civil service salaries, as the establishment needed to provide the desired range of services is larger in relation to total population that might be justified in larger economies which enjoy economies of scale. In that island, remittance income amounts to an astonishing 85 per cent of the value of visible exports.[12] Added to this is the legacy affecting all the Commonwealth Caribbean of the pre-war riots, namely trade unionism. This helped secure relatively high wages, particularly in the public sector. Another difficulty is the administrative inability to absorb, administer and audit aid disbursements even when offered. St Lucia experienced this embarrassing problem in 1976 when a portion of a multilateral aid package had to be foregone as it could not be spent within the regulations during the time limit set. [13]

Then there is the question of credibility as viewed by others. Their aspirations to the unsympathetic appear pretentious and their nationals as ignorant and unsophisticated. Whether or not Montserrat sent the apocryphal telegram to the British government in early September 1939 telling Britain not to worry about the outcome of the newly-declared war as Montserrat was lying four-square behind her, is immaterial. The fact is that it is believed and has gone into the lexicon of small island folklore. Naipaul recounted the words of a Jamaican who, emigrating to England, met small islanders for the first time.

These little dunce breadfruit niggers ... they're going to London, they don't know what they're going to, but when they ask them in London where dem comes from, these yam and breadfruit little niggers, dem's got to say Jamaica, 'cos nobody heard of dem islands. Dem's so small that if you started running on dem and develop speed you'd land up in the sea. [14]

Even the Prime Minister of relatively small Barbados saw fit to insult Eastern Caribbean ministers as 'bandits that I now see masquerading as leaders, presiding over the destiny of the unfortunate West Indian people', [15] although he was referring specifically to the corrupt Eric Gairy of Grenada.

They were also treated to what sometimes amounted to excessive paternalism by an imperial England. They had to be protected and, in turn, the world had to be protected from their demands and begging bowls, and the instability which was alleged to be the more potentially prevalent the smaller the territorial unit. It is not therefore surprising that six of the nine (actually seven as, until 1981, Anguilla was formally joined to St Kitts – Nevis) were the objects of a unique experiment in the history of British decolonialism, that of Associated Statehood status. The story of its genesis and failure as a longterm arrangement (as it was designed to be) highlights better than any other the phenomenon of inadequacy. The islands wanted protection and economic development: Britain wanted to keep them out of world affairs for both its, and their own, good. Neither party got what it desired.

THE HISTORY OF DISADVANTAGE

It is, of course, also true to say that the status, likened to 'internal independence' with residual British reserve powers essentially limited to foreign affairs and defence, emerged at a critical conjuncture in British colonial policy. Colonialism, in the 1960s, was everywhere under attack, most particularly through the medium of the United Nations. The 'wind of change' had also swept through Britain; despite vestiges of nostalgia, few Britons in official positions felt able to be openly proud about imperial possessions. A strong sense of obligation, nonetheless, was felt towards the fate of Britain's oldest colonial possessions. Unfortunately, the constitutional arrangements planned for the eastern Caribbean islands (except the BVI) had collapsed in the bitter aftermath of the illfated West Indies Federation in May 1962. To make matters worse, most were in receipt of British grant-in-aid which necessitated close imperial control of their finances in London's eyes, notwithstanding the introduction of universal suffrage in 1951 and ministerial government in 1956. These constitutional advances, put into effect more quickly than many administrators and local business elites would have preferred because of alleged 'unreadiness' and 'underdevelopment', were made necessary largely by virtue of the impending entry of the islands into the Federation. They were not introduced because of widespread and sustained indigenous pressure at the popular level.

Then ... came universal suffrage, illiteracy being no longer a bar. Whether this at once brought a blessing to the colony ... is a matter of opinion. The masses are still largely uneducated ... and too ready to be swayed by promises (especially) if surreptitiously accompanied by a liberal distribution of rum.[16]

Britain recognised that they were not poor on the scale of, say, Haiti: all bar Dominica are graded category three by the World Bank (twenty desperately poor African and Asian states occupy fifth category status).[17] But, together with the MDC territories, they had undoubtedly suffered benign neglect by Britain. Their strategic importance vanished with the end of the Anglo-French wars in 1815; and their economic trump-card collapsed following the first beet sugar harvest in Britain which brought in its wake depression wider and more penetrating than that experienced in the MDCs. It was worsened by the steady migrant outflow of the educated and most dynamic, prompting Lloyd George to describe them in the early twentieth century as 'slums of Empire'.[18] Consequently, it is not surprising that the widespread riots which swept through the British West Indies from 1935 began in St Kitts. Earlier ones, such as those in Grenada in 1920,[19] were, although barely reported, equally indicative of widespread social distress and frustration. The recommendations of the Moyne Commission, which had been charged by the British Parliament in 1938 to tour the British West Indies and report on the conditions, centred mainly upon the provision of welfare aid. But only £10m. was allocated, leaving very little for the smaller islands.[20]

Far more benefit, in fact, came to those fortunate enough to feature in the Anglo-American 'bases-for-destroyers' deal of 1940, Antigua and St Lucia. The strategic importance of the Commonwealth Caribbean to the USA was made explicit by this treaty, a fact of international life that has remained, and been strengthened, over the years and which no territorial government can afford to ignore. Indeed, the formal annexation of all or part of the Eastern Caribbean chain by Washington was considered before the war and speculation to this effect was renewed with the treaty. However, Roosevelt turned down the proposal, citing the economic burdens on the USA, leaving aside any racial consequences.[21] Despite the investment that flowed from the treaty, an observer in Antigua in 1955 recorded that 'the atmosphere is consistently depressing: physically sombre and silent, socially morose and lethargic'.[22] Only in two islands – St Vincent and Grenada – had the plantation system effectively broken down. For various historical and topographical reasons, they had from 1840 begun to be slowly but inexorably dominated by freeholder peasant agriculture with, first, cocoa and then bananas as the main export crop. For instance, by 1843 the number of freeholders working on two and a half acres or less was 1,360 in Grenada, or about five per cent of the then total population; by 1911, there were 6,332

(10 per cent)[23] and in 1960, an estimated 19,000 (21 per cent).[24] There was, of course, no doubt that they and others of the working class were poor: as a critical report on St Vincent compiled in 1969 by a group of economists from the University of the West Indies commented, 'most of the Vincentians were living in a way which, in terms of material and environmental conditions, could scarcely be far removed from the situation as it was under slavery'.[25] One disturbing fact illustrating this was the evidence of protein deficiency in children: whereas children under five constituted 20 per cent of the population, they accounted for 57 per cent of all deaths. In Dominica, where shareholding had also been established, infant mortality reached such proportions that, in 1952, the British government was finally forced to act. It requested and gratefully received a gift of skimmed milk from the USA, enough to give a crucial one ounce a day to 12,000 impoverished children and babies.[26]

But, poor as the peasantry were, they were proud and independent-minded. It is thus no coincidence that those who first challenged the colonial administrations were from those islands: notably T. A. Marryshow and Uriah Butler in Grenada, followed by the fiery Ebenezer Joshua of St Vincent. Their concerns did not centre upon the grievances and aspirations of only one constituency in one island, such as characterised the actions of Vere Bird and Robert Bradshaw on behalf of the sugar plantation workers in Antigua and St Kitts respectively. Rather, they were concerned with the identification, analysis and alleviation of the deep-rooted dependency in which the islands as a whole found themselves.

It is not difficult to see the results of dependency today. As in the past two hundred years or so, a substantial proportion of traditional exports still depend upon special access and price agreements, a situation as true of Cuba and Puerto Rico as, say, little St Kitts or St Lucia. However, imports of food, as opposed to manufactured goods, are disproportionate when there is so much unused agricultural land and high unemployment. In St Lucia, the cost of food imports in 1980 amounted to 23 per cent of all imports by value; in 1981 in Antigua, it reached 35 per cent, largely due to the demands of the tourist industry. St Kitts, partly fed by the Nevisian peasant farmers, recorded a low of 18 per cent.[27]

DLCC-F

Overall, the trade gap is considerable and as a result, over 80 per cent of capital imports for public sector investment has had to be financed by aid grants and net borrowing.[28] Even in an economy which was being actively diversified and reformed as Grenada's under the PRG after the ravages of the Gairy regime from 1968 to 1979 – where, for instance, the percentage of traditional exports fell from 94 per cent in 1977 to 63 per cent in 1982 and where agricultural production expanded by over 50 per cent in the same period – total imports exceeded exports by EC$151m to EC$50m in 1982.[29] Only by remittances, tourist earnings, aid and credits can the gap be narrowed. Fortunately, only EC$1m, or 3.7 per cent of total export earnings needed to be allocated to interest payments by the PRG, a comparatively remarkably low debt ratio and one attributable to very careful appraisal of investment projects and import needs. By contrast, Antigua, with 60 per cent of GNP and 40 per cent of employment derived from tourism in 1982, was in a far worse position. Its trade balance on visible exports was such that less than 8 per cent of imports could be paid for from this source. The combination of recession in the main tourist markets plus the propensity to import expensive consumer durables and luxury goods has led to a situation where that island, the richest of the Lesser Antilles in the 1960s, could become the first Eastern Caribbean state to become technically bankrupt if IMF terms and conditions continue to be refused.[30]

Psychological dependency, by its very nature, is far less amenable to measurement or assessment than the structural and directed dimensions. But it is the most apparent: indeed, Louis Lindsay identified it as a central concept.

Everywhere and at all times, the emergence and persistence of imperialist domination has been inextricably linked to the operationalisation of techniques which successfully encourage individuals and groups to accept ideas and orientations about themselves and their societies which bear little or no truthful relationships to the concrete or real world situations in which they live.[31]

It also led inexorably to the retardation of a sense of national dignity. Naipaul makes the point that 'living in a borrowed culture, the West Indian, more than most, needs writers to tell him who he is and where he stands [but] most have so far reflected and flattered the prejudices of their race or colour groups'.[32] Lowenthal's comment in this context is also highly apposite. 'West Indians at home', he wrote, 'often wish they were not West Indian.'[33] By extension, it meant it was the responsibility of others to help make them what they wanted to be, at least in materialist spirit.

For their part, the British middle class backbone of the Colonial Service found little difficulty in arguing that its action in abolishing slavery and overthrowing the power of the white planter class was born out of moral principles which underpinned the Christian values of Anglo-Saxon culture rather than anything suggesting economic efficiency. These precepts were institutionalised politically with the progressive introduction of the full panoply of Westminster style government without regard to the islands' small size and population, to the accompaniment of local gratitude. By doing so, political respectability for both metropole and colony was assured. These assumptions were swept aside by the PRG with the suspension of the inherited constitution, the institutions of which had been used so effectively against them by Gairy. Only the Governor-General remained, his signature appearing on 'Peoples Laws' as much as it had done on those formally passed by the House of Assembly. An offer by Barbados Prime Minister Adams to assist in drawing up an electoral list was met with a vituperative attack by Bishop.

Uncle Tom Adams of Barbados still feels he hasn't got enough problems in his own backyard that he can find time to wash his mouth in Grenada's business. Like an expectant dog barking for his supper, he rushes in to please his new master Reagan like all good yardfowls by attacking Grenada.

He ended his attack by hoping 'that those who start wars know how to end them',[34] a rhetorical question whose significance was to become apparent three years later when Barbados was the willing staging point for the invasion. Although it was announced in June 1983 that a commission of experts would prepare a draft revolutionary constitution upon which elections would be based, the 'principled refusal' to go to the country at the behest of others provided a stick of illegitimacy which the PRG's detractors used to great effect. Ironically, it was the suggestion by Trinidad Prime Minister George Chambers that

Bishop's attempt to rebuild relations with the USA would be best served by orthodox elections – which Bishop appeared to accept[35] – that helped precipitate his detention by the hard left of the PRG and which started the chain of events ending in invasion.

THE GENESIS OF ASSOCIATED STATEHOOD

In the context of decolonisation, the combination of poverty, dependency, small size and psychological problems meant only one thing to both the British and the local political elite: the islands could not reach any level of economic and political 'viability' to sustain individual independence. Viability meant, broadly speaking, being 'self-supporting', but this was never defined. Official opinion was restrictive and was in the forefront of attacks upon, for instance, a Labour Party study of colonial policy which unambiguously stated that independence should not be denied to the people of the smallest territory should they desire it.[36] The crux, as a well-placed ex-official wrote, was a 'practical inability' to conduct foreign relations and provide 'adequate defence'; the question was, therefore, who was to provide the wherewithal?[37] At the time, the problem did not encompass the Leewards and Windwards alone since, in 1947, they had agreed in principle to join the Federation. Local leaders saw in this the prospect of self-government but as time, and argument, progressed, they also saw problems. After all, interest in federation between the islands in the 1920s and 1930s, such as was expressed at the Dominica conference in 1932, sprang mainly from determination to transfer political control from white planters and merchants to dark-skinned West Indians. This had, however, been achieved by 1947. Similarly, enthusiasm for federation in 1947–56 was linked to universal suffrage and the constitutional advance of individual islands; this also had been achieved by the time delegates met in 1956 to begin constitution-drafting.

Nevertheless, the small island leaders pressed ahead. Federation was their only option. There was still the prospect of economic development via larger subventions of British aid which they felt sure would be channelled their way by their MDC colleagues. The MDCs would also help alleviate their unemployment as federation implied freedom of movement. But British aid on the scale demanded by the Trinidadian spokesman, Eric Williams – a minimum of £50m. over ten years – was refused, although much of this sum incorporated unspent Colonial Development and Welfare allocations, and grants-in-aid (for budgetary assistance for the smaller LDCs) until 1968, which had earlier been assured.[38] Further, since Britain still adhered to the traditional concept that the acid test of colonies' readiness for self-government was their ability to become financially self-supporting, that prospect looked even less attainable in the future. As for the possibility of any federal aid, the attitude of Jamaica in particular was made clear, especially by the outspoken Bustamante. The Federation meant but one thing: Jamaican taxpayers' money would be used 'for no other purpose but ... to improve the economy of the ... small islands and to deplete the revenue of Jamaica'.[39] It was, after all, contributing 43 per cent of federal expenditure, compared to the 39 per cent of Trinidad-and-Tobago, 9 per cent from Barbados and 9 per cent from all the small units together. For his part, Dr Williams of Trinidad saw no reason to give up his territory's right to limit immigration 'simply because a federation had been established' and particularly as 'it was led by small island politicians with vested interests which were not those of Trinidad'.[40]

The collapse of the Federation with the separate independence of Jamaica and Trinidad and Tobago left a necklace of little island pearls whose string had broken. Their governments' perception of the future was uniform: their political economy dictated a destiny beyond colonial status but all accepted that it had to be short of an independence which everybody agreed they could not sustain. There were two alternatives: a federation with Barbados, or 'unitary statehood' with Trinidad, following Williams' offer to his country's former confederates. Only Grenada took up the latter option, the others spending two years in fruitless negotiations among themselves. The Eastern Caribbean Federation proposals foundered upon the same shoals that wrecked their predecessor. First, Barbados refused to subsidise the six smaller units. Then Antigua demanded widespread powers of veto over financial matters and a weak federal structure, conscious of its rapidly increasing tourist revenues. St Lucia withdrew on the question of postage stamp revenue, supported by Dominica. Barbados then had no option but to proceed to independence. As with the 1958–62 experiment, strife and rivalry were prominent, and issues became more intense. As a historian put it,

As soon as the paeans to the resolution of these factors had appeared, they were deluged by the obituaries and postmortems of a noble idea that passed with the fleeting fascination of a tropical storm.[41]

It also highlighted the difficulties that leaders of small size personalist-dominant political systems found in dealing with each other, let alone in sharing finance, that precious commodity of power and patronage in poor societies. In short, lessons had not been learnt, either by the political elite or Britain. As before, Britain had allowed negotiations to drag on by being unwilling to make any aid commitment which, in its view, would be open-ended. Eventually, and too late, a guarantee of assistance over five years was given, but at a level far below the recommendations of a report which it had itself commissioned.[42]

For its part, Grenada met a similar fate. Williams encountered severe internal opposition, largely on racial grounds with the substantial Indian minority in Trinidad fearing an influx of poor Afro-Grenadians. Not admitting this, his withdrawal was couched in economic terms via a Commission of Inquiry. The potentially severe burden on Trinidadian finances was noted. After all, 'Grenada fits closely the classical description of an underdeveloped country with low incomes, production and productivity, underutilised labour, primitive work practices ...'[43] His representative in the United Nations was more forceful. Unitary statehood with Trinidad would only be possible with large British aid (at one point, referred to as 'reparations'). 'Surely, it is not ex-colonies like Trinidad-and-Tobago which today must be called upon to pay the overdraft due from colonialism.'[44]

Thus Britain had no option but to take matters into its own hands. Colonial status was not possible given the heightened expectations of the elite who wanted some recognisable status for their territories, as did the United Nations. Fortunately for the Colonial Office, an option appeared ready to hand in the associated statehood constitution that had been granted in 1962 by New Zealand to its far-flung Pacific dependency, the Cook

Islands. Also to the point, this had been ultimately approved by the United Nations as fulfilling the requirements of res. 1514 (XV), the so-called Anti-Colonial Resolution, as modified by res. 1541 (XV), which permitted association of one territory to another for certain clearly delineated areas as an alternative to independence, if the population of the associate clearly and unambiguously desired it. The arrangements were discussed and approved by a conference at Oxford University composed of academics, journalists and colonial experts, called by Colonial Secretary Greenwood to consider the future of all the small British remnants of empire.

Association after the Cook Islands example was deemed suitable for the Leewards and Windwards by the conference because it was felt that the lack of potential capability to fulfil international political obligations assumed to exist with membership of the United Nations compounded their severe economic problems. Not only was this 'threshold of viability' too high for them ever to achieve but as 'virtually permanent mendicants' they would be prone to internal instability and international pressures in an area sensitised by the 1959 Cuban revolution. In short, Britain had an obligation to the world community to protect its members from potential political irresponsibility. Greenwood therefore moved quickly against Antigua, St Kitts – Nevis – Anguilla and St Lucia, whose Legislative Councils had in August 1965 voted for internal self-government as the next step in constitutional advancement. They were willing to accept this veto, although St Lucia's John Compton expressed reservations as they were reminded by Britain that, according to its colonial practice, internal self-government was the immediate precursor to independence and was logically temporary.[45] Rather, they were to be offered a long-term arrangement: it was this feature that was behind Britain's refusal to grant associated statehood status to Belize (then British Honduras) on the grounds that, as soon as there was a satisfactory outcome to the territorial dispute with Guatemala, its internally self-governing constitution inaugurated in 1964 would be swiftly converted into full sovereignty.[46] Accordingly, proposals were circulated to all the seven islands in December 1965 and all accepted them in principle except Montserrat. Its government wished to remain a colony, shrewdly calculating that Britain would therby be legally obliged to maintain economic aid rather than act from moral choice.

A series of Constitutional Conferences followed, not entirely without resentment at the extent of British pressure, lack of definite commitment on aid and complete opposition to any amendment to the 1962 Commonwealth Immigration Act in favour of the potential associates. As the Cook Islands model, together with those outside the Commonwealth, Puerto Rico and the Netherlands Antilles, incorporated freedom of movement with the metropole, the latter refusal was particularly resented. Concern was also expressed at the extent of the legal measures that London felt necessary to fulfil its remaining obligations. However, negotiations whittled down the provisions of the original draft which allocated to Britain power to interfere, in effect, in an associate's internal affairs if there was a difference of opinion over external policy. Although a degree of delegated power in this sphere was granted, subject to conditions, the attempt to divorce internal and external affairs in territories whose *raison d'être* almost from the time of their discovery was export production using imported labour, was to prove a dismal failure. As one delegate put it,

It is the astute British pattern to invite everybody and then astutely allow the members to express their views to puerility and then impose their conditions. That is what happened in London.[47]

For the most part, however, agreement was quickly reached as both parties knew that there was no practical alternative. Another delegate admitted as much,

I want to say this: the British did a very nice job making us look inferior [but] what I am not sure of is if some of us are geared psychologically to take the reins of government ... Our worst enemy is in front of us and the biggest enemy is we ourselves.[48]

Only Compton continued to hold out for internal self-government, but had little support from some of his St Lucian delegation. As he explained on returning to Castries,

the St Lucia Government requested ... to proceed to this status of internal self-government, and after a few years in that status to review our position and then declare whether we are prepared to become independent in association with Great Britain or to become independent on our own, or to become independent in association with other territories in the Windward

Islands or in the West Indies. This status Her Majesty's Government refused to discuss with us, telling us that we take or leave the Constitution that had been offered to us. That if we wanted there and then full independence ... they were prepared to give it to us at that London Constitutional Conference, and therefore I have not got much to say at this stage.[49]

With the passing into law of the West Indies Act in February 1967, each acceded to the new status[50] within a matter of days. St Vincent was the exception, remaining a colony until October 1969 due to complex internal political problems centring upon accusations of electoral fraud, the number of legislators permitted under the new constitution and floor-crossing. But no test of public opinion was allowed, although a favourable majority would undoubtedly have been obtained had there been the opportunity. This deliberate omission was a major factor in the eventual decision of the United Nations and its anti-colonialist 'Committee of Twenty Four' not to recognise the status as representing acceptable decolonisation.

From the collapse of the attempts at Federation, the British attitude had been one of paternalism and a wish to dispose of the question quickly. As one MP stated in the poorly attended late night debate on the West Indies Bill,

they are not like other territories which are clamouring for independence: they are terrified of being left alone. We must not be worried about exercising a little paternalism, if I may call it that instead of colonialism.[51]

Similar sentiment caused Britain to incorporate into the arrangements a number of hurdles for any associate who wished to proceed unilaterally to independence, without British permission. Section 10(1) of the Act made the situation clear: the government had to obtain a two-thirds majority in both the House of Assembly *and* a referendum with a 90-day time interval in between. As a Trinidadian newspaper rather condescendingly commented,

this lengthy process was designed to ensure that a government with delusions of grandeur did not saddle a poor Associated State with the burdens and expenditures of Independence, unless the electorate was aware of what it was doing.[52]

But there was an escape clause, section 10(2), designed for Britain alone, but which did not feature in the Cook Islands arrangements. By giving six months' notice, Britain could abrogate the agreement. This was insisted upon by Colonial Office lawyers, by now sharply aware that Britain was shouldering responsibilities without the political wherewithal, for all practical purposes, to fulfil them. It was eventually through this method that each island, starting with Grenada in 1974, requested Britain to permit independence. Ironically, this clause caused considerable concern at the time, several islands wanting firm reassurance that they would not be 'jettisoned': this Britain readily agreed to.[53]

THE FAILURE OF ASSOCIATION

Association failed not because it did not establish a sense of nationalism; the overwhelming reason was that the economic and political expectations of the associates were unfulfilled. It was as if the restrictions put upon their competence in external affairs made them much more conscious of how important external relations were to their welfare and economic development. Not only their perceptions were involved, but more concretely the possibility of radically changed circumstances following British entry into the European Community. Since nearly all their relatively high cost export produce was sold at preferential prices on the British market, this was a critical event. There also occurred in 1973 the fourfold rise in oil prices. As with other poor non-oil producers, this wreaked havoc on their already deficit-prone balance of payments.

The key was deemed to be international personality. Conferred only by sovereign independence, it permitted not only full representation on international and regional organisations but also eligibility for many types and sources of aid funds. To many non-Commonwealth aid givers in particular, they were still British dependencies, whatever the constitutional label, and so fell foul of their assistance regulations. As one expert noted,

had they been independent, they could have been eligible for assistance from sources from the United Nations Special Emergency Fund and from the IMF's special facilities. Moreover as independent countries they would have stood a better chance of attracting bilateral support from some of the sources which came to the rescue of the Most Seriously Affected countries.[54]

Their growing appreciation of this problem brought, first, resentment and thereafter a gradual escalation of demands and complaints, some of which were not entirely justified. For instance, although they were denied representation at the European Community membership negotiations, Britain secured considerable concessions regarding preferential quotas for their products, which often could not, in the event, be fulfilled.[55] Fortunately, Guyana permitted their indirect representation during the talks on trade and aid which eventually led to the 1975 Lomé Convention, the host delegation speaking for them as and when necessary.[56] After its signature, their non-membership meant that they had to rely upon the aid provided for members' dependencies under Part IV of the Treaty of Rome. While this was higher on a *per capita* basis than that given to Lomé signatories, it was, in effect, the only multilateral aid available. It was, it should be noted, considerably lower than that enjoyed by neighbouring French *départements*. As parts of France, they could tap the generous regional assistance and agricultural budgets.[57]

The same disadvantage applied to their activities within CARICOM, where they could not participate in foreign policy discussions, or in other international fora. One such concerned air transport rights. St Lucia, in particular, complained bitterly that it could not be a party to bilateral air agreements and had to rely upon Britain. As 87 per cent of its tourists came from North America, Compton became increasingly concerned that in the Anglo-US negotiations for air transport − the so-called 'Bermuda II' agreement − St Lucia's interest would be lost since Britain was much more concerned with trans-Atlantic and trans-Pacific routes than with those going southwards. Although the truth was that the Associated States did very well out of the agreement,[58] it suited Compton to pursue it for internal partisan reasons. Finally, there were allegations that foreign countries were unwilling to conclude trade and commercial agreements with the associates (this being a delegated competence) because of 'confusion' over their status. Ultimate British responsibility, Premier Walter of Antigua said, meant that 'in nearly every place countries are reluctant to deal with us because they think they're interfering with Britain's external affairs'.[59] This was true in the sense that financial agreements had to be reported to London, and it is difficult to imagine commercial contracts not involving credit obligations. But the allegation seemed to mask the failure to conclude commercial treaties with developed states who were, in reality, sceptical of the profitability of investment in such diminutive territories and the relatively small CARICOM market.

That these economic concerns were paramount can be seen by the relative indifference shown at virtually all levels to the constitutional conundrum of Anguilla in the 1967–69 crisis.[60] The action by British troops in March 1969 to attempt to curtail the secession of the poverty stricken and neglected island from St Kitts–Nevis–Anguilla union was made legally possible on the basis of alleged foreign interference. The Anguillan secessionists, led by Ronald Webster, feared Kittitian rule under the new arrangements and without the restraining hand of Britain. Riots at the time of the inauguration of association led Britain, with the permission of St Kitts Premier Bradshaw, to establish a temporary but separate administration to give time for a settlement to be negotiated. Failure was then attributed to alleged manipulation of Webster by external undesirable Mafia-connected groups, who were also arming his followers. Although this was completely erroneous, it was enough, since the 1967 Act made clear that intra-island affairs within an Associated State involving matters purely domestic between them were strictly internal. The legal crisis began even before the troops landed, when Foreign Secretary Michael Stewart volunteered a statement that 'the Anguillans should not have to live under an administration they do not want',[61] a point heavily stressed in leaflets given out to the 6000 islanders. Putting this into action, albeit reluctantly, meant that Britain drove a coach and horses through its own Act. Only after Bradshaw's death in 1978 were talks on formal separation possible, a situation finally achieved by the Anguilla Act of 1981.

INDEPENDENCE

These difficulties confirmed the total impracticability in the Caribbean context of clearly separating internal and external affairs. Compared to geographically isolated Pacific islands, their exposure to foreign political and economic influences was historically considerable. Gairy recognised this and was the first to insist upon independence. Admittedly, he had opposed association in 1966–67 but this was for purely internal political reasons as he was then in opposition. Once returned to power, he supported it. However, by 1970, he perceived independence to be a useful status and a cheque, particularly in view of his profligacy. He pointed sharply at the ease with which the Bahamas, whose constitutional status as a colony was inferior to that of Grenada, attained independence in 1973. Britain agreed: a referendum was only required if independence was sought against British opposition which was by now certainly not the case, and at his request, section 10(2) was invoked.

Nobody expected, however, the violence which was unleashed. Once a popular union leader and by then a notorious mystic, Gairy had long disregarded his peasant supporters. Such was the broad base of opposition that the business community, clergy, the formal rightwing opposition and the nascent and radical NJM led by Bishop, Bernard Coard and Unison Whiteman found common cause. Forming the 'Committee of Twenty Two', harassments, arson and torture by Gairy's secret police, the Mongoose Gang and the Night Ambush Squad were stepped up: one of those killed was Bishop's father.[62] Mass petitions to London and the concern of neighbouring countries had no effect, the Foreign and Commonwealth Office being well aware that the bulk of the protesters were not against independence as such, but independence under Gairy's leadership. Neither was a referendum practical, as this had not been used in any colony, let alone an associated state. Also, there was the United Nations to consider. As one commentator wrote,

the pressures on any metropolitan power are tremendous. The Committee of Twenty-Four and the anti-colonialists of the Manhattan lobby would want to expel her from the United Nations if Britain attempted to do otherwise.[63]

What happened was to be repeated on all the other islands, although on a far less destructive scale. Opposition groups and, in the case of Antigua and St Kitts, secession movements in Barbuda and Nevis respectively, used the section 10(1) provision as a useful political weapon. Admittedly, some influential elements, mainly businessmen and professional groups, were concerned about the economic capability of their territory to sustain the costs of independence and did not welcome the prospect. But the bulk of islanders, like those of Grenada, either cared little about the issue or preferred independence under another party or leader. Accordingly, opposition groups in all (bar Antigua and St Kitts–Nevis at their second attempt to gain independence) demanded referenda. As Britain was anxious to avoid another Grenada situation and accusations of granting 'premature' independence, long delays ensued despite the protestations of governing parties. They resolutely opposed referenda demands knowing that, in their highly partisan polities, such an opportunity would amount in the electorate's mind to an election, the specific issue to be decided being one of many. In any event, they echoed Gairy's objection: why should they be submitted to that indignity while colonial territories elsewhere were not?

The result was deep frustration, particularly for Dominica and St Lucia. In both cases, Britain pressurised their governments to heed opposition demands. Even this was not enough for Dominica's Freedom Party of Eugenia Charles. With Premier John's agreement, the British chief adviser of dependent territories was dispatched to unravel the state of public opinion. As Britain suspected, he found opinion not to be against independence. He also recorded his judgment of the opposition.

Their uncompromising tactics suggested that they were more concerned to delay or prevent progress to independence under the present government than, by constructive discussion, to obtain the best possible constitutional framework for Dominica's future.[64]

In St Lucia, delays caused by Britain's refusal to use its powers under section 10(2) of the Act until, *inter alia*, a new electoral register had been drawn up, led Compton to vent his frustration publicly.

It is absolutely humiliating and intolerable for a Government that has been elected by the majority of the people of St Lucia since 1964, and has been sustained in office by their confidence since then, to be travelling at great expense of time and money to the UK, and then to trudge up and down the staircases, like so many mendicants seeking favours from a master.[65]

Antigua's experience, however, was different. The opposition, led by Vere Bird, likewise demanded a referendum but was aided by the fact that the 1976 election was due. His Antigua Labour Party (ALP) won, pledging to shelve the issue on the grounds that Antigua's economy could not withstand the cost of independence. However, it was clear that victory came not from that but from the ALP's last minute plan to abolish income tax. Only after winning the subsequent election in 1980 did Antigua proceed to independence in late 1981, justified on the grounds that 'political dependency is now a stigma in the world'.[66]

In St Kitts–Nevis, a similar change of government took place in 1979, not long after the death of the veteran, and in his dying days, pro-independence Bradshaw. Pledged not to proceed to independence, the new People's Action Movement (PAM) government was able to assume power only on the basis of a coalition with the secessionist Nevis Reformation Party (NRP). The significance of this was that the NRP made it clear that the moment independence was requested, it would insist on secession for Nevis and leave the coalition, so precipitating the collapse of the PAM government. In the event, agreement was reached giving a wide range of powers to the Nevis Assembly, including the right of secession at a time of the island's choosing but subject to a referendum, but only after independence had been achieved.[67] The British were forced to agree but made it clear that an independent Nevis could not expect its support.[68] The way was then clear for Premier Simmonds to announce that he would request independence for the bi-island state. He had been under considerable pressure from his mainly urban middle class supporters to seek sovereignty for the same aid and financial reasons as had prompted other leaders earlier. Naturally, the St Kitts Labour Party was furious that an election pledge was upturned, that St Kitts did not have the right to secede from Nevis (and that therefore the labelling of the constitution as 'federal' was erroneous) and that the announcement came via a press interview in Washington, DC. As with so many other opposition parties in the erstwhile associates, the Labour leadership decided to boycott the independence celebrations – the one difference, however, being that they were more pro-independence than the PAM–NRP alliance! In Grenada, there was another, unforeseen, outcome. The opposition to Gairy and, as events proved, a wholly justified fear of what he would do when unrestrained by Britain, prompted the rapid growth in public support for the NJM. This soon assumed the leading role in the opposition following independence and the party's leader, Bishop, began to assume an international stature.

There is little doubt that independence brought some economic benefits, but only with aid. Administrative costs are higher: despite the establishment of the OECs, little has come of its aims for, *inter alia*, joint overseas representation and common services. Only in the question of security has there been action, and that against a fellow member, Grenada. That episode showed decisively that Washington would provide their defence, although with CARICOM, OECS or Organisation of American States participation. More importantly, it also made clear that there would be no distinction made between an external attack, most likely from anti-Western or mercenary forces, and a state of internal instability, coupled with the presence of foreign personnel branded as unfriendly, and deemed to be contagious. Financially, the conversion of the East Caribbean Currency Authority, whose currency operates in all the Commonwealth Leewards and Windwards bar the BVI, into a Central Bank in October 1983 undoubtedly helped the participants to plan and control their economies more effectively. But the promulgation of this reform did not depend upon its members' independence.

The most crucial attribute of independence is, however, the ability to conduct foreign policy. But, as the experience of the PRG made clear, the limits of manoeuvre in what is clearly a US zone of influence are constrained. Faced with the need to combat a Gairy-led mercenary invasion in the days immediately following the revolution, the PRG appealed to Cuba for help when earlier appeals to Grenada's traditional allies fell on deaf ears. Unrelenting opposition to many of the internal policies of the PRG by the US and neighbouring islands, and to its expressions of solidarity with the Nicaraguan Sandinista regime and the El Salvador rebels, together with its support for the Soviet Union in the United Nations,[69] led the leadership to react by stubbornly insisting on its 'principled positions'. Within the general world context of deteriorating relations between the Superpowers, Cold War tensions soon extended to the Eastern Caribbean, despite the PRG's plea for 'ideological pluralism' to be accepted. The agreement by Cuba to assume the lion's share of the work necessary to build the new international airport at Point Salines seemed final proof to the Reagan administration that Grenada would be host to a Soviet airbase unless action was taken. Cuba's contribution was US$40m. (EC$104m.) worth of labour and equipment out of a total expenditure of US$71m. (EC$185m.), using plans first mooted in 1926 and discussed again as late as 1966 by the British.[70] Designed to serve and develop the tourist industry, its facilities such as tank installations were for civilian use. It is therefore ironic that its first military use was by USAF aircraft.

Regionally, the revolution was perceived as an unacceptable virus despite the fact that it was a specific response to the particular circumstances of Grenada and Gairyism. As if to prove the point, subsequent elections in Jamaica, St Vincent, St Kitts–Nevis and Dominica all showed shifts to the right. PRG Foreign Minister Whiteman once estimated that 80 per cent of his time was spent on relations with CARICOM members[71] – if only to heal the many self-inflicted wounds caused by insults and sneers at their bourgeois regimes. Also, helpful discussions at CARICOM Heads of Government meetings in 1982 and 1983 helped to quell regional fears. But his murder together with that of Bishop and most of the Cabinet by elements of the Peoples Revolutionary Army on 19 October 1983 undid all that effort, the invasion beginning six days later.

CONCLUSION

The circumstances surrounding the search for independence by the Associated States, and thereafter the fear that five had of the political and economic experiments of one of their number, give instructive insights into their political economies. The perceptions of the elite and populace about their place in the world were ruthlessly exposed. Open economies with high import propensities, a distaste for agricultural work and widespread exposure to, and contact with, North America and Western Europe, were factors which, when coupled with such Caribbean cultural characteristics as emulation of lifestyles and preferences of others and the 'dog-eat-dog' mentality which is never absent in inter-island relations, helped shape a pervading sense of psychological inadequacy. In one form, this expressed itself as a feeling of helplessness in the face of the impossibility of achieving 'viability', the criteria of which were vague and constantly shifting. Small size and a population which was rapidly growing once most emigration outlets were sealed appeared insurmountable barriers. Non-orthodox strategies were distrusted. The occasional assertions by radical economists who argued that such factors exacerbated rather than caused relative poverty were as ignored as was their advice that, while some options were restricted, even closed, there were others to be explored.[72]

But inadequacy also surfaced in the widespread conviction that their economies were somebody else's responsibility and that it was therefore legitimate to respond to the paternalism and condescending gestures of faraway countries. In these circumstances, it was believed that any attempt at self-reliance or, more radically, structural transformation, was impossible without massive financial inputs within a political and economic environment modelled upon those of North America and Western Europe. But this would have had an opposite effect and serve only to accentuate dependency.

In other words, the island's elites recognised the economic value of independence but appeared not to be interested in its intrinsic worth. One post-independence affirmation of this was Vere Bird's statement at the ground-breaking ceremony of the new US Embassy in the Antiguan capital, St Johns, in early 1982. A strong US 'eagle', he proclaimed, was needed as a 'protector' of the 'little birds' of the Eastern Caribbean, perhaps not realising that eagles were predators whose diet included feathered vertebrates. This led one Antiguan critic to remark that

We were all misled into believing that his long struggle against British control was a serious struggle against colonialism ... It is now clear that it was no more than a lovers' quarrel in which his intention was merely to transfer loyalty and subservience from faraway Britain to the American guy 'next door'. His understanding of independence is, to say the least, highly questionable, if not perverse.[73]

In the wider region, the Memorandum of Understanding signed in October 1982 by all the ex-associates (except Grenada) and Barbados to establish a regional security force, funded and equipped by the USA and British trained, is another manifestation. From the start it was aimed at providing mutual support in the event of a threat to 'democracy' and national security or, as Bird admitted in an unguarded moment, to prevent Grenada-style coups.[74]

But it was precisely in Grenada where the effort to break the mould of inadequacy was the most marked. The challenge to dependency not only materially benefited the ordinary Grenadian but also inculcated a new sense of purpose and national unity. The unexpected extent of military resistance to the invading US forces after their landing on 25 October 1983 did not surprise those who had studied the revolutionay experiment. It would have been far greater had the general population not been in a state of shock after the unwarranted murder of Bishop and his colleagues, and the strictness of the military rule subsequently imposed. As one Grenadian bitterly remarked, 'four and a half years of reforms, of economic and social reforms, is in ruins'.[75] Both the IMF and the EC gave financial assistance to the regime, despite US and British pressure to prevent them. Not only were they dealing with highly motivated economists and technicians but there were also priorities, established audit procedures and sophisticated systems of financial reporting and budgeting. That it was achieved in a context of social welfare, employment and income generating enterprises and public works – such as housing and road construction and repair – and community involvement in decision making, was an inspiration to many in the region.[76]

No wonder, then, that the revolution challenged the pessimistic assertions of political economists such as William Demas that small size governs the process and extent of structural transformation and self-sustained growth. In particular, he argued, it undermined the capacity for continued transformation and social and economic advance. But, only by critically questioning assumptions about the development process, conditioned by norms and political institutions of developed capitalist societies – which he admits 'can impose severe restrictions on the growth process' but nonetheless remain 'intrinsically valuable'[77] – can psychological inadequacy be weakened and finally broken, as well as dependency itself. Only then will independence be meaningful for the ancestors of the thousands of slaves and indentured labourers who were forced to make their home in the little islands of the Commonwealth Eastern Caribbean.

NOTES

1. The general phenomenon of psychological dependence within the colonialist milieu was first discussed by O. Mannoni, *Prospero and Caliban* (1948: translated 1964: New York). The analogy between Robinson Crusoe and Man Friday, and Shakespeare's Prospero and Caliban in *The Tempest*, is the key to the work: each party is expectantly dependent upon the other for security, the coloniser to affirm his superiority complex and the colonised his fawning inferiority.
2. A. P. Thornton, 'Aspects of West Indian Society', *International Journal*, Vol. 15 (1960), p. 120.
3. *Outlet* (Antigua), 6 April 1980.
4. W. Bramble of Montserrat: reported in *The Workers Voice* (Antigua), 19 March 1976.
5. *Advocate-News* (Barbados), 22 Oct. 1983.
6. *Treaty Establishing the Organistaion of Eastern Caribbean States* (Antigua: Government Printing Office, 1981). Reproduced in *Bulletin of Eastern Caribbean Affairs*, Vol. 7, May–June 1981, pp. 16–28. Article 8 and its six clauses are on pp. 20–21.
7. *Daily Telegraph* (London), 26 Oct. 1983.
8. *New York Times*, 27 Oct. 1983.
9. Tourism was seen by British, Canadian and US experts as the only industry which the Eastern Caribbean could develop: Ministry of Overseas Development, *Report of the Tripartite Economic Survey of the Eastern Caribbean, January–April 1966* (London: HMSO, 1967).
10. L. Turner and J. Ash, *The Golden Hordes* (London: 1975), pp. 193–5.
11. Government revenue in Anguilla increased by 44.7 per cent in 1982 due to licence and other fees: Caribbean Development Bank, *Report no. 8/83*, p. 2. For a general discussion on this sector, see R. Ramsaran, 'The Myth and Reality of Off-shore Banking in the Caribbean', *Caribbean Contact*, August and September 1980.
12. *Advocate-News* (Barbados), 28 Feb. 1976.
13. *Financial Times* (London), 28 Jan. 1976.
14. V. S. Naipaul, *The Middle Passage* (Harmondsworth: 1969), p. 30.
15. Errol Barrow, quoted in *West Indies Chronicle*, LXXXX, No. 1527, p. 15 (1973).
16. R. P. Devas, *The History of the Island of Grenada* (St Georges, 1964), p. 164.
17. *1983 World Bank Atlas* (Washington, DC, 1983), pp. 4–5. Dominica is in category four; Britain is in category two.
18. Quoted in E. Williams, *From Columbus to Castro: A History of the Caribbean, 1492–1969* (London: 1970), p. 443.
19. E. Gittens Knight, *The Grenada Handbook and Directory 1946* (Bridgetown: 1946), p. 77. See also P. Emmanuel, *Crown Colony Politics in Grenada, 1917–1951* (Cave Hill: ISER, UWI, 1978), pp. 76–7.
20. West India Royal Commission 1938–39, *Recommendations*, Cmnd. 6174/1940 (London: HMSO); *Report*, Cmnd. 6607/1945 (London: HMSO).

21. *Foreign Relations of the United States*, Vol. III (Washington, DC: US Government Printing Office, 1959), p. 3.
22. D. Lowenthal, 'Economic Tribulations in the Caribbean: A case Study in the British West Indies', *Inter-American Economic Affairs*, Vol. 9, No. 3 (1955), p. 71.
23. E. Gittens Knight, *The Grenada Handbook 1946*, p. 43; p. 70.
24. *Report of the Economic Commission Appointed to examine Proposals for Association within the Framework of an Unitary State of Grenada and Trinidad–and–Tobago* (Port-of-Spain: Government Printery, Jan. 1965), p. 26.
25. H. Brewster et al., *Report on St Vincent* (Cave Hill: ISER, UWI, 1969, mimeo), p. 1.
26. Colonial Office Report: *Dominica, 1953 and 1954* (London: HMSO, 1955), p. 29.
27. World Bank, *Economic Memorandums* for respectively, St Lucia, Antigua and St Kitts–Nevis, 1981 and 1982 (Washington, DC, 1982 and 1983).
28. United Nations, ECLA, *Economic Activity 1981 in Caribbean Countries* (Port-of-Spain, 1982), Part XI, p. 8.
29. *Insight* (London), April 1983.
30. *Insight*, May 1983.
31. L. Lindsay, *The Myth of a Civilising Mission: British Colonialism and the Politics of Symbolic Manipulation* (Mona: ISER, UWI, Jamaica, 1981, Working Paper no. 31), p. 6.
32. Naipaul, *The Middle Passage*, p. 73.
33. D. Lowenthal, *West Indian Societies* (London: 1972), p. 250.
34. *The Nation* (Barbados), 29 Nov. 1980.
35. *The Observer* (London), 23 Oct. 1983 and information from an interview with Prime Minister Bishop, Sept. 1983.
36. Labour Party, *Labour's Colonial Policy: III, Smaller Territories* (London: Transport House, 1957).
37. Sir Hilary Blood, *The Smaller Territories* (London: Conservative Political Centre, 1958).
38. J. Mordecai, *The West Indies: The Federal Negotiations* (London: 1968), p. 305.
39. *Daily Gleaner* (Jamaica), 25 April 1958.
40. Quoted in E. Wallace, *The British Caribbean* (Toronto: 1977), p. 149.
41. F. Knight, *The Caribbean: The Genesis of a Fragmented Nationalism* (New York: 1978), p. 204.
42. C. O'Loughlin, *A Survey of Economic Potential and Capital Needs of the Leeward Islands, the Windward Islands and Barbados* (London: HMSO, 1963). Against a recommended EC\$215m over five years (1964–8), the British offered EC\$75m with no commitment past 1968.
43. Report of the Economic Commission ..., (note 24), p. 73.
44. United Nations, *GAOR*: Doc. A/AC. 109/SR. 9, p. 5 (1964).
45. This was made clear during the negotiations over the acceptance of the British terms: *Report of the Windward Islands Constitutional Conference*, Cmd. 3021/1966, p. 9.
46. *Daily Telegraph*, 4 June 1968.
47. Chief Minister E. T. Joshua, *Proceedings of the St Vincent Legislative Council*, 29 Sept. 1966.
48. McChestney George (Hon. Member for Barbuda), *Antigua Legislative Council Minutes*, App. G, 10 June 1966.
49. *Proceedings and Debates of the Legislative Council of the Island of St Lucia*, Tuesday, 28 June 1966, p. 2.

50. A detailed legal analysis of the Act is provided by M. Broderick, 'Associated Statehood: A New Form of Decolonisation', *International and Comparative Law Quarterly*, Vol. 17, No. 2 (1968).
51. H. C. *Debates*, Vol. 740, Col. 894, 31 Jan. 1967.
52. *Trinidad Express*, 20 Oct. 1972.
53. H. L. *Debates*, Vol. 280, Col. 166, 14 Feb. 1967.
54. A. McIntyre, Sec. Gen. of the CARICOM Secretariat, *Independence and Development in the Leeward and Windward Islands* (Royal Commonwealth Society, 15 Dec. 1976, mimeo.), p. 2.
55. *Financial Times*, 4 July 1982.
56. *Advocate-News*, 23 Oct. 1973.
57. *The Voice of St Lucia*, 18 Oct. 1975 (interview with Rt. Hon. Maurice Foley, MP, Minister of State, Foreign and Commonwealth Office).
58. *Agreement between the Government of the United Kingdom of Great Britain and Northern Ireland and the Government of the United States of America concerning Air Services*, Cmnd. 7016/1977 (London: HMSO), pp. 43–4.
59. *New York Times*, 17 Feb. 1976.
60. T. Thorndike, *Associated Statehood and the Eastern Caribbean Islands*, Social Science Research Council Report no. HR/3553/1, 1978, pp. 18–44.
61. H. C. *Debates*, Vol. 780, Col. 41 (17 March 1969). The invasion began on 19 March 1969.
62. T. Thorndike, 'Maxi-Crisis in Mini-State', *The World Today*, Vol. 30, No. 10 (Oct. 1974).
63. *Advocate-News*, 6 Feb. 1974.
64. *Dominica Termination of Association*. A Report to the Minister of State for Foreign and Commonwealth Affairs by R. N. Posnett. Cmnd. 7279/1978 (London: HMSO), pp. 13–14.
65. *The Crusader* (St Lucia), 25 March 1978.
66. *The Workers Voice*, 18 Jan. 1981.
67. *The Saint Christopher and Nevis Constitution Order, 1983* (London: HMSO), para. 114.
68. *The Labour Spokesman* (St Kitts), 18 Dec. 1982.
69. These complaints were detailed in President Reagan's speech to Congress, reproduced in *The New York Times*, 21 May 1983.
70. Report of the Tripartite Economic Survey ... (note 9), p. xiv.
71. Information from an interview with Whiteman by Drs A. Payne and C. Clarke, Sept. 1983.
72. See, for example, N. Girvan and O. Jefferson (eds), *Readings in the Political Economy of the Caribbean* (Kingston: 1971).
73. *Caribbean Contact*, July 1983.
74. Bird's speech of 27 Feb. 1983 was summarised in *Caribbean Contact*, April 1983.
75. *The Guardian* (London), 28 Oct. 1983.
76. *Grenada Is Not Alone* (St Georges: 1982), pp. 142–3.
77. W. Demas, *The Economics of Development in Small Countries with Special Reference to the Caribbean* (Montreal: 1965), p. 115.

Guyane: A Département Like The Others?[1]

FRANK SCHWARZBECK

With the independence of Belize in 1981, Guyane (also known as French Guiana) is today the last continental country in Latin America, Africa, and Asia, with a considerable surface area (91,000 sq. km) still politically dependent upon a European state. Through it, French sovereignty extends to the mainland of South America, complementing the French presence in other regions of the world: its overseas departments (DOM) and its overseas territories (TOM), plus its 'territorial collectivity', Mayotte.[2] The possession of overseas islands is, of course, not a phenomenon limited to France; it also embraces the United States and Great Britain, although in varying forms. The 'continental case' of Guyane, however, has become unique in the Third World.[3]

Setting aside this general characteristic for a moment, Guyane also presents an interesting case in other respects. It is among those small (in population terms) Third World countries whose numbers have increased in recent years and towards which social scientists are showing increasing interest, particularly in respect of their 'viability'. Does formal independence, which is generally expressed in membership in the United Nations, provide an adequate solution for the mini-states? Is it a better way to tackle their development problems (often more acute than those of larger Third World countries) than continued attachment to the metropole? In not every case would it seem so, with the situation of many mini-states having worsened since the attainment of national sovereignty. And it is within this context that the policies of France appear to have a certain legitimacy: independence is not the only method of decolonization.[4] In certain situations the opposite solution may be more sensible: 'departmentalization' as the 'French solution' to decolonization. A bias towards integration in general, and departmentalization in particular (Algeria), has been a characteristic trait throughout all French colonial history. For a large part of the French Empire, however, this 'French solution' has proved untenable, opposed as it is to the current of history and diametrically against the wishes for emancipation of the elites and populations of these countries. Accordingly, Paris was finally obliged to abandon its rigid attitude and to enter into a more flexible relationship with its former colonies; conceding their right to formal sovereignty the better to preserve its own interest. But for the 'confettis of the Empire' i.e. the DOM and the TOM, the 'French solution' has continued to hold its own.

A 'FORGOTTEN' COLONY?

Decolonization by incorporation has been a postulate advanced by successive French governments up to 1981. It was most rigorously advanced during the 1970s, when the political status of the TOM, and especially the DOM, made them exceptional cases at a time when many small Third World countries were progressively acceding to independence. Paris was untroubled by this fact and quite prepared to go 'against the famous current of history',[5] considering it to be of little benefit to small countries. For Guyane in particular, departmentalization was even more firmly defended. Demands for severance of ties with the 'mother country', an emancipation in the form of a sovereign state, were regarded as an aberration for a colony long 'forgotten', under-populated, under-exploited, non-productive and living entirely off the metropole.

The historical legacy of 300 years of colonization certainly appeared to underline the need for special treatment in the case of Guyane. Rich in potential wealth but never exploited: 'forgotten', but never abandoned, Guyane had conferred upon it a character seemingly unique in the world. Thus the first question raised is: 'Has Guyane been an exception in the history of French Colonialism?' Do the contradictions outlined above justify a metropolitan policy with respect to Guyane which cannot be understood in the light of those measures normally used to tackle the problems of development and underdevelopment in the Third World?

According to official historiography, Guyane was annexed by France in 1604. Perhaps it is more realistic to date effective possession from the end of the seventeenth century.[6] In any case, the country had long been a part of the first French colonial empire and was included from the very beginning.[7] This empire was characterized by the contrast between the extent of its largest possessions (particularly in North America) and their sparse population and meagre economic returns to the metropole. On the other hand, the islands, the numerous French Antilles of that time, played a valued part in Parisian mercantilism. Guyane thus increasingly served as an outlying station for the protection of the southern flank of lucrative commerce with the Caribbean. Its own exploitation seemed hardly necessary, a factor clearly distinguishing it from its neighbouring Dutch colonies (particularly Suriname), the importance of which for Holland was approximately comparable to that of the Antilles for France.[8] Then, in 1763, a radical change occurred. France lost nearly all of its first colonial empire, Guyane became the largest colony remaining attached to the metropole and also, in the same year, the object of 'the most important colonial emigration to take place at one time under the Old Regime',[9] the catastrophic results of which marked the first great episode in the history of the country, with considerable consequences for its future.

The second French colonial empire began with the taking of Algiers in 1830 and the occupation and subsequent 'pacification' of the country. In 1848 France strengthened its grip on the country and confirmed its immediate future as a colony of settlement and exploitation. In fact, Algeria became the most extensive colony of the second empire, eclipsing Guyane's importance in this regard and setting in train the second crucial episode in the history of 'equinoctial France' (as Guyane was also called because of its equatorial location). This was marked by the decision to instal a convict prison in Guyane only a few years after the completion of the territorial occupation of Algeria. Henceforth, the largest colony of what remained of the former empire was economically of even less importance than before. During the period of further expansion of the second empire, and particularly from the 1880s onwards, Guyane became just one among many tropical French colonies, most of which were in West and Equatorial Africa and which were equally difficult to develop in the colonial interest. The 'forgotten colony' in South America, it was scarcely distinguishable from several other 'forgotten colonies' in Africa which were indifferently exploited and of little economic significance for the metropole until after the First World War.

In short, within the general framework, Guyane was not a special case of French colonialism. During the first empire it formed a part of France's larger possessions, although of little economic significance since French interests lay above all in the islands. During the second empire, it formed a part of France's smaller possessions, once more of little economic significance since French interests for a long time focussed on Algeria, and to a lesser extent on Morocco, Tunisia and Indochina. However, if at this general level the case of Guyane proves to be in no way exceptional, a consideration of its more concrete historiography emphasizes three main events which have given Guyane a quite singular destiny. These are the 'episodes' of 1763, 1848–52 and 1946.

The 'episode' of 1763 is known as the 'disaster of Kourou' – an attempt at a massive settlement under the direction of the Duke of Choiseul and designed to compensate for the loss of the first empire. As one historian has noted:

With the rashness characteristic of the era of Louis XV, they had quite simply forgotten that all colonializations based on white manpower in Guiana (English, French or Dutch) had until then failed. If they had sent progressive emigrations to Guiana, starting with some hundreds of men who would have prepared the ground for later arrivals by constructing villages ... But they dumped 10,000 unexperienced emigrants (1763–1764) in one go in a country which was populated by only a few hundred whites. Furthermore, if stocks of provisions had been prepared in advance ... But the unfortunate settlers (half of whom were German-speaking from Alsace and Lorraine) were provisioned with supplies from the metropole which arrived in a pitiable state. Reception villages were not ready and the emigrants often had to sleep on the ground in a humid climate and in a country abounding with dangerous insects! ... Diseases set in very quickly, and a terrible epidemic ... brought the desolation to a climax. Of the figure of 10,446 arrivals, there were more than 6,000 victims.[10]

From this catastrophe arose the reputation, held thereafter, of Guyane as a 'Green Hell' and the 'European's Graveyard'.

Following slave emancipation in 1848 such a reputation was further strengthened with the establishment of a convict prison in the colony in 1851-2. Whereas elsewhere in the Caribbean workers from Asia (particularly from India) were imported to meet the demand for manpower in the plantation economies, in Guyane it was decided instead to 'import' prisoners. Officially, the reasons given were the 'development' of the colony by penal labour and thus the 'rehabilitation' of the convicts. While this aim may have been sincerely held by some well-meaning politicians, it was, in fact, quickly revealed as a cruel hypocrisy. Paris saw it increasingly as a chance to get rid of its 'human garbage'[11] (an intentionally shameful expression) and to empty its congested prisons. The practice of 'doubling' was very obvious in this respect. It required that those condemned to less than eight years forced labour were compelled to stay after their liberation in Guyane for a period of time equal in length to the original sentence; whilst those condemned to more than eight years had to remain in the country for the rest of their life. In essence, this amounted to a renunciation of all productive functions for Guyane, a perversion of colonization, and for around a hundred years the convict prison was Guyane's principal and longest-running role.

The third episode in Guyane's history is the assumption of departmentalization in 1946. Prior to this the country has been described as 'anaemic'[12] — a consequence not only of its penal past but also of the officially tolerated chaos of the 'Age of Gold' which made the colony, for several decades, a French 'California'. After the Second World War, however, everything was to change. Guyane was to be wholly incorporated into the metropole to become 'a department like the others'. It must be emphasized that this incorporation was not enforced by Paris, as had been the case of Algeria nearly a century before. It was sought by the representatives of the four 'old' colonies which now became overseas departments and it had been demanded, above all, by the local left-wing parties who wanted to end colonial injustice and the domination of the white 'plantocracies'. Réunion, Guadeloupe, Martinique and Guyane could well have become overseas territories as happened to most of the French colonies after the Second World War. The French government and the National Assembly were under no obligation to extend departmentalization. Once applied, however, what changes did the new status bring about? Has Guyane become a French *département* like the others?

THE EFFECTS OF DEPARTMENTALIZATION

It is not my purpose to draw up a detailed balance-sheet of the attainments and shortcomings of departmentalization over the last 37 years. The reader should consult the works of Gérard Brasseur,[13] Marie-José Jolivet,[14] and Ian Hamel,[15] which each contain, in their own way, useful discussion of this question. What must be recognized, however, even by the most determined adversaries of Guyane's present political status, is the considerable progress that has been made since incorporation into the metropole, particularly as regards health, education and general living standards. Indeed, as far as these sectors are concerned, Guyane is probably in advance of any country in Latin America.[16] On the other hand, it should not be forgotten that the population of Guyane is very small, at present no more than 80,000 persons.[17] The cost to France of maintaining Guyane is thus not, and never has been, very high. During the second half of the 1970s, the DOM represented only 0.1 to 0.2% of expenditure in the French budget. In addition, about 90% of public money transferred to Guyane returns to the metropole in the form of private revenue. This is due to the tertiary character of the economy, which is essentially one of administration and commercial importation, the one depending on the other. In 1974, for example, 60.4% of the active population were occupied in the tertiary sector (commerce, transport, banking, services); 21.5% in the secondary sector (processing industries, building and public works, public utilities); and 18.1% in the primary sector (agriculture, forestry, hunting and fishing, extractive industries).[18] Such a structure, of course, is the heritage not only of the country's 'penal' past but also the consequence of a schematic departmentalization which has sought to make Guyane 'a *département* like the others', without reference to its specific socio-economic character. Thus the Guyanese standard of living rests on artificial foundations. It is not the product of its own development and it depends almost entirely on the 'umbilical cord' of departmentalization which links it to France.

The hypothesis that Paris has sought to maintain domination of Guyane by keeping it underdeveloped can be dismissed, since departmentalization, as desired by Guyane, presented the best alternative in 1946 and remained unchallenged for some time. Nevertheless, the product of Guyane's early and recent history is a local society which is largely 'parasitic'. Responsibility for this falls on France and it is a situation which complicates every attempt by the Guyanese to break free from metropolitan tutelage. In the event of a break with Paris, those losing would not only be the metropolitan 'bounty hunters' within the *département*, but also the small native elite and many other Guyanese. Any cessation or reduction of French financial transfers would be acutely felt throughout the country. An alternative to this dilemma would be the development of a productive economy which was initiated some years ago but which remains still in an embryonic state. To boost it effectively, however, may require policies of drastic reduction in the tertiary sector which the Guyanese nationalists and the Left are not prepared to seriously consider. At any rate, the question of the development of a productive economy in Guyane does not concern Guyanese interests alone. It also concerns the government in France. Can France allow itself a 'botanical garden'[19] in South America? Of what use is Guyane today and what specific interests does the metropole have in its largest DOM?

FRENCH INTERESTS IN GUYANE

The nature of French interests in Guyane attracted considerable attention, local and international, with the publication in Paris in 1975 of the so-called 'Green Plan'.[20] In his preface to the plan the President of the French Republic, Valéry Giscard d'Estaing, spoke of a country which had only recently shaken off 'the grasp of somnolence'[21] and subsequent actions and statements by both the French Prime Minister, Jacques Chirac, and by the Secretary for the Overseas Departments and Territories at the time, Olivier Stirn, seemed to point to a new awareness of the country and its potential. Since that time Guyane has never disappeared entirely from the news, though increasingly sceptical commentaries have been published contrasting 'great projects' and 'small realisations',[22] and even speaking in recent years of the plan's 'failure'.[23] This is not the place to examine the merits of these arguments or to examine the plan in detail. I have done so at length elsewhere.[24] Rather, my concern is to briefly indicate some earlier dimensions which must be considered in any serious discussion of Guyane at present and in the immediate future.

Forestry resources are far and away the country's principal raw material, the exploitation of which remains of continuing interest to France. Although in the mid-1970s the establishment of a pulping industry was announced, it remained still-born due to fluctuating prices on the world market and to differences between the French government and United States companies as to the financing of the necessary support infrastructure. In the future a renewal of interest in this venture is a distinct possibility with the last Giscardian government revealing a concern focussed on the late 1980s. For the moment, however, the 'conventional' exploitation of Guyanese timber continues and at an ever increasing pace. It is to be hoped that this will be contained within reasonable limits since a repetition of the manner by which forest is presently being exploited in other equatorial regions would soon lead in Guyane to the same irreversible destruction.

As for mineral resources, and contrary to what one might expect from studying the Green Plan, Guyane does not appear overendowed. Bauxite reserves remain limited and only kaolin, on present information, remains a prospect for future development.

The exploitation of maritime resources centres on the shrimping industry. For a long time concentrated in the hands of foreign shipping suppliers, mainly US and Japanese, it is now experiencing greater French participation. At the same time it must be emphasized that this does not constitute a resource of prime importance for the metropole. Shrimps are not an item which France in any sense lacks and which consequently could be an import burden. 'Industrial fishing', therefore, represents an interest for Guyane itself and for its own development. By contrast, another 'maritime resource', the 200 mile zone off the

Guyanese coast, is of interest to France, though it has not yet been fully explored and its economic value is still to be proved.

The European Space Centre at Kourou has attracted much attention and has been written about extensively.[25] I agree with Marie-José Jolivet that the impact of the new town of Kourou has scarcely been of psychological benefit to Guyane.[26] In its present form Kourou represents an alien intrusion: a 'white town' in a Caribbean country, in which both social and racial differences are marked and acute, reflected, not least, in its geographical projection. Additionally, the economic importance of the Space Centre remains relatively limited. In spite of all the declarations made since its establishment, the Space Centre has not succeeded in substituting for the productive economy which Guyane presently lacks. This is so despite the fact that the construction of Kourou has undoubtedly brought some infrastructural improvements to the country, although sometimes in strange ways. Witness here the sudden end of the good quality national highway directly after the launching site of the European rocket, 'Ariane'.

If the Space Centre is only of limited value to Guyane, what is its importance to countries outside? Its economic and technological significance for France and Western Europe is unquestionable. But is it of any military value? An interview with Giscard d'Estaing in 1979 gave the impression that he did not want to entirely rule out a potential function for the French 'Force de Frappe' in Guyane, notwithstanding French adherence to the Treaty of Tlatelolco which seeks to prohibit nuclear weapons in Latin America.[27] Putting this aside, however, it is difficult to see what constitutes French nuclear and strategic interests in Guyane. At what target might any missile be directed if fired from Kourou, bearing in mind that the 'Force de Frappe' disposes of medium range rockets only? Another question concerns the transport of nuclear materials from France via the Caribbean DOM to the South Pacific, utilizing the shortest route to reach the experimental centre in Polynesia. This transport passes by the Antilles and also North America. Is it compatible with the Tlatelolco Treaty? Finally, Guyane does have a military function as a launching base for observation satellites. However, this appears residual rather than crucial, underlining that at least at present the strategic significance of the Kourou Space Centre seems to be less important to France than its economic value.

GUYANE IN A COLONIAL CONTEXT

The above analysis underlines the fact that the Space Centre and the commercial 'Ariane' programme are today the foremost metropolitan interests in Guyane, followed by forest exploitation. But, in order to gain a more exact impression, considerations must be widened beyond specific unilateral French interests in the country to include the other overseas departments and territories. Do the different DOM and TOM have complementary functions which can only be understood within their joint context as French possessions overseas?[28] To determine this, five areas of 'colonial interest' need to be examined.

First, is Guyane of interest to the metropole as a market for its commodities? Because of the country's tiny population this hypothesis can be immediately invalidated and the same applies to all the DOM–TOM collectively. Those small French businesses for whom the DOM–TOM could be of interest do not have sufficient capacity to influence metropolitan overseas policy; and for the larger companies, which can exert pressure, Guyane and the other DOM–TOM are not sufficiently important.

The same observation applies to the question of capital investment. In the Third World, French capital is mainly concentrated in its former colonies in Africa. Until now, and because of the relatively high price of local labour, the French government has encountered many difficulties in encouraging businessmen to invest in the DOM–TOM. Changes in this respect are occurring if at all, only very slowly.

Neither in the recent past, New Caledonian nickel excepted, have the scattered DOM–TOM played an important role as suppliers of raw materials. But this situation is beginning to change. French governments have begun to realize the eventual potentialities of the overseas departments and territories, particularly since the outbreak of the energy crisis. Almost everywhere in the remaining possessions, from the South Pacific to the Indian Ocean, as well as in the Caribbean and near the South American coast, appropriate studies are being undertaken.[29]

It is in a fourth area, however, concerning the possible function of the DOM–TOM as a reserve of labour, that the hypothesis of complementarity may appear to have some validity. It was advanced by Troussier not long after the launching of the Green Plan and posed the question as to whether France was holding back on the industrialization of the DOM–TOM in order to use their emigrant workers in the metropole, while at the same time realizing that it was financially rewarding to carry out 'great' investment projects 'in an empty country with a large potential such as Guyane'.[30] Events since that time have shown this to be false. Guyane has so far seen nothing of the hastily announced 'great' projects and the recession of the 1970s has diminished the urgency of any large-scale exploitation of the department's raw materials. The influx of migrants from the DOM to France has increased since the beginning of the 1960s and by 1980 had reached around the 400,000 mark, some arriving by means of BUMIDOM (the state immigration service) and even more by spontaneous and non-organized immigration.[31] Impelling this, it is now clear, was less the necessity of the metropolitan labour market (which could and did recruit migrant labour from elsewhere) than the growing unemployment in the overseas possession. Indeed, with the recession and unemployment in the metropole, France now has considerable difficulties in the absorption of its numerous immigrants.

Finally, do the remaining DOM–TOM have a role to play in French foreign and defence policy? Has France avoided demotion 'to a rank lower than that of a first power of secondary importance' because of its possessions dispersed 'around the four corners of the globe' as Jean-Emile Vié, former secretary general for the administration of the DOM in the Paris overseas state secretariat, has argued?[32] The role of the Space Centre in Guyane has already been considered. A coral island in Polynesia serves as a site for nuclear tests of the 'Force de Frappe'. Réunion (far more than Mayotte and the small islands in the Mozambique channel) has strategic importance for surveillance of oil-tankers sailing from the Persian Gulf by way of the Cape of Good Hope. To date, and apart from a few periodic protests from the Caribbean community and the Organization of African Unity, the continuation of this French presence has scarcely rippled the international scene. In this respect, the continued adherence of the DOM – TOM to the metropole does not seem yet to be seriously questioned as an external matter. By contrast, internally, there are growing minorities who are increasingly, and insistently, claiming a national destiny for Martinique, Guadeloupe, Réunion and Guyane. In the case of Guyane is a move in this direction, given the consent of France, a feasible alternative to permanent dependence on the 'mother-country'?

ALTERNATIVES FOR GUYANE

From the outset any discussion of this subject is purely academic if one takes seriously the warning by Jean-Emile Vié that should Guyane sever its ties with France then 'annexation by Brazil risks being a formality only'.[33] This opinion is held quite widely amongst the metropolitan French in the DOM. One even hears about maps of Guyane in Brazil clearly outlining the pretensions of the 'giant neighbour'. These maps do not exist as there is no threat of annexation by Brazil. The government in Brasilia would have little to gain and much to lose in the inter-national sphere if it attempted to 'pocket' Guyane in such a way. But if this outcome seems unlikely another 'Brazilian risk' to the country, given the dynamism of expansion and conquest of Amazonia by Brazil, appears a distinct possibility. This is one of Guyane, Suriname and Guyana (former British Guiana) becoming economically 'satellized', undergoing the same fate as Uruguay and Bolivia, much bigger neighbours of Brazil. At present, this risk is not imminent, as Brazil is currently facing enormous difficulties which are slowing down its pace of development and advance in the Amazon Basin. But this will not continue forever. The 'mobile border' (an expression in current use at the Ministry of Foreign Affairs in Brasilia) will inevitably draw nearer to the region.[34]

In order to avoid being 'satellized' by its southern neigh-bour it would be in Guyane's interest to explore the prospects for integration into the Caribbean with which it has many points in common and which are in a way its 'brother countries'. Not everyone recognizes this, not even all those favouring independence or autonomy. The main reason for this is that Guyane has long suffered from an historical isolation which is the result of French policy and which still lasts today. On the political – psychological level this isolation has had consequences which are difficult to overcome.

It can also be explained by the fact that Guyane has a small population which is frightened it will lose its identity if it has too many contacts with its neighbours. There is even a fear of contacts with the other Caribbean DOM! Consequently, the ignorance of many Guyanese of their neighbours is striking. Without any exaggeration it may be said that most of them know Paris, yet almost nobody has been to Georgetown or Port-of-Spain. This attachment to the metropole – which is applicable also to the local *autonomistes* and *indépendentistes* – is clearly incompatible with the demand for independence and autonomy. Guyane is sociologically a small creole country,[35] and so are most of the former British colonies in the region which form the Caribbean Community (CARICOM). The Guyanese ought to be familiar with their development problems and, in particular, with their Common Market; once having acquired formal independence in the form of a sovereign state, they could be confronted with involvement in this as an alternative.

It is not possible here to analyse in any detail the questions of size, underdevelopment or the specific difficulties presently facing CARICOM. From such an analysis it would emerge that regional cooperation has until now brought only modest improvements to the Community members.[36] It is also becoming apparent that obstacles to a self-reliant development for Caribbean countries are not only of an economic nature but also political. In particular the current trend for the United States to see 'a second Cuba' in every attempt by Caribbean countries to break free from a colonial past, is a major obstacle. That is why, in spite of all its economic shortcomings, CARICOM remains indispensable for the states of the region. It gives a certain political protection to these small countries in that it is a larger entity, thus increasing a little their international influence. Even assuming a future reduction of East – West antagonism in the hemisphere. CARICOM will remain a necessity, and an independent Guyane will have to cooperate with its members in one way or another.

CONCLUSION

What does the future hold for Guyane? For the moment, the country can dispense neither with the economic support nor with the international protection of France. Paris should do its best to help the DOM–TOM prepare their own destiny. The metropole owes this to Guyane in particular; to a country which in its roles as 'forgotten colony' and a 'Green Hell' has had to pay the price for the whims of the colonial power. At the same time Paris should not impose independence as long as the majority of the population does not consent. But equally it should do everything to avoid here and in its other remaining 'confettis of the Empire' a 'botched' decolonization such as has already occurred elsewhere.

In 1960 De Gaulle declared at Cayenne that 'it is natural that a country like Guyane, which is in a way set apart and which has its own characteristics, should enjoy a certain autonomy, adapted to the conditions in which it must live'. Before the 1981 elections, François Mitterrand's presidential programme promised to the populations of the DOM 'the administration of local affairs in the perspective of an openly debateable future'.[37] After the elections, Gaston Defferre, Minister of the Interior, and responsible for implementing policies of decentralization, declared: 'The overseas departments are still subject to colonial exploitation, their autochthonous populations are in misery. They need help from France. If we proposed a special legal status for them, they might think that France wants to abandon them, which is not the case'.[38] Therefore, for the moment at least, and according to this declaration, the socialist government in Paris does not seem disposed to create a special statute for the DOM, as it did for Corsica. Instead, they have been included in the plans for reform via the newly created *conseils régionaux*, which have been developed to provide greater local accountability. Although this constitutes a step in the right direction it must be recognized that the issue at stake is not a 'regional' one in a French 'mainland' sense. The people of Réunion, Guadeloupe, Martinique and Guyane are neither Bretons nor Corsicans. They are not Europeans, they live in a different environment. Like the three other 'old colonies', Guyane is a Third World country. Of course, it is French speaking, impregnated with French culture and history, and in the future it will certainly be on friendly terms with France. But it is a country which has to decide its own future, and not a French département in any sense like those of 'mainland' France.

NOTES

1. This chapter draws on my doctoral thesis *Französisch-Guyana. Die letzte Kontinentale Überseebesitzung in Lateinamerika* (French Guiana. The last continental overseas possession in Latin America) presented in 1981 at the University of Hamburg and published in 1982 by the 'Heidelberger Dritte Welt Studien' (Esprint-Verlag, Bergheimer Str. 147, 6900 Heidelberg, West Germany).

2. The overseas *départements* (Réunion, St Pierre and Miquelon, Martinique, Guadeloupe and Guyane) and the overseas territories (French Polynesia, Wallis and Futuna, New Caledonia and the Southern and Antarctic French Territories) can be distinguished in two ways:

    (1) Whereas the TOM has a right to express a desire to change their status and become either overseas départements or independent states, the DOM do not. Any change of their status, with the exception of their conversion into 'territorial collectivities', must be by an amendment of the constitution or through the provisions authorizing the President to submit to a referendum all bills concerning the organization of 'public power';

    (2) Additionally, there are institutional differences between the DOM and the TOM, with the latter enjoying a greater degree of local autonomy. Each has its own statute and is governed under a 'régime of legislative speciality' – French laws are extended to them only in cases of explicit reference. – By contrast, French laws are immediately applicable in the DOM. The legislative régime and administrative organization of the DOM is thus in principle identical to that of the metropole, save that they can be subject to specific measures as necessitated by their particular situation.

    The organization of the 'territorial collectivity' Mayotte has until now been closer to that of a DOM than of a TOM.

3. The only other 'continental cases' – Hong Kong and Macao – are not strictly comparable to Guyane.

4. François Luchaire, *Droit d'outre-mer et de la Coopération* (Paris, 1966), p. 115.

5. Secrétariat d'Etat aux DOM–TOM, *La France et ses Départements d'Outre-Mer* (Paris, 1978), p. 32.

6. A detailed history of Guyane is to be found in Michel Devèze, *Les Guyanes* (Paris, 1968) and in Arthur Henry, *La Guyane Française: Son histoire 1604–1946* (Cayenne, 1974, new edition).

7. For a summary of French colonialism see Xavier Yacono, *Histoire de la colonisation française* (Paris, 1973).

8. See, in particular, Cornelius Ch. Goslinga, *A Short History of the Netherlands Antilles and Surinam* (The Hague, 1979).

9. Devèze, *Les Guyanes*, p. 62.

10. *Ibid.* pp. 63–4.

11. Ian Hamel, *Les Guyanais – Français en sursis* (Paris, 1979), p. 42.
12. Gérard Brasseur, *La Guyane Française. Un bilan de trente années* (Paris, 1978), p. 41.
13. *Ibid*. ff.
14. Marie-José Jolivet, *La Question Créole: Essaie de sociologie sur la Guyane Française* (Paris, ORSTOM, 1982).
15. Hamel, *Les Guyanais – Français en sursis*.
16. On average its living standards are comparable to those in France as can be seen in the number of cars and other expensive consumer durables per inhabitant. In 1979, Guyane had more cars per inhabitant than France. On this see also André Calmont, *Cayenne – La ville et sa région* (Bordeaux-Talence, 1978).
17. Since the begining of the 1980s the population has been growing by approximately 2000 inhabitants a year.
18. Figures on unemployment are disputed. In 1976, official figures showed 10% but as Brasseur has pointed out, this represents only part of reality: 'alongside officially-recorded employment flourish numerous part-time activities described as "jobs", which, without completely supporting the persons depending on them, tide over the unemployed and assure appreciable incomes for others, without any declaration to the social security or to the tax-man' (*La Guyane Française*, p. 141). In 1980, the Gaullist member for Guyane in the National Assembly in Paris, H. Riviérez, estimated the rate of unemployment to be near 30%. *Le Monde*, 31 Dec. 1980.
19. This was a designation used by a senior official in Cayenne during the course of a conversation with the author in September 1979.
20. For details se Secrétariat d'Etat aux DOM–TOM, *Le Plan Vert – Charte de Développement de la Guyane* (Paris, 1976).
21. *Ibid*. p. 1.
22. Jean Octobre, 'Le plan de développement de la Guyane – Grands projets, petites réalisations', *Le Monde*, 1 Aug. 1977.
23. Jean-Emile Vié, 'L'échec du Plan Vert en Guyane', *Le Monde*, 1 July 1977.
24. Schwarzbeck, *Französisch-Guayana*, pp. 153–218. See also Centre d'Etudes de Géographie Tropicale/Office de la Recherche Scientifique et Technique Outre-Mer, *Atlas des Départements Français d'Outre-Mer, 4. La Guyane* (Paris/Bordeaux-Talence, 1979).
25. In addition to articles in scientific reviews, the reader can usefully consult Pierre-Marie Decoudras, 'Kourou-Ville spatiale' (Doctoral thesis, Bordeaux, 1975); and Marie-José Jolivet, 'Essai de sociologie sur la Guyane Française' (Doctoral thesis, Paris, 1978).
26. Jolivet, 'Essai de sociologie sur la Guyane Française', pp. 532–6.
27. In reply to a question as to whether his imminent signature on Protocol 1 of the Tlatelocolo Treaty meant that 'the French department of Guyane is completely excluded from the French nuclear zone' Giscard d'Estaing stated that 'the rights of sovereignty, notably of French military sovereignty, as far as Guyane is concerned, will not be modified by this protocol' (*Le Monde*, 16 Feb. 1979). In signing Protocol 1, France pledged to respect its provisions in respect of non-Latin American countries within the zone of the treaty.
28. For an earlier statement of this question see Jean-François Troussier, 'La Guyane en questions', *Revue Tiers-Monde* (Paris, 1976), pp. 721–37.
29. See Commissariat Général du Plan, *Rapport du Comité DOM–TOM, Préparation du 8eme Plan* (Paris, 1980).
30. Troussier, 'La Guyane', p. 737.
31. Commissariat Général du Plan, *Rapport du Comité DOM–TOM*, p. 8.
32. Jean-Emile Vié, *Faut-il abandonner les DOM?* (Paris, 1978), p. 134.

33. *Ibid.* p. 137.
34. For an official analysis of the development programme of the Brazilian Federal Territory of Amapá, contiguous to Guyane, see Ministerio do Interior – Território Federal do Amapá, *Il Plano Nacional de Desenvolvimento. Programa de Acáo do Governo para o Território do Amapá (1975–79)* (Brasilia, 1975).
35. This term applies to 80% of the Guyanese population. The 'creoles' are the descendants of Africans brought to the Caribbean by the slave trade. 'Whites could have intermingled with them, so that anthropologically all skin complexions come together, but on the whole it is the negroid characteristics that stand out' (Brasseur, *La Guyane Française* p. 32).
36. See, for example, the Group of Caribbean Experts, *The Caribbean Community in the 1980s* (Georgetown, Guyana, 1981).
37. *Le Monde*, 8 May 1981.
38. *Le Monde*, 17 July 1981.

An Economic Policy for Martinique

JEAN CRUSOL*

The problem of economic development in Martinique is one of the most delicate to have faced any Caribbean nation in the last thirty years. It arises from a threefold crisis which compounds Martinique's difficulties; a crisis of colonialism, a crisis of a plantation economy and the contemporary world crisis.

Since the problem of economic development has been formulated in this way, it is first necessary to specify as precisely as possible the implications of these three crises for a small country with a population of 325,000. In the following pages the specific economic and social characteristics of Martinique are examined and its strengths and weaknesses are highlighted. A strategy of development with some chance of success can only be drawn up on the basis of an understanding of these strengths and weaknesses.

I THE THREE CRISES

1. The Crisis of Colonialism

Since its establishment as a French colony in the seventeenth century and up to the Second World War, Martinique has had a strictly colonial status, characterised by a centralisation of decision-making powers in the colonial nation and institutional and juridical discrimination against the island and those native to it. The incorporation of the island as an administrative *département* of France, introduced in 1946, which extended French law and institutions to the island, was intended to suppress all forms of discrimination, and to allow Martiniquans to reach full political maturity as French citizens. Since this

* Translated from the French by Tina Page.

period there has undoubtedly been progress in this direction, but *départementalisation* also succeeded in reinforcing the centralisation of decision making powers. After three decades of *départementalisation*, the Martiniquans have lost a large part of their control over their own destiny even though they have gained access to the economic and political advantages of a developed European society.

The crucial decisions concerning the economic, social, cultural and political development of the area during the last thirty years have for the most part been taken by Paris. Frustration born of this has nurtured nationalist ideology among large sectors of the population. And whatever the different forms this nationalism took among different social strata, every impartial observer would agree that the claim for more local power has been the most striking feature of political life over the last twenty years.

It is not only politically necessary to satisfy the demands for more local power, it is also the principal means through which the population preside over their own development. The Socialist government which took power in France in May 1981 has clearly realised this. It understood the urgent need for reform by transferring more important powers to Martiniquans, allowing them to take responsibility for their own development. For that reason, the government, following the experience in Corsica, went ahead with applying its decentralisation measures well before it decentralised the *départements* in mainland France. Since 20 February 1983 Martinique has a new *Conseil Régional*, a regional assembly elected by proportional representation on the basis of universal suffrage, with a left-wing majority. The law which transfers functions to government institutions, at the time of writing still under discussion, gives the *Conseil Régional* important powers in economic, social and cultural development. These powers, when added to those already given the *Communes* (local municipalities) and *Conseils Généraux* (the legislatures of the *départements*) by the decentralisation laws of March 1982, constitute a set of means for development without precedent in colonial history. If used effectively, these measures could assure the development of Martinique. This, of course, presupposes that the new decision makers have a good grasp of the characteristics of Martinique's economy and of the nature of the crisis of the plantation economy which has been experienced for nearly twenty years.

2. *The Crisis of the Plantation Economy*

To start with, Martinique possesses the principal structural characteristics of the island plantation colony: its economy specialises in a small number of primary goods for export, sugar cane, bananas and pineapples; the country is heavily dependent upon the outside and particularly upon the economy of France; a tiny minority of the population, principally composed of whites, controls the essential levers of the economy – land, commerce and industrial capital.

In the Caribbean this type of economy has been in crisis since the 1960s at least. Competition from other regions such as Europe, Africa, Central and Southern America and Asia has provoked a progressive decrease in the price of traditional primary goods over the past twenty years. New economic activities, very often brought into the country by foreign firms, and the unionisation of the workforce have caused an increase in production costs. The competitive position of Caribbean countries has, in fact, deteriorated. This deterioration was accelerated in Martinique by the introduction of the social welfare and fiscal legislation linked to *départementalisation*. This crisis has been marked by the decline, over a long period, in the level of traditional agricultural exports.

The generally pursued strategy to cope with the surplus labour resulting from this in most of the Caribbean islands since the 1960s has been to diversify agricultural production and to develop new industries (import substitution or export promotion) and/or the tourist industry. There has also been emigration insofar as there have been opportunites for it. In Martinique it appeared as if nobody had to find solutions to the crisis. The absence of any real local power of decision-making pushed the responsibility upwards to the authorities in mainland France. In what appeared to be a solution, the authorities were happy to inject more and more public money into the island's economy and to encourage a large outmigration to mainland France. Thus, in the course of the last 20 years, Martinique has become transformed from an economy principally based upon agricultural exports into one in which the principal motor is the public sector. In other words, the crisis of the plantation economy was solved neither by agricultural diversification nor by a structural transformation of the economy. Production fell and with it employment. The total number of people in employment went from 92,000 in 1961 to 83,000 in 1980, with a consequent rise in the unemployment rate from 21 per cent to more than 25 per cent over the same period despite the emigration of more than 5,000 people per year.

Today Martinique has a completely unbalanced economy. The growth rate of the Gross Domestic Product has only been achieved by public spending. Public spending constituted almost 60 per cent of GDP in 1980 and the public sector employed directly more than 30 per cent of the workforce. Moreover, more than 70 per cent of employment depends indirectly on economic activity arising from public spending. But this spending is not financed by the island's own economy but rather to the extent of over 80 per cent by transfers from France; this translates into a chronic balance of trade deficit with exports covering barely one fifth of imports.

The task of seeking to put such a profoundly unbalanced economy on a firm footing is formidable enough in a favourable international economic climate. Yet the search for a solution takes place in the context of the international crisis that has troubled the world since the early 1970s.

3. The World Crisis

During the 1950s and 1960s the conditions for world growth were relatively favourable. The developed as well as the under-developed countries were able to benefit from them. The developed nations, using technologies available since the war, had at their disposal cheap raw materials and energy as well as expanding home and foreign markets. The developing nations benefited during this fortunate period, albeit proportionately less than the developed nations, through making available cheap raw materials and energy used by the industrial areas or by attracting capital from large industrial corporations which were relocating parts of their production.

Although primarily motivated by the possibility of exploiting a cheap labour force, tax advantages or access to proteced markets, this relocation allowed the creation of some additional employment as well as the (marginal) transfer of technology to underdeveloped countries. The arrival of the world crisis meant several important changes to this picture.

First, it brought a sharp increase in competition among developed nations as well as between developed and underdeveloped nations in all markets. In struggling with the difficulties posed by the crisis, each country adopted increasingly aggressive strategies to ease its own particular problems. The most powerful nations, and particularly the most powerful among these, the United States, adopted increasingly egotistical attitudes towards the rest of the world.

Second, in order to maintain or gain a sharper competitive edge, governments resorted to austerity measures which decreased demand and reduced the growth in markets. For the world as a whole the scope for growth has become limited.

Third, the effects of the return of relocation of industrial activity to low labour cost countries have been felt in the industrialised countries. Competition with low labour cost nations totally destroys the traditional industries of the industrial nations.

Fourth, the refusal by certain of the Third World nations to accept prices for their raw materials which were both too low and decreasing puts an end to the possibility of world growth based on cheap energy and raw materials.

Finally, in those countries with sufficient levels of unionisation, the refusal by workers to accept a reduction in real wages as an adjustment to the crisis has produced an increase in wage costs. In this context, the constraints on the development of a very small country which in happier times had benefited from a growth based upon resources which it did not produce, are heavy. Such a country must, in fact, take over political responsibilities at a time when the international conditions are least propitious, indeed hostile, and has to develop new products at a time when the competition is particularly fierce and when the markets are in recession. In this context, Martinique has no important comparative advantage over others, it has no technological tradition and no significant level of primary energy sources.

II DEVELOPMENT POLICY FOR MARTINIQUE

These are the principal handicaps. Are there any trump cards that can be played? Curiously enough, the first of Martinique's trump cards in the contemporary situation is its small size. This means, in fact, that its needs (in terms of markets and capital) are small and turn out to be negligible in the context of the great world economic powers. These needs can be satisfied without too much trouble for the larger countries.

The second of Martinique's trump cards derives from the high level of domestic product per capita, even though this is produced by artificial means. Nevertheless, it creates a relatively important domestic market which opens the possibility for the important development of non-exchanged goods under conditions of natural protection, as well as import substitution, above all in the areas of agricultural foodstuffs and non-durable consumption goods. In this context it is helpful to remind oneself that the island imported more than 500 million francs' worth of foodstuffs in 1982.

The third trump card is the existence of an infrastructure which is relatively more developed than that of most neighbouring Caribbean nations, as well as a relatively highly educated population which undoubtedly gives it an aptitude to learn sophisticated techniques.

The fourth trump card is its position in the Caribbean: its proximity to American and Latin American markets. Since Martinique is institutionally a part of France it has a particularly interesting position among European and American economies. This position can be judiciously exploited as a favoured location in the Latin American and Caribbean area for scientific and technological cooperation as well as a springboard for the development of economic and commercial relations not only with Latin America and Caribbean nations, but also with North America and Africa.

Bearing these considerations in mind, the general direction of a policy of development should be as follows:

First, it is imperative to seek a greater degree of social justice. The extreme inequalities that currently exist slow down the development of a firm social consensus – an essential precondition for social stability and therefore for Martinique's development. This quest for greater social justice must be translated into agrarian policy, fiscal policy and incomes policy.

Second, it is imperative to seek to reduce dependence on other countries. This implies on the one hand measures designed to reduce in relative terms the reliance on external sources to fund public expenditure, and on the other hand measures aimed at reducing the share of imports in current consumption. This policy would only be possible insofar as the local public authorities could take decisions affecting a larger portion of total public revenues and expenditures. This would be possible after a decentralisation of financial powers.

Third, it is imperative that a policy reshapes Martinique's relationships with the other two French *départements* in the Caribbean towards closer economic integration, and develops closer cooperation with other neighbouring countries in the Caribbean.

Fourth, a bold new technology policy must be established. Martinique, in fact, suffers from serious handicaps to its development: relatively high salaries, the absence of an industrial tradition and the reduced size of its home market. It could only redress these shortcomings through a highly dynamic policy of technology and technical innovation.

Fifth, the strategy must include a larger degree of workers' participation in their firms' decisions. This involves, on the one hand, a need for a system of providing workers with information about the management of their firm (about its profits as well as its problems) and, on the other hand, incentives to set up cooperative enterprises based upon the democratic participation of workers in the decisions of the firm.

The above constitute broad approaches which should be included in development policies. Yet in practice and in the short and medium term a certain number of these concrete measures must be taken, and new institutions should be set up or old ones reformed in order that such decisions can be applied.

The first problem to be faced is that of the reform of the land system. Although the large landowners, in response to the crisis in the plantation economy, have in the course of the past twenty years parcelled out parts of their land, this process did not constitute a rationalisation of agriculture. Of the 85 per cent of lands owned by large landowners in 1960, there remains only 50 per cent given over to property of over 100 hectares in size. But the 35 per cent of land parcelled out was divided into very small plots for construction rather than medium size properties of between ten and thirty hectares (the optimal size in the region) for agricultural production. The reform of the land system, which could allow for the creation of a large sector of medium-sized holdings and bring to an end the traditional polarisation between large holdings and small plot farming, remains to be undertaken. It presupposes the existence of an institution capable of agricultural reform, free of the influence of the large landowners and which could have the task of expropriating with compensation land which is not being used, or used inadequately, of buying large areas of land put on the market and selling it off again in economically optimal sizes. This policy of land reform is not alone sufficient to solve the problems of agriculture. It must be accompanied by a policy of financing farmers and of creating greater access to modern techniques and to cultural innovations. It is also imperative to attack the problem of the commercialisation of agricultural products – export products as well as those destined for the domestic market. To achieve this it is necessary to set up offices for each type of product which would be able to stabilise farmers' incomes by entering into stable price contracts with them (for export production) and by organising the domestic market (for local consumption).

The second problem is the development of industry. Here, it is useful to recall Martinique's peculiar position in this respect. Most of the Caribbean islands began to industrialise in the 1950s, at a time when their wage rates were still relatively low, when the market for labour intensive goods was buoyant and when the developed countries were experiencing rapid growth. Martinique had to begin industrialising with wage rates almost as high as those of France itself (as well as the social insurance costs), without an industrial tradition at a time when the market of the developing countries has been increasingly conquered by the new industrial nations and all this in the middle of a world crisis. In this set of conditions the results could only be limited.

The industrial development of Martinique can only be accomplished to the degree that its people make judicious decisions about technological matters. The constraints imposed by wage levels lead to research into relatively labour-saving technologies. The absence of traditional sources of energy (oil and gas) gives rise to a particular effort to explore new sources of energy. The saturation of the markets for traditional industrial goods leads to research for gaps in the market with products demanding a great degree of adaptability and a certain level of educational qualification among those who produce them.

In these last two issues, Martinique is not without advantages. The education development policies of the last 20 years have produced a new largely literate generation which, even if not technically educated, has a capacity for such technical education. On the question of new sources of energy, serious research has already been started. Interesting results concerning the harnessing of wind and solar power have already been put into effect. Martinique is already exporting products and technology in this field to other countries in the area. Moreover, the infrastructure put in place over the last 20 years represents an undoubted advantage.

In order to stimulate economic development it is important to establish a policy of incentives and industrial promotion. Up until now, incentives have consisted of tax relief to companies seeking to locate in Martinique. But Martinique's experience as well as that of other countries in the region and elsewhere have demonstrated that it is not tax relief that attracts or creates real industries (that is, those really able to transform) but rather profitability and the wish to take risks which might eventually pay off. In spite of the fact that generous tax relief schemes have been on offer for the past 20 years or more, the industrial sector has not expanded to more than six per cent of Gross Domestic Product and industrial employment has only accounted for around 4,500 of Martinique's workforce. To ensure profitability it is necessary to develop the qualifications of the labour force in order to increase productivity; to improve and adapt the infrastructure in order to lower production costs.

The creation of the desire for taking industrial risks is more difficult. It concerns issues relating to the mentality and culture deeply engrained in the population. In this respect there is hardly any other solution than demonstration followed by imitation. In the first instance it is necessary for the community to take responsibility for the risks; it may later benefit from development. The solution is to create a development agency capable of launching public enterprises. After the profitability of such enterprises has been demonstrated, they can be sold to the private sector or a workers' cooperative. In pursuing this policy of industrialisation aimed first and foremost at the promotion of local initiative, external and foreign initiative must not be neglected, still less ruled out. Foreign initiatives, as we know, have the advantage of guaranteeing capital, technology, know-how, external and domestic outlets (insofar as firms which sell on the local market may decide to produce in Martinique) all at the same time. Nevertheless, in this respect it is important to be highly selective — to encourage the importation of forms of investment which leave the greatest possible margin for flexibility and produce the fastest and largest spread of technology and know-how. In any case, the experience of a number of newly industrialised nations has clearly shown the dangers of high levels of dependence, without any significant technological or economic gains, which may result from too permissive a policy of foreign investment.

The potential of tourism for the development of Martinique is not negligible. This sector directly accounts for 2,000 jobs and its turnover in 1982 was above that of agriculture. Its rate of growth has been relatively high over the past decade. There has been a threefold increase in the number of people taking their holidays in Martinique. Meanwhile, the number of visitors to the island remains relatively small in comparison with other Caribbean nations. Barbados, for example, which is half the size of Martinique has twice the number of visitors.

The potential for the tourist development of Martinique remains considerable. All the more so because the relatively unspoiled nature of its beauty spots, the influence of French culture and the presence of French goods, plus the high quality of its infrastructure, make it outstandingly attractive in the Eastern Caribbean region. But the contemporary development of the tourist industry displays certain weaknesses. The effects of tourist income throughout the economy are weak and there is insufficient penetration of the important North American market.

In order to increase the spread of revenue from tourism, it is important to help the local ownership of hotels, to encourage the construction of the small and medium sized hotel and, above all, to develop local products (material and cultural) which could find an outlet in the tourist sector. In order to increase the penetration of the North American market, promotional activities could be stepped up. The efforts devoted to the French and European market have already borne fruit, and there is no reason why similar efforts in the North American market should not pay off too.

Development policy would also have to seek a better integration with the surrounding region. The region can be thought of as three circles: first, the other French *départements* of the Caribbean; second, the islands which are signatories to the Lomé Convention; finally, the Caribbean basin and the American continent. Each of these regional groupings has some sort of 'institutional proximity' to Martinique. Guadeloupe and Guyane are part of the same institutional structure. It is already possible to bring about a level of integration of markets and production in these territories as well as a better division of labour thanks to more *rapprochement*, the developments of an inter-regional transport system and collaboration in some planning processes.

The islands which are signatories to the Lomé Convention are also potentially close to Martinique. In fact, Martinique is part of Europe and, in consequence, the Lomé arrangements regulate the economic, commercial, technological and scientific relations between Martinique and these countries too. Up till now producers in Martinique have only seen the negative side of this relationship (remember that reciprocal arrangements risk favouring Caribbean producers in Martinique's domestic market), but the geographical position of Martinique may allow it, in return, to play a role as an intermediary in economic and technological matters between Europe and the Lomé nations. Moreover, in the relatively well developed technologies, Martinique may draw advantages from a developed infrastructure and its institutional integration into Europe.

However, the search for greater cooperation with the countries which have some sort of institutional proximity to Martinique does not prevent Martinique from developing closer relations with the other countries in the region. Above all, given the direction of France's policies towards the developing nations, opportunities for commercial development should come from the direction of Cuba and Latin America.

CONCLUSION

The task of devising a development policy for Martinique under contemporary circumstances calls for an exceptional amount of realism. Very small economies with high standards of living cannot remain content with their domestic market. These cannot provide the resources or the goods on the scale necessary for a high level of productivity. The conquest of foreign markets is therefore a necessity. But the days of strategies for development based solely upon exports (raw materials, industrial goods and tourism) passed by with the advent of the world crisis. Maybe this is a temporary situation, but in the short to medium term, the use of such strategies is problematic. To ensure the development of an island like Martinique, which possesses neither traditional raw materials nor other comparable assets, but which must nevertheless preserve and increase its standard of living, demands a particular effort of imagination combined with realism.

In these circumstances, there is no simple route for Martinique's development. One must try to exploit all opportunities. The first possibility is to seek to satisfy the basic needs of the population. Given the tastes of the population imported from outside, a policy of import substitution must be accompanied by vigorous measures to change people's tastes. A second priority is to export to regional and international markets. In this sphere, Martinique must seek to profit from its advantages: its geographical position, its level of education, the quality of its infrastructure, its position as an integral part of the institutions of a country with a high level of industrialisation and technological development.

The next decade must be devoted to correcting the most flagrant sources of instability in the economic structure and to reduce dependence on public transfers from France. The

institutional means of such a policy will come from decentralisation. But the political and psychological means which will
allow the mobilisation of energy and enthusiasm will only be
produced if the participation of workers in both economic and
political decisions is guaranteed.

The Social and Political Thought of Aimé Césaire and C.L.R. James: Some Comparisons

JOHN LA GUERRE

The purpose of this chapter is to compare the theoretical positions of James and Césaire on what must be regarded as two of the most crucial issues in the social and political thought of the colonial intelligentsia, namely, the race factor and colonial revolution. There can be no doubt that discussions of negritude and the nature of colonial revolution have been two of the most enduring themes to occupy the attentions of colonial radicals. Negritude emerged out of the experience of slavery and colonialism. It was, as Sartre argued, the antithesis of the racism that was inherent in colonial rule. Colonial revolution, with its concomitant of political independence, had its roots not only in a desire for freedom but also in a determination to redress some of the injustices that accompanied colonial rule.

James and Césaire were both products of Empire. James grew up in Trinidad, a British West Indian colony. Césaire was born and grew up in Martinique in the French West Indies. They were both shaped by the respective forces of differing imperialisms – British and French. The French Empire rested on the assumption that the French had a 'mission civilatrice' in the colonies; that their Empire was 'one and indivisible'; that the colonies were merely 'overseas France'; and that the object of colonial policy was to lift colonials to the level of metropolitan standards of culture. The British, on the other hand, beyond occasional dicta and 'Lugardisme' were never able to work out a coherent theory of colonial rule along the lines of the French. They stumbled from precedent to precedent leaving a great deal of policy in the hands of the 'man on the spot'. They nevertheless had some ideas as to what they wanted to achieve in their various colonies. They shared with Mill the assumption that representative government was something to be achieved, not imposed, by a Great Power. Hence the recurring emphasis on gradual constitutional advance. They shared, as well, a belief that certain standards went with 'good government'; in practice the values – and prejudices – of the British ruling class. The term 'fit to rule' was the embodiment of this thinking. There was one cardinal principle, however, from which the British hardly ever wavered. Unlike the French, the British felt that their duty was to lead their dependent peoples to self-government and eventually into independence. For this reason British colonies were spared some of the constitutional experiments of the French in Africa and the West Indies. As will become clearer later in this chapter, these clashing conceptions of Empire were crucial to the responses of James and Césaire to the experience of colonial rule.

JAMES ON RACE

James was unusual in his attitude to the question of race. He grew up in Victorian Trinidad but his grandparents had been allowed to rise to positions normally reserved for whites. His reading fare at an early age came to include pieces like the *Review of Reviews, Tit-Bits*, the *Strand Magazine, The Pickwick Papers* and *Vanity Fair*. To a large extent his attendance at the prestigious Queen's Royal College in Port-of-Spain served to vaccinate him against the pressures emerging out of the wider society. He was later to write:

The race question did not have to be agitated. It was there. But in our little Eden it never troubled us. If the masters were so successful in instilling and maintaining their British principles as the ideal and norm (however much individuals might fall away) it was because within the school, and particularly on the playing field, they practised them themselves.[1]

And yet, inevitably, James was drawn into some of the racial controversies that characterised the thirties in Trinidad. Albert Gomes, a Portuguese radical and future author of the book *Through a Maze of Colour*, had urged the black man to 'bare your fangs as the white man does. Cast off your docility. You have to be savage like a white man to escape the white man's. But the white man won't spare your neck.'[2]

It was the publication, however, of an article by a European Professor at the Imperial College of Tropical Agriculture, located in Trinidad, which sought to prove that Negroes were inferior in intelligence, that struck a nerve and provoked James to reply. He wrote:

I am not 'touchous' on the race question. If at times I feel some bitterness at the disabilities and disadvantages to which my being a Negro has subjected me, it is soon washed away by remembering that the few things in my life of which I am proud, I owe, apart from my family, chiefly to white men, almost all Englishmen and Americans, men some of them of international reputation, who have shown me kindness, appreciation and and in more than one case, spontaneous and genuine friendship.[3]

It should be immediately obvious that at this stage at least James was taking a personal view of racism. It is of importance, too, to note that James was also claiming that at a personal level there were few obstacles to genuine relations between himself and whites of international standing. It should also be noted that the subject for James's first work, *The Life of Captain Cipriani: An Account of British Government in the West Indies* (1932), was not a black personality but a white creole who had caught the local imagination by his radical championship of the cause of the 'barefooted' man and his defence of black soldiers during the First World War.

Yet at the same time James was already well aware of the achievements of men like Booker T. Washington, W.E.B. DuBois, James Weldon Johnson and Toussaint L'Ouverture. The social and political ideas of personalities such as these exercised considerable influence on the social and political ideas – and aspirations – of the emerging colonial intelligentsia. It is not surprising to read then that James was considering writing a book on Toussaint L'Ouverture. Ever since 1815 Toussaint and the state of Haiti, in an age of dependence and subordination elsewhere, had become points of reference for colonial radicals. Toussaint had defeated a mighty European Power. In so doing he had, in the opinion of other colonial intelligentsia, vindicated the African race.

It is, accordingly, not surprising that as soon as James arrived in England in 1932 he should become immersed in a study of Toussaint. Yet the form and emphases that the work took were very much influenced by the fact that James had by then become a follower of Trotsky. The very title of the work became *The Black Jacobins* and its many theses derived from Trotsky's reading of the works of Marx.

The Black Jacobins was, however, not addressed to West Indians but to the African nationalists in Paris and London who were engaged in the struggle for independence. Robert Hill was thus right to point out to Singham that *The Black Jacobins* was conceived as 'the principal contribution to the debate going on inside the International African Service Bureau along with Padmore, Kenyatta and others, on the *Strategy for the African Revolution*'.[4]

For James, however, the revolution in Haiti had little to do with the vindication of a race. The song linked with the voodoo cult, argued James, was no different from the songs the Jews in Babylon sang. The racial discriminations in Africa, James writes, were 'matters of Government policy, enforced by bullets and bayonets, and we have lived to see the rulers of a European nation make the Aryan grandmother as precious for their fellow-countrymen as the Carib ancestor was to the Mulatto. The cause in each case is the same – the justification of plunder by any obvious differentiation from those holding power'.[5]

Thus, for James, the root cause of the various discriminations suffered by both Jews and blacks was economic exploitation. Racial stereotypes were mere rationalizations. Not many would share this view. Anti-semitism and the concentration camps that went with it derived from more deep-seated sentiments. Like many a Marxist, colonial and otherwise, James believed that there was 'a materialist basis' to race prejudice. James selects a quotation from Marx's *The Eighteenth Brumaire* to prove his point:

Upon the different forms of property, upon *the social conditions of existence as foundations*, there is built a superstructure of diversified and characteristic sentiments, illusions, habits of thought, and outlook on life in general.[6]

On this common derivation of prejudice, he concludes, small whites, big whites and bureaucracy were united against the mulattoes. Yet it should be pointed out that the historical origins of an institution or a sentiment do not necessarily explain its continuing existence. Engels, it will be recalled, had warned against excessive emphasis on economic factors to the exclusion of factors such as race, geography and climate.

James tells us that in Haiti there were no white servants; that there was a pecking order of racial contempt – the whites holding the mulatto in contempt while the latter in turn held the Negro in even more contempt; but significantly, he admits that it was racial rejection in France as well as in San Domingo that drove the mulattoes to revolt; that mulattoes were tired of persecution and lynchings by small whites.[7] James dismisses as nonsense the claim that the whites refused to concede rights to the mulattoes because of race prejudice. Why, he asks, did not Charles I and his followers behave reasonably towards Cromwell? It is, of course, not easy to weigh the respective influences of racial, economic and political factors. Discussions accordingly posed in terms of 'economics' or 'race' tend to miss the complexity of the question.

Political conflict, for James, has little to do with race. He reminds his readers on the French Revolution that whites had fought whites. He writes:

Had the monarchists been white, the bourgeoisie brown, and the masses of France black, the French Revolution would have gone down in history as a race war.[8]

The lesson, for James, is obvious. Conflict is rooted in class interests not race sentiments. In making the Haitian revolution the blacks, for James, had not necessarily vindicated a race, but had played their part in the destruction of European feudalism begun by the French Revolution with its slogans of liberty and equality.[9] In short, the Haitian revolution, far from being a racial uprising, was a chapter in the great French Revolution. If the mulattoes were unstable, argued James, it had little to do with their oft-cited blood. Instead it was due to their peculiar position in society.

If racism had its basis in politics and economics, then what was the way out? James points out that although the capitalists of Britain and America were racists, they were the first to compliment Toussaint.[10] Yet it needs to be pointed out that race prejudice runs throughout classes; that the working classes are more inclined than the capitalists to suffer from assumptions of racial superiority. For James the struggle and achievement of independence was causing race prejudice, 'the curse of San Domingo' for two hundred years, to vanish fast. Negroes and mulattoes were holding some of the highest positions in the country. Americans were marrying mulatto women, and negro players had begun to appear in the theatres.

Yet it should be noted that Americans were marrying mulatto not black women. And yet James could not completely ignore the race factor. He had written:

The race question is subsidiary to the class question in politics, and to think of imperialism in terms of race is disastrous. But to neglect the racial factor as merely incidental as [is] an error only less grave than to make it fundamental. There were Jacobin workmen in Paris who would have fought for the blacks against Bonaparte's troops.[11]

James must then be seen as one who is inclined to accord some degree of influence to the race factor. But he believes that it is fatal to make it fundamental to political conflict. James can accordingly be criticized for not exploring the importance of the race factor in specific situations as subsequent writers have done. To assert that the race question is subsidiary to the class question in politics is too abstract an approach. Had he recalled the warning by Engels that ideas sometimes acquire a force of their own he might have explored a different perspective on the Haitian revolution.

In much the same way, James's approach to the Italian invasion of Abyssinia was one based on an assumption of harmony between colonial and metropolitan workers. Whereas the black intelligentsia, both in London and Paris, were declaring that the race war had begun, James had urged the Independent Labour Party (ILP) of Britain, of which he was a member, that they work towards an alliance between metropolitan and colonial workers. He declared:

It is necessary to support the anti-imperialist mass movements arising among 'coloured' peoples in all countries in connection with the Abyssinian crisis, and to create a firm alliance between the international working-class movement and suppressed peoples.[12]

He thus failed to recognize the extent to which the metropolitan workers shared the assumptions of colonial rule. John McGovern, a leading member of the National Council of the ILP, argued that the quarrel between Mussolini and Haile

Selassie was one between dictators. Yet it must be pointed out that earlier the ILP had agreed to ally with the Abyssinian people in their struggle against imperialism and had proposed sanctions by the British working class against Italy. Such a position represented a complete *volte-face* that was no doubt dictated by the impending General Elections. It was also a tacit surrender to some of the prejudices of the British voter. On the whole James was opposed to the apostles of negritude and Black Power. He believed that African and colonial liberation would come from armed uprising, not from *salons littéraires* or Pan-African Congresses. He had written:

from the people heaving in action will come the leaders; not the isolated blacks at Guy's Hospital or the Sorbonne, the dabblers in *surréalisme* or the lawyers, but the quiet recruits in a black police force, the sergeant in the French native army or British police, familiarising himself with military tactics and strategy, reading a stray pamphlet of Lenin or Trotsky as Toussaint read the Abbé Raynal.[13]

This was a most devastating indictment of the black colonial intelligentsia and their approaches to colonial liberation. On James's reasoning they were disqualified because they were isolated from the masses. Yet it was the graduates of the Sorbonne, Oxford, Cambridge, London and Guy's Hospital who were destined to lead the anti-colonial forces and to become the beneficiaries of the transfer of power to local rulers. In extremely few cases were the army and police force the crucial determinants of the decision to hand over to local rulers.[14]

CÉSAIRE ON RACE

If the race factor was subsidiary to James, it was of central importance to Césaire. Indeed Césaire, along with Damas and Leopold Senghor, is widely accepted as one of the creators of negritude. Negritude, in its French expression, was essentially a claim to a distinctive culture and personality on the part of Africa and the Africans of the Diaspora. Yet the major premise of the French Empire was its policy of assimilation into French culture. Perhaps because of this the revolt in the French case was more cultural. Césaire was also by profession a poet–politician.

Césaire's thesis was on Negro literature while the greater part of his output as a poet is concerned with Africa and the descendants of Africa. His critiques of colonial rule and race relations are essentially literary in character. They inevitably, however, involve Césaire in discussions which have to do with problems of alienation and the personality.[15]

Césaire is proud of his race, of the first Negro Republic of Haiti 'where negritude stood up for the first time'. He is critical of the French middle class West Indians because of their 'false culture'. Blacks for him are indeed the wretched of the earth. Colonialism made the Negro into a thing. He is critical of doctrines like rationalism. He is disenchanted with Western science and philosophy. He is far more concerned to refute the alleged intrinsic superiority of the West.

Yet Césaire is quick to point that his negritude is not a self-contained cultural prison. He writes:

My negritude is not a stone, deaf to the clamour of everyday life. My negritude is not a speck of stagnant water on the dead eye of earth. My negritude is neither a tower nor a Cathedral.[16]

He believes that there is mutual benefit in the sharing of cultural experience. Césaire is therefore far more concerned with values. As an artist he believes that 'decolonization' is largely a cultural phenomenon.

Two works by Césaire – *Une Saison au Congo* (1966) and *La Tragédie du Roi Christophe* (1962–3) – are concerned specifically with the problems of Africa and African independence. He is, however, far more taken up with the extent to which political liberty has brought about changes in the material and moral conditions of people demoralized by colonial rule. What is exciting about Haiti is not, as it was for James, the fact that it made a revolution; it was because Haiti was the only real representative of Africa in the West Indies. He confesses:

I am a West Indian ... it is Haiti which has remained more African than the rest since it has been independent since the 18th century. the features of the black continent are therein to be found almost intact, voodoo, for example ...[17]

For Césaire, then, colonial rule is at bottom a naked form of economic exploitation which entails, inevitably, the relegation to inferior positions of the mass of black people. On the basis of economic exploitation, argues Césaire, there is erected a superstructure of ideological rationalizations which have as their common aim the exploitation of the Negro. Césaire is not, however, concerned with black workers, but with black people.

It was in his *Discours Sur le Colonialisme* (1950) that the relationship between colonial rule and racism was more sharply defined. *Discours Sur le Colonialisme* was essentially an attempt at a Marxist interpretation of colonial rule. Colonies, according to Césaire, were the inevitable accompaniment of the development of bourgeois society. Its necessary corollary was racism; and so it followed that all colonial powers practised racism. Hitler was condemned, not because of a crime against man himself, but because Hitler had done it to whites. Césaire wrote:

It is a crime against the white man; it is a humiliation of the white man, to have applied to Europe the colonial methods which have so far been reserved for the Arabs of Algeria, the coolies of India and the Negroes of Africa.[18]

For Césaire, then, France had no greater cause for boast than Germany. Since both possessed colonies both were forced into the practice of racism. Indeed, argues Césaire, the 'rights of man' was mere sloganry. In the writings of philosophers like Renan and in the public utterances of politicians like Sarrant, there was already a Hitler in evidence. While it must be conceded that there is a world of difference between the ovens of Birkenau and Dachau and the subtler forms of racism practised by the British, Césaire is concerned to demonstrate that racism was inherent within the concept of Empire.

It is in his famous *Lettre à Maurice Thorez* (1956) that Césaire makes his position as a 'man of colour' more explicit. Marxist though he is, Césaire is concerned to show that the anti-colonial struggle is different from that of the worker involved 'against French capitalism'. Colonial struggle therefore obeys a different logic. Perhaps for this reason Césaire believes that even as radical an organization as the French Communist Party suffers from some of the prejudices of the rest of the society. Césaire was critical of the French Communist Party because of

its inveterate assimilation; its unconscious chauvinism; their current, though understandable conviction — which they share with bourgeois Europeans — of the omnilateral superiority of the West.[19]

In accusing the French Communist Party of sharing with bourgeois Europeans some of the assumptions regarding the 'omnilateral superiority of the West', Césaire identified one of the most crucial questions concerning the relationship between communism and the colonial intelligentsia. Colonial intellectuals rallied to the communist parties the world over because they were the only political organizations to call for the independence of colonies. When they were subsequently transformed into political parties attempting to capture political power by electoral means, they were led, however inevitably, to pander to the prejudices of the wider electorate. Indeed, notwithstanding professions of international working class solidarity, as James found out over the Abyssinian issue, communist parties in the advanced countries were sometimes as 'chauvinist' in their policies as the colonials whom they accused of chauvinism.

For Césaire the force of nationalism was too powerful to be subjected to international fiat. Every nation, according to Césaire, was the carrier of a 'peculiarity' because it was the embodiment of a peculiar history. He wrote to Thorez of the

peculiarity of our 'position in the world' which cannot be confused with any other; peculiarity of our problems which cannot be reduced to any other problem; peculiarity of history studded with so many vicissitudes and which she alone can know; peculiarity of our culture, one which we wish to live out in an increasingly authentic manner.[20]

It may be argued that this was an assertion by a member of the colonial intelligentsia stunned by the revelations of Stalin's atrocities. Yet this was a theme that went way back into Césaire's early poetry. For Césaire's position is that a people embodies a peculiar culture and history. To envelop them into the procrustean formula of a proletariat or 'international working class' is to be guilty of cultural intolerance – a short step from racism.

Césaire agrees, therefore, with James, that colonial rule and the race problems that go with them are problems with 'bourgeois capitalism'. James, however, is more avowedly Marxist because he reduces the problem to one of class. Race relations for him is a problem of stratification. The relations between black and white are essentially the problem of oppressor and oppressed. In the case of Césaire, racism is much broader than a question of economics. While he agrees that colonialism necessarily produces a race relations problem, he believes that it is much more than a problem in stratification. In short, race relations for Césaire could not be reduced to a problem between classes. The force of culture, personality and values combine to make the relationship between races a very complex one. This is why Césaire and James differ so fundamentally in their prescriptions for the problems of colonial liberation.

JAMES ON COLONIAL LIBERATION

For James, the problem of colonial liberation and decolonization is part and parcel of the wider problem of human liberation from the common enemy that is capitalism. Whether in London or in Port-of-Spain, capitalism for James is one and indivisible. The solution then is 'world revolution'. Indeed this is the message of *The Black Jacobins*. As James confesses in the preface to the Vintage edition, the concluding pages 'were intended to stimulate the coming emancipation of Africa'. In his study of the Haitian Revolution James had

sought not only to analyse, but to demonstrate in their movement, the economic forces of the age; their moulding of society and politics, of men in the mass and individual men; the powerful reaction of these on the environment at one of those rare moments when society is at boiling point and therefore fluid.[21]

Yet this is only the method − not the purpose − of the book. *The Black Jacobins* must be read not as a thesis on the Haitian Revolution but as a contribution to the debate that was taking place during the thirties in the camps of internationalism, communism and the black intelligentsia alike.

James was concerned, above all, to challenge the notion widely held in Pan-Africanist circles that the subjection of colonies to continuing imperial rule was at bottom the domination of one race over another. It is not that James was unaware of the practice of racism inherent in colonial rule. To those who had in their international policy overlooked the problem, he had written:

Lenin in his thesis to the Second Congress of the Communist International warned the white revolutionaries − a warning they badly needed − that such has been the effect of the policy of imperialism on the relationship between advanced and backward peoples that European communists will have to make wide concessions to natives of colonial countries in order to overcome the justified prejudice which these feel toward all classes in the oppressing countries.[22]

Where he differed from the rest of the colonial intelligentsia was in attempting to demonstrate that the issue was one of economics, not race, that race derived from economics.

For him 'political treachery' was not a monopoly of the white race but one of 'programme, strategy and tactics' and 'not the colour of those who lead it, their oneness of origin with their people, nor the services they have rendered'.[23] He felt compelled to remind his colleagues in the Pan-African Movement that the Black Jacobins in Haiti were playing their part in the destruction of European feudalism begun by the French Revolution and liberty and equality; the slogans of the revolution meant far more to them than any Frenchman.[24] He pointed out how, on the declaration of Haitian independence by Dessalines, private merchants of Philadelphia presented him with a crown whilst his coronation robes came to Haiti from Jamaica on an English frigate from London. He writes:

Thus the Negro monarch entered into his inheritance, tailored and valeted by English and American capitalists, supported on the one side by the King of England and on the other by the President of the United States.[25]

In short, politics has to do with who possesses power, not race per se.

Yet we might ask whether the Haitian revolution was about feudalism or the slogans of liberty and equality. Could it not equally be interpreted as a revolt by a subjugated race who saw their chance in the vacuum created by the revolutionary developments in France? For colonial revolutions have their own logic and their own agenda. James had noted the anti-white feelings that accompanied the triumph of Toussaint. He wrote:

these anti-white feelings of the blacks were no infringement of liberty and equality, but were in reality the soundest revolutionary policy. It was fear of the counter-revolution.[26]

For James, then, anti-white sentiments so characteristic of revolutions are the expression of more fundamental political fears and rivalries. The Haitian Revolution had to be seen in the context of the French Revolution and of the place of a colony such as San Domingo in the French Empire.

As far as James was concerned, the slave trade and slavery were the economic basis of the French Revolution, but it was the French bourgeoisie that pressed the button that brought the Black Jacobins to the stage. The destiny of the colony was therefore inextricably bound up with the metropole. Revolution, like Empire, was one and indivisible. It may be retorted that this was a view relevant only to James's reading of the Haitian revolution. But as is evident throughout the pages of *The Black Jacobins*, James was addressing his theses to contemporary events and personalities. Thus he wrote of Africa gaining its independence by armed rebellion:

Nor will success result in the isolation of Africa. The blacks will demand skilled workmen and teachers. International socialism will need the products of a free Africa more than the French bourgeoisie needed slavery and the slave trade.[27]

Colonial revolution then for James was part and parcel of 'world revolution'. In this respect James was sharing the various positions on the subject held by his mentor Trotsky. Trotsky, it will be recalled, as the advocate of 'permanent revolution', had advanced the view that the socialist revolution in Russia could not survive unless revolution abroad was pursued with equal vigour.[28] James saw the colonies as locked into the web of internationl capitalism. The World War was the opportunity for those seeking freedom in the colonies, since war weakened the ruling class. James accordingly urged the freedom fighters of his day:

Turn the imperialist war into a civil war. Abolish capitalism. Build international socialism. These are the slogans under which the working class movements and the colonial peoples will safeguard the precious beginning in Russia, put an end to imperialist barbarity, and once more give some hope in living to all overshadowed humanity.[29]

James's message then to colonial radicals was that they should turn the World War into a civil war within countries, and on its ruins to build international socialism. The clue to colonial revolution lay in the state of metropolitan revolution. Since ultimate power over a colony rested with the imperial power the best hope for freedom lay in the breakdown of power in the metropole. For this reason, the various metropoles became the centre of gravity for most colonial radicals. Although after the experience of the First World War Lenin had begun to advance his theory of the 'weak link', radicals from the 'periphery' turned their labours to the centre in the belief that once capitalism was broken there colonial freedom necessarily followed. This is why James put so much faith in the international movement and why he was seen as the ideologue of Trotsky's Fourth International. Whereas Lenin and his followers had revised their theses in the light of the outburst of patriotic fervour during the First World War, James was confident that in the case of the Second World War 'the War will begin as a conflict between nation and nation. The end of it will be the beginning of an era of conflict between rulers and ruled'.[30] Indeed, James's explanation for the failure of the international working class to obey Marxist predictions was that it was due 'chiefly to inexperience and the lack of a revolutionary international'. Colonial and metropolitan revolutions were for James indivisible. The one was inextricably bound up with the other since both were locked in a common economic and political mould.

CÉSAIRE ON COLONIAL LIBERATION

For Césaire, on the other hand, colonial revolution is by its very nature *sui generis*. He holds that capitalist society 'at its present stage, is incapable of establishing a system of individual ethics', and argues that 'at the end of capitalism, which is eager to outlive its day, there is Hitler'.[31] He thus agrees with James that racism derives from capitalism. Where he differs is in his perception of the relationship in terms of colonizer and colonized. He wrote:

Between colonizer and colonized there is room only for forced labour, intimidation, pressure, the police, taxation, theft, rape, compulsory crops, contempt, mistrust, arrogance, self-complacency, swinishness, brainless elites, degraded masses.

No human contact, but relations of domination and submission which turn the colonizing man into a class-room monitor, an army sergeant, a prison guard, a slave driver and the indigenous man into an instrument of production.[32]

Césaire argues colonial rule and its effects are not confined to class but to the whole complex of attitudes towards colonial subjects. Colonial rule, he reasoned, had brought a new ontology into existence, dehumanizing everyone with whom it came into contact:

> Not only sadistic governors and greedy bankers, not only prefects who torture and colonists who flog, not only corrupt check-licking politicians and subservient judges, but likewise and for the same reason, venomous journalists, goitrous academicians wreathed in dollars and stupidity, ethnographers who go in for metaphysics, presumptuous Belgian theologians, chattering intellectuals born stinking out of the thick of Nietzsche, the paternalists, the embracers, the corrupters, the back-slappers, the lovers of exoticism, the dividers, the agrarian sociologists ...[33]

Colonialism, then, was not only the enterprise of a ruling class. It was as much a looting by all kinds of people from sociologists to judges. What is Césaire's prescription for escape from so total an experience? He recommends that Europe undertake

> on its own initiative ... a policy of nationalities, a new policy founded on respect for peoples and cultures – nay, more – unless Europe galvanizes *the dying cultures, or raise up new ones* ... Europe will have deprived itself of its last chance and, with its own hands, drawn up over itself the pall of mortal darkness.[34]

Discours Sur le Colonialisme, it must be recalled, was first published in 1955 at a time when the greater part of the colonial world was still ruled by the respective imperial powers. It is interesting that Césaire should call on Europe and fix responsibility on them to resurrect the dying cultures of the colonial world. But as a poet and a 'man of culture' it is understandable that he should place so much emphasis on culture. Even Lenin, for all his Realpolitik, has begun to recognise that transformation from a capitalist to socialist form of organisation was no easy transition. Marxists of varying persuasions believed that all that was necessary was 'a dictatorship of the proletariat' and 'control of the commanding heights of the economy', along with an appropriate foreign policy. Yet, as Lenin observed, socialism was also a matter of values and culture. Economic relations were not the only relations into which men entered, however crucial they may be. It is not that Césaire jettisoned the proletariat or that he abandoned the goal of a classless society or that he denied the universal mission of the proletariat. What he believed was that until such time as the classless society comes, a force was needed to rescue societies from the bourgeoisie and the machine. That force was culture.

It was, however, in his famous *Lettre à Maurice Thorez*, and more specifically in his work *Toussaint L'Ouverture* (1961), that he came to address the specific nature of colonial revolution. In his remarks to Thorez he announced that

we men of colour, at this particular point of our history have, in conscience, become aware of our own distinctive position and are ready to assume at all levels and in all fields the responsibilities which flow from this 'prise de conscience'.[35]

As George Padmore found out during his experience with international communism, 'men of colour' do have a distinctive position, unity in the ranks of the proletariat between black and white being the exception rather than the rule.

For Césaire the anti-colonial struggle was more complex than that of the French worker, struggling against 'French capitalism'. For this reason it could not be regarded as 'a part or fragment in this struggle'.[36] It also meant that the correct strategy in the anti-colonial struggle was one that embraced 'the widest as against the narrowest' of social movements.[37] To subordinate one's policy to the metropolitan Communist Party of France was to transplant into local politics [Martinique] the issues and policies of metropolitan France and in so doing create artificial divisions within colonial society.

The first contention of Césaire was that colonial society was different from that of the metropole. This is obviously a fair comment. The lines of cleavage in colonial society are different from those in France and England. Whereas, in the latter, the rulers belong substantially to the same culture, in the colonies it was different. Colonial rule, almost by definition, involved rule by an alien culture. Stratification was also based, not as in the metropole on economic criteria, but on racial attributes.[38] And in colonial society the proletariat is small and underdeveloped. Class struggle, accordingly, has a different meaning in the metropole. In colonial society its appeal is limited to some sections of the intelligentsia and trade union elites. This is why in colonial and ex-colonial societies appeals to racial sentiment have been so powerful in influencing social and political behaviour. Garvey was far more feared than the combined forces of the Pan-African intelligentsia. For this reason Césaire is right to conclude that the colonial struggle was different from that of the French worker involved against French capitalism. The inevitable corollary was that it could not therefore be regarded as a 'fragment' of metropolitan struggle. Colonial revolution could not come either from the metropolitan workers, or from an alliance between the two, since they both developed from different premises and proceeded along different lines. Thus a vital link of the Marxist chain – the necessity for international working class solidarity as a prerequisite for colonial revolution – had been severed.

Worse still, for Césaire, dependence on metropolitan ideology and organizations such as the Communist Party meant creating artificial divisions within the anti-imperialist movement. Of course, Césaire may have been here confusing the doctrine with the church, that is, Marxism with the Communist Party. Metropole and colony at a very general level may both be in the grip of capitalism. Both may be enduring the problems of ruler and ruled. But here the similarities end. A colony may be a source of raw material, an outlet for the manufactured goods of the metropole. The issues between them vary since they were located at different stages of economic and cultural development. Race may be a more salient factor in the colony and there may not necessarily be a harmony of interest between the working classes of both countries. To import the issues of the metropole into the politics of the colony is to create artificial divisions and to misinterpret the feelings of important groupings. This is why so many revolutions have to be imposed on colonial peoples. The kind of revolution that Césaire had in mind differs fundamentally from the imposed revolution.

In *Toussaint L'Ouverture* Césaire elaborated more critically on these themes. For Césaire, Haiti posed the characteristic problem of the twentieth century – the colonial problem. An analysis of the Haitian revolution is accordingly an analysis of the colonial problem. He wrote:

Saint Domingue is the first country in modern times to have posed in all its reality for the reflection of men – the colonial problem – the great problem of the 20th Century in all its complexity – social, economic, racial.[39]

His method of analysis was to see the Haitian Revolution on its own terms, that is, as a specifically colonial revolution. His purpose is best put in his own words. 'I have tried', he wrote,

to delineate the characteristics of a colonial-type revolution. I stress colonial because the worst error would be to consider the Saint Domingue revolution purely and simply as a chapter in the French Revolution. On the contrary, if one was tempted to confuse a Revolution occurring in an independent country, the study of events would suffice to guard against such an absurdity.

It is important to understand; there has been no 'French Revolution' in the French colonies. There has been in each French Colony, a specific revolution born out of the occasion of the French Revolution, deriving from it, but developing according to its own laws and on particular objectives. Nevertheless, one point in common between the two phenomena – the rhythm. In France – the Constitutionalists, Girondins, Jacobins – each party played its role in office and pushed the Revolution to a point where – exhausted – it was forced to stop; the relay is then taken up by the boldest ally, who supersedes it, becoming in its turn a moment soon to be bypassed.

It is the same line of development that one finds in the Sainte-Domingue revolution; whites then mulattoes, then negroes, one pushing the other and incarnating with increasing intensity the different 'moments' of the anti-colonial revolution.'[40]

In this extended quotation lie Césaire's substantive theses on colonial revolution. The purpose of the book was to tell us why, of all the groups in Saint Domingue, the Negroes – those with the most widespread suffering – succeeded.[41] Against those like James and other Marxist-oriented writers in France who were inclined to see the Haitian revolution as a chapter of the French Revolution, he had to warn that revolutions in dependent and independent countries followed a different logic. Each had their different impulses and objectives. There was one point, however, which they shared, namely, that both revolutions went through phases with succeeding leaders carrying the struggle a stage further. In Saint Domingue, however, it was the Negroes who achieved the ultimate victory under Dessalines. How was the victory to be explained?

For Césaire the outbreak of the French revolution meant different things for the different racial groupings in Saint Domingue. To the planters it represented political and commercial liberty; for the mulattoes it meant political liberty and

equality but for the Negroes it meant simply freedom. For the
bourgeoisie in France the dilemma was whether to pursue the
politics of principle or the politics of interests. The politics of
'interests' won out – those of the colonists and the metropoles.
Does this mean that the French Revolution had no effect on
the colonial revolution? Far from it, argues Césaire. In the first
place, it was a catalyst since it disturbed the existing equilibrium
among classes. In the second place, it proclaimed the principle
of the rights of man and people. What Toussaint did was to
carry forward the rights of man to the right of men to nationhood. It was the achievement of Toussaint to have transformed
a formal right into a real right and to 'have inscribed the revolt
of the black slaves of Saint Domingue into the history of
universal civilization'.[42] But there was one flaw in the politics
of Toussaint. According to Césaire, he was more concerned
to treat his people from an abstract universal than to grasp
the peculiarity of his people in order to bring them to the
universal.[43]

There can be no doubt that colonial revolutions have been
influenced by metropolitan upheavals. The metropole can be
a source of ideas and principles; it can provide allies – and in
more recent times arms and training. Césaire is right to point
out that whilst there are similarities with metropolitan development, the foundations of colonial revolution may be quite
different. Metropolitan revolutionaries may be prepared to die
for the rights of man or the right to have 'no taxation without
representation', but colonial revolutionaries may be moved by
other impulses. In some cases the impulse may be religious, such
as the desire to protect Islam; in others it may simply be, as
Fanon pointed out, to get into the settlers' shoes; and in yet
others, simply a desire to be ruled by people of their own race.
The terms of revolution differ between Port-of-Spain, Fort-de-
France, London and Paris.

Césaire can be accused of being too schematic in his view
of the stages of the Haitian Revolution. The fact that it was
the blacks who eventually gained control of the state may have
had little to do with liberty and equality. It may very well be
that Dessalines represented Negroes in a way that neither
mulattoes nor whites could. Césaire, it seems, was so mes-
merized by the power of Hegel's dialectic, that, despite his plea

for recognition of the particularity of the colonial situation, he was inclined to cast it in terms of the Hegelian conception of history.

It is indeed remarkable that although James and Césaire emerged out of contrasting empires they agreed so much on the nature of racism and colonial revolution. They both agreed that race relations between blacks and white emerged out of colonial rule and slavery. For James, however, the race problem was subordinate to the class question. Barring occasional pleas for a study of Negro history, his study of the Haitian Revolution and his various theses before Trotskyite gatherings, James has been more concerned with the achievement of socialism than with the recitation of cultural themes. Césaire, on the other hand, has been one of the creators of negritude. From the *Cahier* of 1939 to *Toussaint L'Ouverture* of 1961 Césaire had been concerned with demonstrating the 'peculiarity' of the black man. His is a search for man. Perhaps the difference between James and Césaire is the difference between the activist and the artist. Césaire is less moved by competing ideological systems. He is far more concerned with a humanist enterprise in which the alienation of man will cease.

Differences such as these go a long way towards explaining their approaches to colonial revolution. For James, colonial revolution was part and parcel of metropolitan revolution. Since the motive of revolution was economics and since metropole and colony were locked into a single economic system, colonial independence was dependent on the breakdown of capitalism and bourgeois government in the metropole. The theatre of revolution was therefore the metropole. Marx and Engels, it will be recalled, had recommended precisely this course. Colonial and other revolutionary movements in the under-developed world were advised to await the achievement of socialism by the metropolitan proletariat. It was, however, Lenin who had identified the weak link in the colony and backward country, and on this basis made the Russian Revolution. Colonial revolutions, for James, were not about race but about classes and economic interests.

For Césaire, colonial revolution is never a chapter of metropolitan revolution. The latter may act as a catalyst or impetus but the pace and pattern of colonial revolution is *sui generis*. For Césaire, colonial revolution is best seen as the unfolding of liberty. Is not this a reification of Hegel's idea? Is it not too teleological a view of colonial revolution? Yet Césaire is right to emphasise that colonial revolution has its own agenda and priorities. Metropolitan revolutionaries may have been too quick to discern socialist ideals in colonial revolutionaries. Disenchantment with the failure of socialist revolutions in their own countries have led them to write off their own proletariats and to fasten their hopes on colonial revolutions. Hence the attraction initially of Russia, then Cuba, Nicaragua and until recently Grenada. When colonial revolutionaries at last reassert themselves and try to come to grips with their own problems the metropolitan Left reacts as if a fraud had been perpetrated on them.

In conclusion it may be said that in many ways James is typical of the metropolitan revolutionary who sees colonial revolution as the delayed achievement of a proletariat asserting itself according to Marxist predictions. Césaire, by contrast, is concerned to show that colonial revolution is fundamentally a colonial phenomenon. It may demonstrate some similarities with metropolitan revolutions but its pace, content and aspirations will be dictated not by Marxist ideology but by local circumstances and history.

NOTES

1. C. L. R. James, *Beyond a Boundary* (London, 1963), p. 10.
2. *The Beacon*, July 1931.
3. Quoted in La Guerre, *The Social and Political Thought of the Colonial Intelligentsia* (ISER, Jamaica), p. 84.
4. Singham in his review 'Notes Toward a Theory of Black Politics' published by Guild of Undergraduates (Mona) for C. L. R. James Symposium.
5. C. L. R. James, *The Black Jacobins* (New York, 2nd Edition: 1962), p. 43.
6. *Ibid.*, p. 44 (my emphasis).
7. *Ibid.*, p. 96.
8. *Ibid.*, p. 128.
9. *Ibid.*, p. 198.
10. *Ibid.*, p. 227.

11. *Ibid.*, p. 283.
12. *The New Leader*, 17 April 1936.
13. James, *The Black Jacobins*, p. 377.
14. James left London in 1938 on a lecture tour of the USA and remained there until the early fifties. The American experience did modify his views on the importance of the race factor in politics. In substance, however, the primacy of class considerations was retained. Reasons of space prevent its inclusion. Interested readers may turn to the writer's *Social and political Thought of the Colonial Intelligentsia* (ISER, 1982), pp. 104–21.
15. For this section on Césaire I have drawn generously on a recently published work *Enemies of Empire* (Extra-Mural Department, UWI, 1983).
16. Aimé Césaire, *Cahier d'un Retours au Pays Natal* (Paris, 1939; Présence Africaine, 1956), p. 71.
17. Interview with Jacqueline Sieger in *Afrique*, Oct. 1961, No. 5, pp. 64–7.
18. Aimé Césaire, *Discours Sur le Colonialisme* (Présence Africaine, 1955) (4th Ed.), p. 13.
19. Aimé Césaire, *Lettre à Maurice Thorez* (Présence Africaine, 1956), p. 8.
20. *Ibid.*
21. James, *The Black Jacobins*, p. x.
22. *Ibid.*, pp. 286–7.
23. *Ibid.*, p. 106.
24. *Ibid.*, p. 198.
25. *Ibid.*, p. 370.
26. *Ibid.*, p. 261.
27. *Ibid.*, p. 377.
28. For an extended discussion of Trotsky's views on world revolution see Baruch Knei-Paz, *The Social and Political Thought of Leon Trotsky*, pp. 302–33.
29. C. L. R. James, *World Revolution, 1917–1936. The Rise and Fall of the Communist International* (London, 1937), p. 421.
30. *Ibid.*, p. 9.
31. Césaire, *Discourse on Colonialism* (translated by Joan Pinkham), p. 15.
32. *Ibid.*, p. 21.
33. *Ibid.*, p. 33.
34. *Ibid.*, p. 61 (my emphasis).
35. *Lettre à Maurice Thorez*, p. 8.
36. *Ibid.*, p. 9.
37. *Ibid.*
38. See Lloyd Braithwaite, *Social Stratification in Trinidad and Tobago* (ISER, Trinidad).
39. Césaire, *Toussaint L'Ouverture* (Présence Africaine, 1961), p. 22. Except where otherwise indicated the translations are those of the writer.
40. *Ibid.*, pp. 22–3.
41. *Ibid.*, p. 23.
42. *Ibid.*, p. 310.
43. *Ibid.*

Cultural Dualism and Political
Domination in Haiti*

DAVID NICHOLLS

For William Wilberforce, Thomas Clarkson and others who
fought for the abolition of slavery, Haiti was seen as a test case;
the story of her independence, of black self-government, would
demonstrate conclusively the wisdom of their programme.[1]
Opponents of emancipation, like James Franklin, also regarded
Haiti as significant, providing an exemplification of the kind
of situation that would exist if slavery were abolished in the
British colonies.[2] The former group tended in consequence to
paint a somewhat rosy picture of the situation in Haiti, while
the latter exaggerated the undesirable features of life in the black
republic. Throughout the nineteenth century up to the present
day, Haitians have seen their country as a symbol of black
independence and dignity while, on the other hand, much of
what is said and written about the country by foreigners contains
a significant degree of racial prejudice. Most accounts of Haiti
are therefore highly coloured by the preconceptions and commitments of the authors. Nevertheless it is, I think, possible to make
a more or less disinterested, if provisional, assessment of the
history and present condition of the country and of the French
legacy in Haiti.

'The power of the mighty,' observed Thomas Hobbes, 'hath
no foundation but in the opinion and belief of the people.'[3]
All political domination rests to a large extent upon a hoax –
upon a confidence trick. No government could stand for long
without a whole collection of myths, symbols and beliefs which
– with their supporting institutional structures – reinforce its
claims to obedience on the part of its subjects. Here I want to
look at the role of two interconnected strands in this cultural
complex: religion and language, seen as a consequence of

colonialism and of the system of slavery which was integral to it. First, however, it is necessary to say a few words on the historical context.

French troops were finally expelled from the western third of the island of Hispaniola towards the end of 1803 and the independence of Haiti was proclaimed. Naturally in the early years there was a considerable degree of anti-French feeling among Haitians of all classes. A minority was in favour of reaching some kind of settlement which recognised French suzerainty, but the majority of both black and mulatto leaders insisted that full independence from the former metropolitan power was essential. Yet the legacy of French colonialism remained.

ECONOMY

In the first place the colonial economy had been tied to that of France. It was centred on the large scale production of a few crops: sugar, coffee, indigo, cotton for export to Europe. Agriculture was dominated by huge plantations, particularly in the North and Artibonite. After independence the former free coloureds or *affranchis* (known after emancipation as *anciens libres*) owned much of the property; some they had inherited, other plantations they seized when the white owners fled. Most of the former white-owned plantations were nationalized and in the early years, under Pétion (and later under Christophe), many of these estates were given to members of the army or sold in lots of various sizes. It is frequently suggested that by 1820 there were no large plantations left in Haiti. This is not so. Senior army officers and other members of the elite continued to own enormous tracts of land which they attempted to cultivate with wage labour. Yet plantation agriculture ceased to dominate the economy. Large numbers of former slaves squatted on vacant, state-owned property and began to cultivate crops for local consumption. The export of sugar fell dramatically. In this respect Haiti has differed from the pattern which has predominated in other parts of the Caribbean. Even today in Haiti landless wage labourers make up a remarkably small percentage of the population, though the number of rural Haitians unable to support themselves from their own land is growing.[4]

In 1825 President Boyer accepted as a condition of the French recognition of Haitian independence an enormous indemnity of 150 million francs to be paid to the dispossessed French land owners. Haiti had to borrow large sums from Europe to pay the first instalment of this debt and thus began significant foreign financial involvement in the Haitian economy. This was reinforced by the arrival of large numbers of foreign merchants who have dominated the commerce of the country throughout the nineteenth century to the present.

CLASS, COLOUR AND REGION

With respect to the class and colour situation in Haiti today, regarded as a legacy of French colonialism and slavery, I do not want to say much here.[5] Crudely the general (though not total) coincidence between colour and class can be said to date back to colonial times. As most of the slaves were black, so most of the poor are black today. As most of the *affranchis* were mulatto, so today most of the rich are light skinned. This is a familiar feature of Caribbean social structures and its roots in the system of slavery and manumission are evident. It may also be worth mentioning that regional differences in the colour composition of the population, having significant political consequences, also date back to colonial times. The South was the last region to be developed, partly because of a terrain relatively unsuitable for large plantations; in this region the *affranchis* became strong in colonial times and here the mulatto leaders of the revolutionary and early independence periods had their power base. In the election of 1957 this was the region where Duvalier's principal opponent, the mulatto businessman Louis Déjoie received the bulk of his support.

POLITICAL AND MILITARY

Political and administrative aspects of the French colonial system have also been bequeathed to independent Haiti and persist into the present day. Colonial government was centralised, authoritarian and dominated by the military. The governor general was invariably a military officer. This pattern persisted throughout the nineteenth century, though a degree of decentralisation occurred as a result of bureacratic inefficiency and the inability of governments to control the activities of local army leaders. It was not until 1913, over a hundred years after independence, that Haiti had its first civilian head of state. Much of Haitian life manifests the influence of militarism. Many of the voodoo spirits, for example, are portrayed in military costume, and one of the principal figures in the voodoo liturgy is *la place* (from *Commandant de la Place*). The power of the local *chef de section* ensures a strong military element in rural administration. Efforts by the US during the occupation of Haiti from 1915 to 1934 to secure a non-politicised military failed and the army emerged once more in 1946 as the arbiter of events. One of the achievements of François Duvalier has been to remove the army from its position as an independent and frequently determining variable in the political life of the country.[6] Since his death the military has continued to be controlled by the presidential palace. This is not, of course, to say that it will not once again play an active political role sometime in the future.

I wish now to turn to two aspects of Haitian life which have been powerfully influenced by its French colonial heritage. These are the connected phenomena of religion and language. In speaking of religion and language I do not simply refer to the fact that Roman Catholicism is the official religion of the country as French is its official language. The peculiar dualism, religious and linguistic, which is found in Haiti, predates independence and reflects the ambiguities of the colonial sytem of domination.

CREOLE AND FRENCH

French is and has always effectively been the official language of Haiti and no serious attempt has been made to challenge its status. Henry Christophe told Wilberforce that it was his hope and intention eventually to substitute English as the official language of Haiti but it is unlikely that he would have been able to do so. Despite being the official language, however, only about five per cent of the population speak and write French fluently, though somewhat more are able to understand spoken French. The true oral language of the country is *créole*, which is spoken by all Haitians but is written and read by relatively few. The general level of illiteracy of about eighty five per cent is the highest in Latin America. During the nineteenth century serious claims were made by Haitians to a literary tradition distinct from that of France; yet this literature was written almost entirely in French.[7] The linguistic dualism found among the elite in Haiti is technically called diglossia. All members of the Haitian elite, and also other professional people, speak both French and *créole*. On formal and public occasions they will speak French and will normally speak with their children in French in order to help them to learn this indispensable means of social acceptance. Informally they will generally speak *créole* or will move from one language to the other even within a single sentence. Jokes and stories are almost always told in *créole*. The fact that elite groups are able to handle both languages gives them considerable power over the monolingual masses, a power not willingly to be relinquished.

It is a notable feature of the period of the US occupation that Haiti's French language and culture became a source of pride to nationalists who were resisting North American imperialism. In the 1918 constitution French was formally proclaimed the official language of the country, partly as a gesture of defiance to Haiti's uninvited guests. This is somewhat similar to the way in which Puerto Rican nationalists today revert to the culture and language of an older imperialism in reaction to the over-whelming presence of the USA in their country.

Créole is a French-based language, similar to that spoken in the French Antilles, in Dominica, St Lucia and parts of Trinidad. It has much in common with the *créole* spoken in Louisiana and with the popular language of Mauritius. Much of the vocabulary is derived from French though sentence construction is radically different. Various theories have been suggested to explain the origin of *créoles* and pidgins.[8]

a. Early theorists suggested that *créole* was the product of attempts by African slaves to imitate the language of their masters or that the white slave owner or seaman deliberately taught a simplified form of his language to a people he believed to be inferior.

b. Another theory is that this patois developed in three stages: the slave attempted to copy the language of his master or foreman, the white man simplified his language in imitation of the slave and finally the slave imitated the French-speaker's own modification of his language.

c. A third hypothesis rejects the idea that *créole* was developed on the plantation, ascribing its origin to the lingua franca, spoken by seamen and traders of the seventeenth century, known as Afro-Portuguese pidgin. The French sailors later replaced Portuguese words with French words and it was then acquired by the slaves who further developed the language.

Most experts today agree that *créole* developed as a result of attempts by African slaves to communicate with their masters and with each other. The role played by Afro-Portuguese, the influence of African languages and the mode of dispersion of the language among the islands remain matters of contention.

Although the *créole* spoken in Haiti today manifests minor regional variations, it presents a high degree of standardisation. There is, however, a significant distinction between *gros créole* of the countryside and the somewhat more French-sounding *créole* of Port-au-Prince. This raises the vexed question of the form in which the language should be written. There are two extreme positions. The first is that spelling of *créole* words should be phonetic. The other view is that they should be spelled as nearly to the French as possible. This is not the occasion to enter into the technical aspects of this debate, but it is worth saying a word about some of the wider social implications.

Those who advocated French spelling saw *créole* as a stepping stone to learning French and believed that if it was written in phonetic form it would be difficult to move on to French. Today, however, it is generally agreed that *créole* is a distinct language and should be written phonetically, though there are some disagreements about the best system to use. Many advocates of the vernacular argue that *créole* should be recognised as an official language of Haiti, together with French and that it should be taught for its own sake rather than merely as a means to learning another language.

Naturally the French government is keen to maintain French as an official language of Haiti and to ensure that *créole* remains a subordinate means of communication. They have an active

Institut Français in Port-au-Prince and have financed a large pedagogical centre to forward their interests and to form, in the words of a confidential memorandum to the French government, 'a sort of foreign legion of the French language, devoted to our cultural and political interests, within the Haitian administration itself'. An article in a prestigious French journal recently celebrated Haiti's alleged 'fidelity to France and her language' as more than mere sentiment. The author of this article – on Haiti as a part of '*la francophonie*' – does not so much as mention the fact that *créole* is spoken in Haiti. No uninitiated reader would guess that a mere handful of the population is able to converse fluently in French.[9] Today, however, the French government appears to have accepted the need for literacy in *créole* as part of a bilingual education programme.

Most of the educated elite of Haiti also wish to maintain French as the official language of the country for obvious reasons. Speaking Haiti's official language puts them in a position of domination with respect to the mass of the population. It is one means of ensuring the continued hegemony of a small bilingual class.[10] Many of those involved in the early years of the Duvalier regime wrote about the importance of *créole*, as followers of the so-called ethnological movement. Some small changes have been made, so that court cases at the lower levels are now conducted in a language which the participants can understand, and some primary school teaching is done in *créole*. A rather more serious attempt to challenge the predominance of French in the educational system of the country is being made at the moment. The proposal to make *créole* the language of the first four years of primary education was put forward by the government. This was greeted with fierce opposition from the educated classes and from some of the religious orders. The Department of Education had, however, failed to make adequate plans for the training of teachers who could operate the proposed scheme and for the provision of teaching materials, thus giving ammunition to opponents of the reform. The plans have since been suspended and the minister responsible, Joseph Bernard, has been sacked and replaced by Franck St Victor who, though favouring reform, is prepared to make compromises on the issue.

Despite his populist and anti-elite stance, François Duvalier almost invariably addressed mass rallies in French rather than in *créole*, implicitly recognising the importance of maintaining this instrument of domination. Middle class black Haitians who had in the past argued for a more extensive use of *créole* have lately been among the most resolute defenders of the traditional role of French, since they have themselves secured a share in social and political power.

The linguistic problems of Haiti have been exported to those countries where Haitian migrants have settled. Susan Buchanan has recently shown how conflicts over whether to use French or *créole* in the liturgy of a New York church reflect social tensions in a migrant community. The minority, led by a book-keeper and a social worker, are portrayed as arguing for the retention of the French mass as part of an attempt to maintain their leadership position in the Haitian community. This group also saw a knowledge of French as a status symbol, distinguishing Haitians from other New York blacks, as belonging to a superior culture. The pro-*créole* group, on the other hand, 'rejected the French identity and the idea of whiteness as superior to blackness', though they too wished to dissociate Haitians from US blacks.[11]

With respect to the political importance of *créole* two other points should be made. First that in the late seventies when, under pressure from the USA, a limited degree of opposition was permitted, *créole* was naturally the medium of the most effective criticisms of the government. *Créole* plays, such as *Pèlin Tèt* by Frank Etienne, containing thinly disguised attacks on the regime, were enormously popular, and the *créole* broadcasts of Jean Dominique, Compère Filo and others contained hard-hitting and effective attacks on aspects of the administration.

Secondly, it is noteworthy that one of the most powerful elements in the pro-*créole* lobby has been the protestant missionary movement. This movement, largely financed in recent years from the USA, has done most of its work in the countryside and has naturally worked almost exclusively in *créole*. Though it would be wrong to suggest a conscious and concerted conspiracy between US business interests, the state department, and the protestant churches, these missions have indeed constituted an important arm of US penetration in Haiti. It is significant that much of the pressure for the educational reforms referred to above has come from the United States, with financial backing from the World Bank.

One of the most influential attempts to construct a *créole* orthography was, however, the work of a Northern Ireland Methodist, O. H. McConnell who, in collaboration with Frank Laubach, produced in 1940 a phonetic orthography which has been widely used. The fact that this orthography took rural, or *gros créole*, as the standard pronunciation has sometimes been resented by *créole* speakers from the capital. The story is told of the maid who left her literacy class in Port-au-Prince because the word for 'egg' which she had pronounced 'zeu' (nearer to the French) was spelled 'zé'; she inferred that the purpose of the literacy classes was to impart a rural form of *créole* which she regarded as inferior.[12] Today the vernacular is widely used in the liturgy of the Roman Catholic church and the *créole* monthly *Bon Nouvel* with a circulation of some 30,000 is published by the church. *Créole* journals are also published by catholic groups in New York, the Bahamas and elsewhere, perhaps the best known being *Sèl*.

As Albert Valdman has argued,[13] there are two possible language strategies to be followed in Haiti. Either there must be a massive effort to transform French into the vernacular language by means of mass adult and child education programmes, or *créole* must be accepted as the (or at least an) official language of the country. The enormous cost of the former, both financial and in terms of social resistance, makes it an unlikely option. Nevertheless the second possibility would also encounter opposition, not only from the bilingual elite, but also from the monolingual population, who might interpret the move as an attempt to keep them as second class citizens by effectively closing one of the principal doors out of the rural maze. With the increased migration of rural Haitians to the USA and the Bahamas, however, English is coming to be seen as more useful than French as the linguistic pathway to salvation among the masses. It should be stressed, in conclusion, that compared with many countries in the world Haiti's linguistic problems are relatively simple and there is every reason to believe that a determined and consistent national programme over fifteen or twenty years could raise substantially the level of literacy and provide a solid basis for improved secondary education.

CHRISTIANITY AND VOODOO

The second form of cultural dualism I want to discuss is the phenomenon of christianity and voodoo. As in the case of language the dualism is not that of a simple either/or but rather a situation in which many people adhere to both.

Catholicism is the official religion of Haiti and has been recognised as having a privileged position in almost every Haitian constitution since 1806. The *concordat* of 1860 formalised the relationship between the Haitian government and the Vatican and marked the beginning of a period in which foreign clergy and nuns came to dominate the educational system. By 1881 there were 74 priests and a considerable number of sisters working in the republic. Prior to the *concordat* a few private and state schools existed, but these were soon overtaken in importance by the catholic schools. Until recently little attempt has been made to incorporate local culture, such as the *créole* language or the music of the *tambour*, into the christian liturgy. Latin and French were used in church and the music was European. The church hierarchy generally identified itself with the francophile mulatto elite and was frequently in conflict with governments of a *noiriste* tendency, like those of Salnave and Salomon, which were dominated by freemasons who were sometimes also protestants.[14]

There is plenty of evidence to demonstrate that successive French governments have seen the activity of missionaries, most of whom were from France itself, as a crucial aspect of its policy of cultural imperialism. The French naval commander, Admiral Alphonse de Moges, wrote to Foreign Minister Guizot in 1843: 'we must retake Haiti, not by the force of our arms but by frankly aiding this new republic by our influence ... by the sending of honourable and numerous clergy'. During the period of the US occupation the French government looked to the Catholic priests and sisters to maintain French cultural influence in the country. The clergy, wrote the French minister in Port-au-Prince, are 'precious collaborators of our political propaganda'.[15]

Voodoo is an amalgam of various African religions which has also incorporated elements of christianity. It is concerned with the worship of God (*bondié* or *grand mèt*) and the spirits (*loas* or *mystères*, as they are called). The cult frequently involves possession by one of the *loas*, who is said to 'ride' the devotee. The practice of voodoo also requires making certain sacrifices to the spirits. In Europe voodoo is frequently misunderstood and used as a term for black magic. This is not to deny that magic is involved in the practice of voodoo; it is often practised together with the religion and voodoo priests (*houngans*) may also act as magic-men (*bocors*).

This is not the place to enter into details on the esoteric aspects of the cult and in any case I am not competent to do so. I wish here merely to make some brief comments on the social and political importance of voodoo in the life of Haiti.[16] Whether the slave revolt of 1791 began with a voodoo ceremony, as tradition has it, is a vexed question among historians, but it does not seem to me unlikely that it did. The religion certainly provided a source of solidarity, by reminding slaves of their African past and by bringing them together for cultic ceremonies.

Throughout the nineteenth century voodoo remained the popular religion of the Haitian people, despite persecution of the cult by governments, black and mulatto, and in the face of aggressive missionary work by catholic and protestant churches. There was, for example, in the 1890s an active 'Ligue Contre le Vaudou'. Not only were most Haitian governments keen to suppress the religion, but also intellectuals, whether from the mulatto liberal tradition or from the *noiriste* camp, were unanimous in their condemnation of voodoo. Some of them, in writings directed to a foreign audience, even denied the existence of voodoo, for it was seen as uncivilised and out of accord with the European model which all nineteenth century Haitians accepted. (They did, however, remind their foreign readers that superstition was not a prerogative of African people and that some Haitian superstitions had European origins.)

It was only with the ethnological movement, beginning in the first decade of the present century, that Haitian intellectuals began to take voodoo seriously as a part of the national heritage. This theme was taken up by a number of young middle class *noiristes* in the nineteen thirties, among whom was François Duvalier. These men emphasised the African roots of Haitian culture, and voodoo was seen as an integral part of this. This *noirisme* was fought by members of the mulatto elite and by the Roman Catholic hierarchy, who saw it as a challenge to the system of domination of which they were the representatives. This battle culminated in the so-called 'anti-superstition' campaign of 1941–2, in which the church, backed by the government of Elie Lescot, conducted a massive attack on the voodoo religion, involving not merely an oath against voodoo practices being administered to the faithful, but also the physical destruction of voodoo temples and sacred objects. Threats of violent resistance from devotees of the cult, however, led church and government to back down and terminate the campaign. This issue was by no means resolved, and emerged again during the government of Estimé (1946–50) who was thought by the church to be sympathetic to voodoo.

The Roman Catholic hierarchy generally backed Duvalier's principal opponent, the mulatto elite businessman, Louis Déjoie, in the election of 1957 and in the period from 1960 to 1966 the government of Papa Doc conducted a sort of *Kulturkampf* against the church, expelling bishops, priests and nuns and imprisoning many others. In 1966 agreement on a revised *concordat* was reached with the Vatican and a new indigenous hierarchy was appointed. The new bishops were the result of a compromise between church and government but were generally prepared to back Duvalier's regime. When Duvalier came to power in 1957 ten of the eleven bishops were foreign; by the time of his death all but one were Haitians.[17]

It has been suggested that the backward state of the country is partly due to the fatalistic attitude cultivated by popular religion in Haiti, voodoo and catholic. One writer refers to 'a catholicism of resignation' which has been taught by the church and which is reflected in the popular *créole* hymns published by the hierarchy.[18]

Since the death of Papa Doc in 1971, however, the bishops have on occasion cautiously raised objections against some of the more outrageous activities of government ministers, such as the export of blood to the United States by a company owned by Luckner Cambronne. More recently the church has been vocal in the defence of human rights. In a more long term perspective clergy have taken the lead in many parts of the country in projects for community development. These activities have been criticised by some opponents of the regime as reinforcing the *status quo*. Certainly many of the projects are administered in a somewhat paternalistic fashion, but it is likely that the long term effect will be to raise the social and political consciousness of rural Haitians, leading them to question many institutions and practices hitherto taken for granted. Voodoo is still widely practised not only in remote country areas but in the capital and in other towns. It is therefore quite wrong to suggest that 'the antagonism town/country coincides with the antagonism catholicism/voodoo'.[19]

One important aspect of the religious scene is the greatly increased activity of protestant groups in the last decades. Some of these protestant sects are indigenous but, as already mentioned, many have their headquarters in the USA, from where they receive financial backing. While it is undoubtedly true that a number of these christian groups have improved the conditions of health, sanitation and agriculture in the countryside, others have been more concerned to forward US interests and to buy up tracts of land at low prices from peasants, for their own profit. One government minister referred to these protestant missions as a 'fifth column' inside the country and the Roman Catholic church has become alarmed at their proselytising activities.

The attitude of most protestants towards voodoo differs significantly from that generally adopted by catholics. The latter have tended to adopt a fairly lenient policy, encouraging their members to give up the practice of voodoo, but not insisting on a radical break with traditional ways. Priests have in the past pointed out that the *loas* can be thought of as christian saints and there is even a sort of identification between voodoo spirits and particular christian saints: Erzulie Fréda with Our Lady, Damballah with St Patrick, Ogoun with St James the Great and so on. Even Bishop Paul Robert, an implacable opponent of voodoo who was one of the leaders of the 'anti-superstition' campaign, could write: 'There exist in voodoo, practices which are able to assist us wonderfully in understanding the sense of the christian calling and even of the priestly and religious vocation.'[20] The attitude of the Roman Catholic church in Haiti has thus been somewhat ambivalent with respect to voodoo, occasionally resorting in panic to repression and confrontation, but normally attempting gradually to wean its lay people from the cultic practices at the same time as infusing these practices with christian content.

Protestants, in contrast, have generally adopted a much more radical approach, insisting that converts make a complete break with all voodoo practices and beliefs, burning or otherwise destroying cultic objects in their possession. Illustrative of the difference of approach is the debate about the best translation for the Greek word *kyrios*, or 'Lord'. The nearest equivalent in *créole* is *grand mèt*, but as we have already noted this is a term central to the voodoo liturgy and is derived from the system of domination in a slave-owning state. Protestants have in general studiously avoided this term, preferring a word quite unfamiliar in *créole: ségnè*, which is used, for example in the *créole* translation of the Psalms in *Bon nouvèl pou tout moun*, published by the protestant Alliance Biblique Universelle. Roman Catholic and Episcopal (Anglican) churches have, however, used the term *grand mèt* widely in *créole* hymns and translations of the liturgy, when referring to God the Father, and to Christ.

CONCLUSION

Haiti cannot, of course, be understood simply in terms of its colonial legacy and any attempt to do so, ignoring the deep and widespread African inheritance of the people, will come to grief. In this chapter I have therefore been concerned with only part of the story, though one which is central to Haiti's history.

The linguistic and religious dualism found in Haiti are to be seen as bequests of the colonial regime. Not only does this bequest involve those things brought from France and passed on to the colonial subjects: the French language and the christian religion. *Créole* and voodoo are also a part of the colonial legacy and furthermore the peculiar dualism in both language and religion is itself related to the ambiguities of colonial domination. The rejection of colonialism and slavery by a considerable number of the population was often combined with a recognition that preferment and even survival involved the adoption of certain aspects of the dominant culture. This is a familiar phenomenon in the anglophone Caribbean too, as C. L. R. James himself has pointed out and also, in certain respects, exemplifies. Yet the dualism both in religion and in language takes a somewhat different form in Haiti from that found in the Commonwealth Caribbean. This is due to a number of factors: the predominance of catholicism with its peculiar approach to the phenomenon of voodoo, the fact of 180 years of political independence and the less direct impact of European colonialism, and the relatively weak educational system which leaves large sections of the population untouched. While it is generally true to say that the *créole* language and the voodoo religion are associated particularly with 'the masses', as French and catholicism are with the elite, important reservations need to be made. As we have seen, members of the elite are fluent in *créole* and it is also true that they are familiar with voodoo beliefs and practices. The role of the maid, and other domestic servants, is crucial here. The children of elite families spend much of their time in the company of black servants from whom they learn *créole* and who pass on to them knowledge of the religion of their ancestors.

A vivid illustration of the linguistic ambiguity occurred in my house in Oxford, where we have a large and aggressive macaw sitting on a perch in the hall. The wife of a well-known Haitian playwright and poet came to see me some time ago. Her husband writes much of his work in *créole*, but I noticed (though without great surprise) that she was talking to her children in French. As she was leaving, the bird said in a loud and clear voice: 'bye bye'. Now as anyone who knows Haiti will be aware, 'bye bye' is the *créole* form of saying farewell. The lady looked at the bird, somewhat reproachfully as she might have done to one of her children and replied 'au revoir'. I could not resist the remark: 'zwazo-a pa kapab palé fransé, selman kréyol'.

NOTES

* I am grateful to Albert Valdman, Leslie Griffiths and Gertrude Buscher for some helpful comments on an earlier version of this paper. A slightly modified version appears in David Nicholls, *Haiti in Caribbean Context* (London, 1985).

1. See W. W. Harvey, *Sketches of Hayti from the Expulsion of the French to the Death of Christophe* (London, 1827; reprinted Frank Cass, 1972) and Z. Macaulay, *Haïti ou renseignements authentiques sur l'abolition de l'esclavage* (Paris, 1835).

2. See J. Franklin, *The Present State of Hayti* (London, 1828; reprinted Frank Cass, 1972).

3. T. Hobbes, *Behemoth* (London, 1889; reprinted Frank Cass, 1969), p. 16

4. See 'Dynastic Despotism: from Father to Son', in David Nicholls, *Haiti in Caribbean Context*.

5. See 'Caste, Class and Colour' published in *ibid.*

6. See Kern Delince, *Armée et politique en Haïti* (Paris, 1979) and J. H. McCrocklin, *Garde d'Haïti, 1915–1934* (Annapolis, 1956); also David Nicholls, 'On Controlling the Colonels', *Hemisphere Report* (Trinidad), July 1970.

7. R. Berrou and P. Pompilus, *Histoire de la littérature haïtienne*, (Port-au-Prince 1975f). I discuss some of this literature in *From Dessalines to Duvalier* (Cambridge, 1979), chapter 3.

8. See Albert Valdman, 'The Language Situation in Haiti' in R. P. Schaedel, ed., *Research and Resources of Haiti* (New York, 1969), pp. 155f; more recently Valdman in Jean Perrot, ed., *Les langues dans le monde ancien et moderne* (Paris, 1981). also L. Todd, *Pidgins and Creoles* (London, 1974), chapters 3 and 4.

9. Paul Dumont, 'De la colonie à la francophonie', *La Nouvelle Revue des Deux Mondes*, mai 1973.

10. See L. Hurbon, *Culture et dictature en Haïti* (Paris, 1979); also D. Bébel Gisler and L. Hurbon, *Cultures et pouvoir dans la Caraïbe* (Paris, 1975).

11. S. H. Buchanan, 'Language and Identity: Haitians in New York City', *International Migration Review*, 13:2, 1979, pp. 298f.

12. A. Valdman, 'The Language Situation in Haiti', p. 175. It should, however, be noted that McConnell himself saw his phonetic orthography as facilitating an ultimate transition to French. The rural pronunciation is today generally accepted as the norm for written *créole*.

13. A. Valdman, 'The Linguistic Situation of Haiti', in C. R. Foster and A. Valdman, eds., *Haiti – Today and Tomorrow* (Lanham, Md., 1984), pp. 79f.

14. See David Nicholls, *From Dessalines to Duvalier*, pp. 117f.

15. A. de Moges à Guizot, 3 juin 1843, Archives du Ministère des Affaires Etrangères (AAE) Corr Pol, Haïti 10, f. 390; and L. Agel au Ministre, 2 juin 1921, AAE Amérique 1918–1940, Haïti 15. Also 'Le clergé français, soit séculier, soit régulier, propage ici notre langue et nos idées; de plus, il jouit d'une grande influence dans tout le pays.' Agel au Ministre, 8 juin 1920, AAE Amérique 1918–1940, Haïti 15.

16. For more details on the social role of voodoo see L. Hurbon, *Dieu dans le vaudou haïtien* (Paris, 1972); H. Courlander and R. Bastien, *Religion and Politics in Haiti* (Washington, 1966); A. Métraux, *Le vaudou haïtien* (Paris, 1958).

17. See David Nicholls, 'Politics and Religion in Haiti', *Canadian Journal of Political Science*, 3:3, 1970, pp. 400f. François Duvalier tells his version of these events in *Mémoires d'un leader du tiers monde* (Paris, 1969).

18. Claude Souffrant, 'Un catholicisme de résignation en Haïti', *Social Compass*, 17:3, 1970, p. 428.
19. Ibid., p. 428.
20. Paul Robert, *Difficultés et ressources* (Gonaïves Haïti, 1952), p. 20.

Contemporary Educational Issues in the Commonwealth Caribbean

COLIN BROCK

In this chapter an attempt is made to illustrate the overwhelming influence of the legacy of colonialism on contemporary educational issues in the Commonwealth Caribbean. Educational patterns and problems are reviewed with special reference to the pressures and constraints of demographic and geographic factors; the development of systems after independence; and questions of regional co-operation in respect of public examinations and the provision of higher education.

While concentrating on the Commonwealth Caribbean, it is understood that this collection of political entities is also subject to wider hemispheric influences that affect educational provision in terms both of ideology and practice. Clearly the term 'regional' may be variously defined in the Caribbean context, but on the other hand it is in no small measure due to educational legacies and links that the Commonwealth Caribbean remains one of those definitions.

Education will be viewed here in its widest sense, though with most consideration being devoted to the manifestations of the formal strand, compulsory and post-compulsory. It is important, however, to remember that most education is informally acquired throughout life, and that both formal and informal variants include miseducation, an important element of which is the mystique and regard afforded to the process. Most societies in the world suffer from exaggerated expectations in respect of organised education and the totems of accreditation. They have contracted the 'diploma disease';[1] a condition which is itself a potent legacy of colonialism. The idea of 'education as transformation'[2] is unrealistic except in certain political contexts which in general do not exist in the Commonwealth Caribbean, though the Cuban model must not be forgotten and has been influential, notably in Grenada from 1979 to 1983.

THE LEGACY OF COLONIALISM FOR EDUCATION IN THE COMMONWEALTH CARIBBEAN

The development of educational systems in the territories of the British Empire was obviously influenced by attitudes and policies in respect of Britain itself, and especially England as the dominant component of metropolitan Britain. As is well known, the battle for the provision of universal schooling was waged throughout the nineteenth and early twentieth centuries against the resistance of much of the establishment, including the established church and many of the other churches. Universal primary provision was grudgingly conceded in 1870, and universal secondary schooling decreed in 1944. Empirical and partial traditions of education in England contrast sharply with more strongly developed rational philosophies in her erstwhile colonial rivals. Indeed an examination of the comparative effectiveness of different factors leading to the abolition of slavery would probably find some parallel in respect of those leading to the popular provision of schooling. That is to say, the pragmatic was more influential than the altrustic. A basically literate labour force for factory industry was made necessary by nineteenth century technical advance, and the location of the 1944 Education Act within the period of the Second World War is more than coincidental.

With respect to the former British West Indies this metropolitan disregard for the education of the masses was made total during the period of slavery itself, and after abolition manifested itself differentially according to quirks of sectarianism and paternalism.[3] While slavery obtained, no attempt was made to provide schooling, except on the part of a few maverick priests who were summarily dealt with as a result. Given the opposition of the established church to the provision of popular schooling in England this was not surprising. Towards the end of this period, the impact of inter-colonial conflict and the rise of non-conformist churches began to create opportunities for individual initiative, and with abolition these multiplied and became more formalised under official mission auspices. Since in each colony there were a number of competing missions in operation the outcome varied according to the particular mix of churches. The potential of the teacher for developing and supporting sectarian interests became evident in the scramble to establish denominational teacher training colleges. D'Oyley[4] graphically illustrates this in respect of Jamaica by listing no fewer than twenty-five foundations between 1832 and 1897 spread across seven denominations.

Colonial education legacies also have spatial dimensions. Differential locations and concentrations of mission and church schooling developed in the rural context have been replicated and ramified through the process of urbanisation.[5] For example, Clarke[6] and Goodenough[7] have illustrated the educational contribution to multicultural urban ecology in San Fernando and Port-of-Spain respectively. The spatial legacy is also evident on a wider scale in terms of 'the formal education system as a structural element in center-periphery cultural relations'.[8] That is to say, the formal system tends to act against innovations in education that might be more appropriate for local and national development.

Because of the creation of totally new societies through the slave-based plantation economy, very clear social divisions were engendered along the lines of the emerging social class structure in England, but with the additional indicator of colour. Although slave communities had no educational provision, the plantocracy often ran kindergartens for their own children and included children of mixed race arising from miscegenous relationships. Through this paternalistic access, the creole sector of West Indian society embarked on an educationally advantageous route which has in general helped to maintain and enhance their social positions. The dwindling white plantocracy did establish some prestigious secondary schools, but normally sent their children to metropolitan boarding schools, this being to some extent a function of territorial smallness. As selective secondary (grammar) schools were established in the late nineteenth and early twentieth century, usually by the denominations, so white and creole sectors were disproportionately represented in them. Again a very close parallel to the relationship between types of secondary schooling and social class in England, with similar built in replicatory mechanisms. Miller has illustrated this well in relation to Jamaica.[9]

As Lowenthal has shown,[10] West Indian societies are stratified by colour as well as class. This relates not only to the creole dimension but also to the legacy of indentured labour immigration as a replacement plantation population. This has had its educational effects, not only in terms of particular curricular variations (in areas such as social studies, civics and religious education), but also with respect to differential educational achievement. 'East Indians', for example, are no longer tied to a particular type of agricultural occupation, and figure strongly in commercial and professional fields, especially in Trinidad where their social and educational advancement has long been supported by adherence to the Presbyterian mission from Canada.[11] Differential patterns of urbanisation as between black and Asian elements of Trinidadian society, especially within the Port-of-Spain–Sangre Grande corridor, are beginning to throw up some difficult educational problems. Indeed in some schools even the choice of certain subjects and the teaching of them exhibit racial correlates, to say nothing of the relationship between colour, class and ethnicity in respect of selective secondary education. Minority groups such as Levantines and Chinese often exhibit distinctive educational profiles.

Language is probably the cultural indicator most centrally related to the educational process, and here there are certainly problems deriving from the colonial experience. The practice during the period of slavery of fragmenting African cultural groups and also not allowing the acquisition of English, resulted in the development of various forms of creole. With standard English being the official educational medium there has obviously been a discrepancy between the language of the home and the language of the school. This is not uncommon in former colonial territories in other parts of the world, but the fact that the social language is a less developed variant of the educational medium makes for extra and different difficulties in the West Indies as compared with, say, Indian Ocean and Pacific island nations. In the cases of St Lucia and Dominica, where the social language is a form of patois, there can be additional problems especially in relation to regional curriculum development initiatives.

One must next consider the political legacy of colonialism in respect of education. This has both ideological and organisational dimensions. The political context of the formative period of education systems in the 'British West Indies' was that of Crown Colony government. In practice this meant that each Governor or Chief Administrator had complete control over his particular colony. So, added to the particularity of each colony in ethnic, racial or religious terms was the legacy of a succession of idiosyncratic 'oddballs'. Some such officials left education entirely in the hands of local interested parties, others exercised prejudices derived from personal experiences far removed from those of their charges. As a result of all this, although each territory acquired a broadly similar system based on the English model of universal primary and highly selective secondary education, in detail there were by the mid-twentieth century many significant international as well as internal differences.

The received ideology was competitive, which in educational terms meant the domination of the primary curriculum by the demands of the examination for grammar school selection. In turn, the grammar school was dominated by the style and content of the 'Cambridge Overseas' and the ultimate in glittering colonial prizes, the 'Island Scholarship'. Despite the odds, the efforts of grammar school pupils were concentrated on the hunt for marks. They 'played' the curricular system, inherited from England, selecting fields most susceptible to cramming. This in general enhanced the status of classics and literature. Genuine hardship would be experienced by many families anxious to bid for an opening in metropolitan higher education for one or more of their offspring. As Williams[12] pointed out, 'one would have to consult the records of people's co-operative banks and local money lenders', rather than educational reports, to appreciate the practical effects of such an elitist system on individual families in the West Indies.

Given the origins of the educational model implanted in the 'British West Indies', it is not surprising to find that in addition to the aforementioned characteristics, it was also profoundly sexist. The schooling of boys enjoyed considerably more financial backing than that of girls, and differences in curriculum as between the sexes were clearly designed to perpetuate traditional differences of social and economic role. In the context of some of the social legacies of slavery these differences were, and sometimes still are, distinctive and resistant to change. Cole reports that there is even evidence of the patronising and invidious practice of applying lower standards and demand of girls as opposed to boys.[13] This attitude and practice has been something with which pupils of West Indian origin, and of both sexes, have had to contend in British schools. It engenders low self esteem and a relatively poor educational profile.

The political scale of the colonial operation was international and metropolitan, with two types of migration being fundamental to it. First, the migration to higher education in Britain and the possibility of working there or in some other part of the then Empire in a professional field. Second the opportunity to migrate within the British West Indies for similar roles. It has been suggested that the only demonstrable success of the highly selective system of schooling in the region in question was to effect the escape of the chosen few. Given post-colonial restrictions on migration to Britain and within the Commonwealth Caribbean the legacy of this system is one of anachronism.

A parting political legacy of the colonial education era was the nature of the establishment of a local university. During the period of classical colonialism a number of attempts had been made to set up such a college, notably in Bermuda, Barbados and Jamaica. These proved abortive due to lack of support from the white and creole classes who preferred to enjoy the established facilities and status of Oxford, Cambridge and London. In the event it was not until the mid-twentieth century that the University College of the West Indies was founded, and as Braithwaite[14] has observed, it was a profoundly colonial and paternalistic 'parting gift'. He identified two wings of this educational albatross if such it was: financial and curricular. The former refers to the fact that since the British government made a capital grant, 'local legislatures and politicians never came to grips with the serious problems of financing a university in the area'. The latter refers to the fact that affiliation to London in the first instance 'guaranteed the middle classes that the "standards" to which they were accustomed would not be violated'. More importantly perhaps it meant that the opportunity to create a radically different style of post-compulsory education in the special context of the West Indies was overlooked.[15] Of course, the idea of apprenticeship of new university institutions by starting off as University Colleges of London was customary at that time in Britain (at the time of the founding of the University College of the West Indies (U.C.W.I.), in 1948, the University College of Hull was itself still under London tutelage, having been founded in 1928), but the application of this system to such foundations as U.C.W.I., University College, Ibadan, and Makerere in Uganda was unfortunate given the extraordinary inertia of the British university model.

I shall return later to some consideration of the regional role of U.W.I., but it is now necessary to turn from the bases of colonial legacy in education to some of the contemporary contextual problems with which these received systems have been faced since 1945.

EDUCATION AND HUMAN ECOLOGY IN THE CONTEMPORARY COMMONWEALTH CARIBBEAN

The term 'human ecology' is here taken to indicate the integrated outcome of geographical, economic and demographic influences. To begin with, educational systems are products and agents of political systems, and in spatial terms at least very much affected by changing patterns of political geography. The University College of the West Indies was founded in the pre-Independence era, but as Payne has shown, with the assumption that the components of the British West Indies would come closer together rather than the opposite.[16]

As it turned out, the emergent and expanding systems of education in the period since 1945 have had to cope with a number of significant political changes. Ten years after the foundation of U.C.W.I. came independence for the British West Indies in the form of a Federation which lasted only four years, dissolving in 1962. The four strongest components, Jamaica, Trinidad and Tobago, Guyana and Barbados soon became individually independent, leaving the other territories to revert to colonial status. The medium scale islands acquired internal self-government as Associated States from the mid-1960s, and, beginning with Grenada in 1974, have successively proceeded to full independence. The microstates mostly remain as colonies. This is well known, but the effect of almost constantly changing relationships between West Indian states during the 1960s in particular certainly constrained the potential for development and reform of individual education systems at a time of relative affluence and plentiful aid income.

The acquisition of political independence has resulted in the expansion of education systems for a number of reasons. First, and especially in the 1960s, many developing countries accepted current theories relating investment in formal education and the achievement of economic growth. This has widely proved to have been unfortunate, though perhaps less so in the West Indies than in larger and poorer Third World countries. Second, early post-independence governments were keen to utilise education in the promotion of feelings of national identity and cohesion. National education systems everywhere have among their prime functions that of political control mechanisms. Third, the localisation and expansion of the public service sector after independence required the generation of additional educated manpower. Perhaps most potent of all was the popular demand for increased educational opportunity, to which politicians with an eye to personal party advancement were keen to accede. The mystique of formal education was of course one of the cultural legacies of colonialism.

In practical terms, most Commonwealth Caribbean governments took their lead from Jamaica especially in respect of raising the general level of schooling. A survey by Roberts and Abdullah[17] with reference to the situation in 1960, clearly showed that despite fairly long-standing universal primary provision, the educational ceiling profiles of the adult (15 +) populations of most West Indian territories were rather modest. They also exhibited considerable variation as between countries. For while Barbados had only 1.8 per cent of its adult population without any experience of schooling, St Lucia had 26.2 per cent. Between these two extremes lay Trinidad and Tobago (11.3), Dominica (13.4) and Jamaica (16.8). The proportion with a ceiling of primary education ranged from 89.1 per cent in St Kitts – Nevis to 69.7 per cent in St Lucia; while the range for a ceiling of secondary schooling was from Barbados (15.9 per cent) to St Lucia (3.3 per cent). Secondary schooling at that time meant 'grammar school'.

The Jamaican response to the evident need to raise the general level of school experience was to institute a Junior Secondary sector, and this policy was followed by many other Common-wealth Caribbean states. However in all cases the necessary con-comitants of such a policy, namely the delaying of selection until the end of this sector and also the generation of sufficient fund-ing to make the new sector universal, failed to materialise. The Jamaican case is well described by King,[18] where the junior secondary schools were effectively appropriated by the selective inertia of the system to become a secondary modern equivalent, euphemistically renamed 'New Secondary Schools'. Elsewhere, the incomplete nature of the new sector rendered it selective by default, and they became 'division two' grammar schools.[19]

The lost opportunity of the junior secondary sector in these countries is a significant issue in respect of post-Independence considerations of human ecology and educational provision in small island states. Referring back to the elitist and metropolitan orientated legacy, the insertion of a complete new sector between universal primary and selective secondary could have provided the opportunity for radical curriculum reform.[20] The need for a shift towards very localised themes and circumstances is a direct outcome of the changing political structures outlined above. The old system suited a situation of professional emi-gration, regional or metropolitan. It is not only the tough immigration controls of the United Kingdom, Canada and the U.S.A. that have changed the situation, but also similar controls quite naturally instituted by each newly independent Caribbean state. The political parameter now obtaining is the national one, and given the small scale of most of the countries involved, this has increased both the constraints and the demands on the educational systems of each island. So instead of a radical junior secondary network becoming the focus of new community based educational programmes, they have been sucked into the inertia of the selective colonial legacy.

In most countries of the Commonwealth Caribbean at the present time we find the potentially explosive combination of an increasingly qualified and specialised educational output and an ever enlarging pool of young unemployed. Bennell and Oxenham[21] estimate that within the Caribbean 'unemployment is 20–25% of the labour force and this rises to around 50% in the 15–19 age cohort in many states'. The received educational attitudes and structures are grotesquely inadequate to meet this challenge, and yet finite insularity and demographic increase combine to require a radical response in the not too distant future.

Small demographic, economic and geographical scale severely constrains educational provision both qualitatively and quantitatively unless certain conditions operate. In a survey conducted under the auspices of the Commonwealth Secretariat,[22] it became clear that a limited number of small countries seemed to prosper on the basis of their historical and geographical position, and relatively high degrees of spatial compactness, internal infrastructure and diversity in the economy. Cases in point are Mauritius, Malta, Barbados, and to a lesser extent, Fiji. These attributes enable Barbados to absorb not only the quantitative output of its long standing and extensive system of education, but also find a correspondence between the diffuse skills associated with a relatively academic output and the flexible requirements of a large tertiary sector in the economy. Unfortunately this is not a model that can be emulated by other small Caribbean countries, unless, like the Cayman Islands, they got in on the early days of the tax haven act, and are very small in population total.

The other small states of the Commonwealth Caribbean must confront the necessity of increased involvement in subsistence agriculture and any other local economic orientations that may be possible. Both tourism and plantation agriculture will continue, but neither carries the prospect of either stability or significant employment opportunity. In such a situation the internal human ecological legacy, including its education component, requires radical reappraisal on a community basis. An experiment was taking place along these lines in Grenada, including a complete restructuring of the teacher education programmes. Unfortunately this radical project in community education[23] has been effectively aborted by the invasion of Grenada by the U.S.A., but the necessity for locale-specific approach to island educational provision may not have been lost on its Windward neighbours.

Of the Commonwealth Caribbean states, only Jamaica exceeds the population threshold of two million regarded by the Commonwealth Secretariat as the upper limit for a 'small country'. As such, and due also to certain regional and resource attributes, it is able to sustain a complete national education system, leaving aside its involvement in the University of the West Indies. Even so, the disparities of the wider Commonwealth Caribbean can be found mirrored within Jamaica with its class based system of education. Guyana, by population and economy, ranks as a small country. Its enormous land area, however, provides a range of resources for potential economic diversity, and to its credit, the University of Guyana operates a range of flexible sub-degree programmes designed to effect a correspondence between educational output and economic structure. Trinidad's educational provision has been greatly enhanced during the past decade by its oil income, and increasingly diverse economy. As in Barbados, there is a capacity to absorb the products of an academic schooling, but its particular ethnic mix in relation to attainment and occupation is beginning to prove problematical, as mentioned above.

So there is clearly an educational gulf as well as otherwise between Jamaica, Trinidad, Barbados, Guyana and most of the other territories. Problems of smallness have much to do with it. A new perception of the role of education in tight insular circumstances, as well as of its content and method is required, and this probably means an enhancement of non-formal and adult education in relation to the compulsory sector. This requires political courage as well as skill: as Bennell and Oxenham observed, 'official efforts to reformulate fundamentally educational objectives generally lack the political commitment required'.[24] This has also to do with the politics of the curriculum. Shifting environmentally based components from the periphery to the core, as I have advocated elsewhere,[25] would be difficult to achieve due to the received mystique about 'subjects' and their relative status.

In addition to problems of internal scale and ecological legacy, small Commonwealth countries in the Caribbean and South Pacific, due to their clustering and colonially derived connection, find themselves in a regional relationship. Certain educational activities, at least as traditionally perceived, operate at this level and will be considered next.

SOME REGIONAL ISSUES IN CARIBBEAN EDUCATION

Two dimensions of educational activity in the Commonwealth Caribbean will be selected for discussion, with wider contextual issues always in mind.

First there is the question of public examinations at school level. The colonial legacy in this respect was the operation and status of the 'Cambridge Overseas' G.C.E. 'O' and 'A' level and to some extent its London equivalent, which provided certain indicators of achievement and status that had significant meaning in Commonwealth Caribbean societies. However, despite a degree of localisation of syllabus and examination content, this form of metropolitan validation proved increasingly unwelcome in the post-colonial context. The old Commonwealth countries had long since developed their own local examinations, and the developing countries of West Africa cooperated in the replacement of 'Cambridge Overseas' by the West African School Certificate. In the various territories of the British West Indies local secondary certificates had been developed, but ranged widely according to content and level, and in any case traditional inter-island friction would have prevented any one of these becoming the regional norm.

So in 1964, the Second Conference of Heads of Government of Commonwealth Countries (Georgetown) decided to establish the Caribbean Examinations Council (C.X.C.). In the event it took eight further years of negotiation before an Agreement setting C.X.C. in motion was actually signed. Since 1972, the Council has experienced all the vicissitudes common to any 'federal' enterprise in the Caribbean, but so far it has survived. The first examinations were held in 1979, in Caribbean History, English, Geography, Integrated Science and Mathematics. In 1980, Agricultural Science, Office Procedures, Principles of Accounts, Principles of Business, Typewriting and Spanish were added, and in 1981, English Literature and Social Studies. The following subjects are becoming available in the 1980s: Industrial Arts, Physical Sciences, Music, Art and Craft, French, Home Economics and Business Education. Two levels are operated: the 'basic', designed to relate to employment following the compulsory period of formal schooling, and the 'general' which is intended as a foundation for further study. Some subjects are available only at one or other of these levels, and as yet there is no equivalent/replacement for the Cambridge 'A' level.

C.X.C. has been faced with problems on a number of levels, each symptomatic of wider influences on the system. First it has been regarded with considerable hostility by many parents who value the traditional credibility of the Cambridge examination. Given the aforementioned elitism and selectivity of the system, this set of clients comprises mainly middle-class professionals — an articulate and influential group. On the other hand, the examination has been criticised for being too similar in content and level to its metropolitan forebear! Indeed, on the basis of 1979 results of pupils taking both C.X.C. and G.C.E., the former proved to be more difficult than the latter in all subjects except Geography.[26] Third, problems have been experienced over international co-operation in respect both of agreement over syllabus content and also of equity of marking of scripts as between candidates from different islands. Insularity is proving a difficult nut to crack. Indeed partly due to these traditional 'rivalries' C.X.C. has had to maintain two headquarters, one in Barbados, the other in Jamaica, with predictable consequences in terms of cost. This relates directly to the next problem, that of funding and logistics. Any regional venture in the Commonwealth Caribbean is frought with problems of co-operation and cost, as the ill-fated Federation itself illustrated. Whether C.X.C. will suffer the same 'final solution' remains to be seen.

In fact an interim solution has been found, the implications of which will lead on to consideration of wider regional influences. As funds began to run out in 1979, an agreement was signed with U.S.A.I.D. to run a joint 'Caribbean Educational Development Project' which would maintain and even develop the system into the mid-1980s.[27] This includes a secondary level curriculum development sub-project, and also provides a data processing facility for C.X.C.; support for large-scale in-service education for teachers; funding and advice on the development, evaluation and dissemination of new materials for the classroom. Not surprisingly this support carries with it certain cultural and ideological implications and constraints.

The other regional issue to be considered here is that of further and higher education. Mention has already been made of the paternalistic legacy inherent in the mode of foundation of the University of the West Indies. Its subsequent evolution, even maintenance, has been subject to the conflict between local, national, regional and metropolitan scales of consciousness and interdependence.[28] Within the Commonwealth Caribbean group of sponsoring nations there are almost endemic problems of funding in relation to perceived problems as well as benefits arising from continued involvement.

As mentioned above, Guyana has its own university, having opted out of the U.W.I. community. The remaining client countries may be divided into those who host campuses and those who do not, the former comprising Jamaica (H.Q.), Trinidad and Tobago, and Barbados. Campus countries, for obvious reasons, derive greater benefit from the university. There is greater accessibility for their potential students since travel costs are comparatively small and living at home is possible. They also enjoy the multiplier effects of the presence of a large employer of local labour and the substantial input of miscellaneous student spending to their local economy. On the other hand these three countries contribute disproportionately to the funding of the university.

Another problem perceived by non-campus countries is the appropriation of its talented students by the university itself or by the economies of the campus countries. Given the generally enhanced opportunites for professional work in the M.D.C.s, they have in effect become regional metropolitan substitutes for the erstwhile migration of graduates to Britain. Although each non-campus country has an extra-mural centre, there is a general feeling among this group that they should have a bigger territorial stake at the undergraduate stage. Consequently there has been a move to establish tertiary facilities in some of the smaller countries where the first year or two of university study could take place. The College of the Bahamas is seen by some as a promising model, given the experience it has developed in relation to links with university programmes in Florida. The Morne Fortune Higher Education Complex in St Lucia could also move in this direction, though it is unlikely that every client state of U.W.I. could provide and support this level of facility.

The basic structure of U.W.I. remains as originally designed, namely that certain 'general' subjects should be available on each of the main campuses, while certain technical or professional programmes should be concentrated on one campus only. Consequently, there is medicine at Mona, law at Cave Hill and most of the agriculture at St Augustine. With Trinidad now enjoying considerable oil revenues, there seems to be an injection of national funds in relation to developing medicine and law, and possibly other fields, there. Will St Augustine become the University of Trinidad and Tobago and leave U.W.I.? If so, or in any case, will either Mona and/or the College of Arts, Science and Technology next door become the University of Jamaica? If these possibilities come to pass, or even if they do not, what future lies in store for Cave Hill? An Eastern Caribbean function perhaps, or merger with the 'public sector' of Barbadian further education which is already very highly developed? Payne contends that 'much looser links between the campuses may be the only condition on which the University can survive at all as a regional institution'.[29]

British university foundations, and U.C.W.I. was certainly that, are institutional phenomena with considerable capacity for inertia and survival, but in the context of the wider Caribbean and the range of outside influences at work, greater flexibility of approach in respect of client countries will be required. As Carrington,[30] a leading educationist at U.W.I. has indicated, the university has failed to perceive the significance of adult and continuing education: 'Part of the reason for this is the maintenance of the inappropriate tradition that university activity requires a campus base.' A similar point has been made by Peter-Williams in respect of the nature and funding of research.[31]

CONCLUSION

The contemporary Caribbean is in a state of flux. Perhaps it has always been so, given its locational and strategic significance. Systems of education reflect stronger political and social forces, and the legacy of the colonial educational model, implanted at a time of relative stability in the 'British West Indies' is proving increasingly dysfunctional especially at secondary and tertiary levels. There are strong parallels to be observed in comparable small island situations, notably in the South Pacific, that could repay research in comparative education. This would be true at national or regional level, and help to focus attention on the urgent problems produced by smallness and the need to co-operate in educational fields.

Educational provision is a major political activity, and radical responses to the sort of problems outlined above carry their own ideological and political ramification. Grenada's attempt to strike out on a path traditionally at odds with the colonial inheritance and with strong philosophical and practical support from Cuba, was obviously a matter of acute interest and concern to the U.S.A. One of the responses of the U.S.A. to such influences is to increase its own support for, and involvement in, all kinds of educational projects in the region. Its willingness to bale out C.X.C. and related curriculum development at secondary level is a prime example.

To its credit, U.W.I. gave strong and imaginative professional and accreditational backing to the Grenadian reforms, so perhaps it will also play a fuller part in the network of regional activities undertaken by the Association of Caribbean Universities (U.N.I.C.A.). Certainly a greater focus on the acute problems of small countries would be a welcome reorientation of the thrust of university work, and U.N.I.C.A. is actively aware of the urgency of the ecological problems such states are facing.[32] Whether it is a disinterested body in the academic sense, or a C.I.A. cover, is the sort of question to which the mostly small Commonwealth Caribbean countries should address themselves as they seek an indigenous/regional alternative to the colonial educational legacies of the Old World.

Beckford has suggested that 'the most intractable problem of dependent societies is the "colonised" condition of the minds of the people'. Such is the legacy of colonial education in the widest sense. While seeking solutions to urgent local problems, and identifying new roles for educational provision, most Commonwealth Caribbean countries are well aware of the overtures of new forms of colonialism. Some are internal, some are regional, others global — but they all come bearing educational gifts. Hard political decisions will have to be made, and as far as education is concerned there is not a very strong track record in this respect among the countries of the Commonwealth Caribbean. But to be fair to them this is probably another colonial legacy. Geopolitical realities in the Caribbean Basin are a formidable complex within which the Commonwealth members have to survive. Still carrying the educational baggage of their British colonial experience, they must now it seems prepare for new educational incursions from both North and Latin America. The future is unclear, but whither politics leads, education must follow.

REFERENCES

1. R. Dore, *The Diploma Disease* (London, 1975).
2. C. London, 'Education as Transformation: A Case for the Caribbean', paper presented to the Fourth Annual Conference of the Association of Caribbean Studies, Havana, 1982.
3. C. Brock, 'Education and the Multicultural Caribbean', in: T. Corner (ed.), *Education in Multicultural Societies* (London, 1984), pp. 156–96.
4. V. D'Oyley, 'Plans and Progress in Nineteenth-Century Jamaican Teacher Education', in: V. D'Oyley and R. Murray (eds.), *Development and Disillusion in Third World Education*, Ontario Institute for Studies in Education, 1979, pp. 5–32.
5. M. Cross, *Urbanisation and Urban Growth in the Caribbean* (Cambridge: 1979).
6. C. G. Clarke, 'Residential Segregation and Intermarriage in San Fernando, Trinidad', *The Geographical Review*, Vol 61, No. 2, 1971, pp. 198–228.
7. S. Goodenough, 'Race, Status and Urban Ecology in Port of Spain, Trinidad', in: C. G. Clarke, (ed.), *Caribbean Social Relations*, University of Liverpool Centre for Latin American Studies, 1978, pp. 17–45.
8. W. W. Anderson, 'Dependency Relations and Structural Obstacles to Development Education in the British Caribbean', paper presented to the Fourth Annual Conference of the Association of Caribbean Studies, Havana, 1982.
9. E. Miller, 'Education and Society in Jamaica', in: P. M. E. Figueroa, and G. Persaud (eds.), *Sociology of Education: A Caribbean Reader*, (Oxford: 1976), pp. 47–66.
10. D. Lowenthal, *West Indian Societies* (Oxford: 1972).
11. J. T. Harricharan, *The Work of the Christian Churches among the East Indians of Trinidad: 1845–1917* (Trinidad: 1976).
12. E. Williams, *Education in the British West Indies*, (Trinidad: 1950).
13. J. Cole, 'Official Ideology and the Education of Women in the English-Speaking Caribbean, 1835–1945, with Special Reference to Barbados' in: J. Massiah (ed.), *Women and Education*, Institute of Social and Economic Research (Eastern Caribbean), University of the West Indies, Cave Hill, Barbados, 1982.
14. L. E. Braithwaite, 'The Role of the University in the Developing Society of the British West Indies', *Social and Economic Studies*, Vol. 14, No. 1, 1965, pp. 75–96.

15. G. A. Peter-Williams, 'Constraints on Establishing Credibility in Higher Education: the Case of the University in Developing Countries, *Caribbean Journal of Education*, Vol. 8, No. 3, 1981, pp. 278–321.
16. A. Payne, 'One University, Many Governments: Regional Integration, Politics and the University of the West Indies', *Minerva*, Vol. XVIII No. 3, 1980, pp. 474–98.
17. G. W. Roberts, and N. Abdullah, 'Some Observations on the Educational Position of the British Caribbean', *Social and Economic Studies*, Vol. 14, No. 1, 1965, pp. 144–54.
18. R. King, 'The Jamaican Schools Commission and the Development of Secondary Schooling', in: V. D'Oyley and R. Murray (eds.), *Development and Disillusion*
19. C. Brock, 'Structural and Curricular Developments at the Junior Secondary Level on the Caribbean Island of Saint Lucia', paper presented to the Bi-Annual Conference of the Comparative Education Society in Europe, University of Valencia, 1979, mimeo, pp. 11.
20. C. Brock, 'Junior Secondary Innovations in Nigeria and Saint Lucia: A Comparative Study', in: B. Gorwood (ed.), *Intermediate Schooling*, Aspects of Education No. 32, University of Hull Institute of Education, 1984, pp. 54–65.
21. P. Bennell and J. Oxenham, 'Skills and Qualifications for Small Island States', in: *Report of the Commonwealth Foundation Seminar on the Development of Appropriate Skills and Qualifications Required to Serve the Community in Small Island States,* Commonwealth Foundation, 1982, pp. 83–101.
22. C. Brock, *Scale, Isolation and Dependence: Aspects of Education in the Island Developing and other Specially Disadvantaged States of the Commonwealth*, Commonwealth Secretariat, 1984.
23. C. Brock, and R. Parker, 'School and Community in Situations of Close Proximity', in: K. Lillis (ed.), *School and Community in Less Developed Areas* (London: 1984).
24. P. Bennell and J. Oxenham, 'Skills and Qualifications for Small Island States', p. 97.
25. C. Brock, 'Education, Economy and Employment in Small Commonwealth Countries', in: J. K. P. Watson (ed.), *Youth, Education and Employment: an International Survey*, 1983, pp. 122–45.
26. *CXC News*, Vol. 1, No. 2, 1981, p. 3.
27. S. Griffith, 'Report on the CXC/USAID Secondary Curriculum Development Project', *Caribbean Journal of Education*, Vol. 8, No. 3, pp. 322–31.
28. A. Payne, 'One University, Many Governments'.
29. *Ibid.* p. 495.
30. L. D. Carrington, *Education and Development in the English-Speaking Caribbean: a Contemporary Survey*, UNESCO, 1978, p. 83.
31. G. A. Peter-Williams, 'Constraints on Establishing Credibility in Higher Education', p. 294.
32. J. Bonnet and E. L. Towle, 'Energy/Environmental Management: a Broad Perspective for the Islands of the Caribbean', *Caribbean Educational Bulletin*, Vol. VIII, No. 3, 1981, pp. 13–33.

INDEX

INDEX

Abyssinia 206–7, 210
Adams, Tom 151
African, Caribbean and Pacific
    Countries (ACP) 6, 57, see
    also 89–119
Anguilla 142, 145–6, 160
Antigua and Barbuda
    dependency 142–3, 149–50
    politics 12, 148, 153, 155,
        161–3
    sugar 35–6, 43, 91
Association of Caribbean
    Universities (UNICA) 255
Associated States (141–70);
    10–11, 90, 246

Bahamas, The 2, 83, 161, 231,
    253
Barbados, (62–88) 8, 46, 245–6
    agri-business bourgeoisie 5,
        69–71, 80–5
    education system 247, 249,
        253–4
    plantation system 63, 66,
        68–9, 72, 75
    plantocracy 62, 66–7, 84
    relationship with Eastern
        Caribbean 146, 151, 153,
        166
    sugar 6, 72, 75–7
    tourism 82–3, 197
Beckford, George 1, 255
Belize (formerly British
        Honduras) 2, 46, 48, 155,
        171
    sugar 3, 44, 57, 89, 98
Bennell, P. 249–50
Bermuda 83, 245
Best, Lloyd 1

Bird, Vere 149, 162, 166–7
Bishop, Maurice 9, 133–4, 145,
    152, 161, 164–5, 167
Blaize, Herbert 133–4
Bradshaw, Robert 149, 160, 163
Brazil 182
Britain
    aid 144, 150, 152–4, 166–7
    and Associated States 152–65
    and Caribbean sugar industry
        56–7, 65–6, 89–92, 94–5
    and Sugar Protocol 95–7,
        102–5
    cultural influences 19–20,
        24–5, 202, 241–3
    imperial system 201–2
    political influences 8, 10–11,
        13, 17, 131, 142, 244–6
    see also 120–40
British Guiana (now Guyana)
    63–5
British Honduras (now Belize) 8,
    65, 91
British Virgin Islands (B.V.I.)
    142, 147, 164
Buchanan, Susan 231
Burnham, Forbes 9
Bustamante, Sir Alexander 128
Butler, Uriah 'Buzz' 149

Canada 25, 58, 243, 248
Caribbean
    agricultural sector 46, 59
    culture and identity 2, 17–28,
        143
    decolonization 8–17
        see also 141–70
    dependency 1, 11–12, 15,
        140–52, 165–8

Caribbean contd.
  education 23–6
    see also 240–57
  electoral politics 9–10, 124–37
  industrial sector 45–6
  independence 12, 141, 152–3,
    158–65, 171–2, 182–3
  political pluralism 127, 137
  race and class 1, 17, 71,
    202–11
  race and politics 131–2, 135–6
  social sciences 1–2
  sugar industry 3–8
    see also 33–61
Caribbean Basin Initiative 8, 56
Caribbean Community (CARI-
  COM) 145, 159, 164–5,
  183
Caribbean Examinations Council
  (CXC) 251–2, 255
Cayman Islands 249
Césaire, Aimé (201–21), 18–20
  on class 209–11, 215–17
  on colonial liberation 214–21
  on culture 207–8, 215–16
  on race 207–11, 220
Charles, Eugenia 144, 162
Chambers, George 151
Coard, Bernard 133, 161
Créole 226–32, 236–7, 243
Colonial intelligentsia 201, 207,
  210, 212
Colonial liberation 18, 20, 201,
  207, 211–20
Colonial system 27–8
Commonwealth Sugar Agree-
  ment (CSA) 56–7, 90–9,
  115
Communist Party of France
  209–10, 216–7
Compton, John 155–7, 159, 162
Confédération Internationale des
  Betteraviers Européens
  (CIBE) 93, 113
Conseil Général 16, 189
Conseil Régional 16, 184, 189
Constitution-making 120–4
Cook Islands, The 155–7

Cuba 16, 56, 65, 149, 164–5,
  199, 221, 255

Déjoie, Louis 225, 234
Demas, William 167
Democratic Labour Party (DLP)
  (Trinidad) 132
Départements d'Outre Mer
  (DOM) 171–2, 176
  French interests in 180–2
  politics in 13, 16–17, 184–5
  sugar 6–7, 90
    see also 171–200
de Smith, S. A. 123
Dessalines, Jean-Jacques 212,
  218–9
Dominica 12, 34, 126, 154, 162,
  165, 227, 243, 247
  dependency 142, 144, 147
Dominican Republic 66
Duvalier, François 21–2, 225–6,
  230, 234

Education (240–57)
  colonial legacy 241–6, 251–3
  curriculum development
    251–3
  economic and social develop-
    ment 246–51
  gender differentiation 244–5
  political issues 244–6, 255–6
  regional issues 251–4
  size 249–50
Electoral systems
  and democratic costs 129–30,
    132–4
  in Grenada 132–4
  in Jamaica 127–30
  in Trinidad 131–2
Emmanuel, Pat 134
European Economic Community
  (EEC) 6–7, 15, 77, 85,
    144, 158, 167
  and Sugar Protocol 57–8,
    89–119
  and sugar regime 92–4,
    102–4, 111, 115
European Space Centre 179–81

France
  and Caribbean sugar industry
    6–7, 66, 68, 91
  and Sugar Protocol 93, 113
  cultural influences 19–20, 22,
    207, 228–9, 232, 236–7
  imperial system 172–6, 201–2
  in Martinique 188–90
  political influences 8, 13–17,
    232
  see also 171–200
French Guiana (see Guyana)

Gairy, Sir Eric 12, 133–4, 146,
    151, 161, 163
Gomes, Albert 202
Grenada
  and independence 153–4, 158,
    161–2, 246
  dependency 142, 145, 148
  elections 132–4, 137
  People's Revolutionary
    Government (PRG) 143,
    150–1, 164–5
    see also New Jewel Move-
    ment
  politics 9–13, 126, 163, 221,
    249
  sugar 34, 42–3
Grenada National Party (GNP)
    133–4
Grenada United Labour Party
    (GULP) 133–4
Guadeloupe 8, 17, 64, 70
  departmentalization 175–6
  plantation system 64–5
  sugar 3–4, 35, 50–1, 57–8
Guyana (formerly British Guiana)
    2, 46, 159, 182, 246, 250,
    252
  and Sugar Protocol 89, 91,
    95, 98–9
  politics 9, 126, 135–6
  sugar 3–4, 35, 50–1, 57–8
Guyane (171–187) 2, 8
  and Green Plan 177–8, 181
  departmentalization 175–7
  economy 14–15, 176–7

French interests in 177–82
  history 14, 172–6
  politics 13–15

Haiti (formerly Saint Domingue)
    (223–239) 66, 147, 203,
    208, 217
  economy and social structure
    205, 224–5
  history 20–1, 223–6
  identity 23, 230
  language 226–32
  religion 22–3, 232–6
  revolution 204–6, 211–2,
    217–9
Hamel, Ian 14, 176

Independent Labour Party (ILP)
    (Britain) 206–7
Insanally, S. R. 99
International Sugar Agreement
    (ISA) 8, 55, 92, 103, 110,
    114

Jackman, Oliver 99, 111, 113
Jamaica 46, 48, 152, 165
  and Sugar Protocol 58, 89,
    91, 98, 101, 106, 109
  education system 25–6,
    242–3, 245, 247–8, 250,
    253–4
  electoral system 9, 126–30,
    135
  sugar 3–4, 35, 41, 51, 63, 65
Jamaica Labour Party (JLP) 9,
    127–8, 135
James, C. L. R. (201–21) 18–20,
    237
  on class 205–6, 213–4, 220–1
  on colonial liberation 211–14,
    220
  on race 202–7, 220
Jolivet, Marie-José 176, 179
Joshua, Ebenezer 149

Knight, Franklin 2

Levin, V. I. 214–5, 220

Lewis, Gordon 2
Lomé Conventions, The 97, 108,
    112, 115, 159, 198
  safeguard clause 98, 114
  Stabex 106, 113
  see also 89–119
Lowenthal, David 151, 243

Mahler, Vincent 7
Manley, Norman 128
Manley, Michael 128, 130, 135
Marryshaw, T. A. 149
Martinique (62–88, 188–200)
    201, 216
  agri-business bourgeoisie 5,
    69–71, 80, 83–5
  agricultural diversification
    77–8, 80–1, 190–1, 194–5
  and the world crisis 191–2
  departmentalization 188–96
  development policy 15–16,
    193–200
  economy 190–1
  identity 18–19
  industrialization 195–7
  plantation system 66–7, 72,
    190–1
  plantocracy 62–68 passim, 84
  politics 16–17
  sugar industry 6, 77–80
  tourism 197–8
Marxism 204, 209, 217, 220–1
Michels, Robert 135–6
Migration 6, 13, 17, 28, 181,
    190–1, 245, 248
Mintz, Sidney 20, 28–9
Mitterrand, President 15–16, 184
Modernization 122–3, 137
Montserrat 34, 43, 142, 146, 155

Nationalism 2, 143, 158, 210
National identity 18, 23–4
  and constitution-making
    121–2, 136–7
Naipaul, V. S. 28, 146, 150
Negritude 19, 201, 207–8
Netherlands, The 27, 90, 173
Netherlands Antilles 156

Nevis 34, 43, 161, 163
New Jewel Movement (NJM) 10,
    12, 124, 133–4, 143, 145,
    161, 164
  see also Grenada
Noel, Lloyd 134
Nwabueza, B. O. 123

O'Neil Lewis, James 99
Organization of Eastern Caribbean
    States (OECS) 144, 164
Oxenham, J. 249–50

Padmore, George 216
Parti Progressiste Martiniquais
    (PPM) 18
Payne, A. J. 246, 254
People's National Movement
    (PNM) (Trinidad) 10,
    131–2
People's National Party (PNP)
    (Jamaica) 9, 127–8, 135
Protestantism 23, 230, 232–6
    passim
Puerto Rico 56, 65–6, 83, 149,
    156

Radix, Kenrick 134
Reagan, President 56, 129, 145,
    165
Rippon, Geoffrey 90–1
Roman Catholicism 22, 231–7

Saint Domingue (now Haiti) 20,
    66, 205–6, 212, 218–9
St Kitts – Nevis 8, 46, 146, 148,
    160, 247
  and Sugar Protocol 57, 89,
    91, 98
  dependency 142, 149
  independence 12, 141, 155,
    161–5
  sugar 3, 35–6, 43–4, 48, 51,
    58
St Lucia 64, 126, 148, 153, 227,
    243, 247–8, 253
  dependency 142, 144, 146,
    149, 159

St Lucia contd.
  independence 12, 155, 162
  sugar 35, 42−3
St Vincent 12, 35, 157, 165
  dependency 142, 145, 149
San Domingo (see Saint
  Domingue)
Seaga, Edward 128, 130, 135
Shearer, Hugh 106
Singham, A. W. 204
Smith, M. G. 1−2
Stone, Carl 130
Strachan, Selwyn 133−4
Sugar (33−88) 3−8, 27, 54
  beet sugar 55, 57, 80, 90,
    93−5, 102−115 passim, 148
  costs of production 4, 6, 49,
    51−2, 57−8
  economic development 4,
    33−4, 49
  employment 4, 35−6, 48−9,
    54
  export earnings 3, 52, 75−8
  government intervention 4, 49,
    59, 76−7, 79−80
  production in
    Barbados 36−7, 72, 76
    Belize 44
    Guyana 37−41
    Jamaica 41
    Martinique 79−80
    St Kitts 43−4
    Trinidad 42
  productivity 50−2, 72−5
Sugar Protocol (89−119) 4, 7−8,
    57−8
  access to 96, 100−5
  and force majeure 7, 98,
    100−2
  as aid 110−111
  negotiation of 95−7
  prices 96−8, 105−9
  quotas 57−8, 96, 98, 100−2
  review 112−15
  terms of 97−9
Suriname 2, 89−90, 98, 100−1,
    173, 182

Tate and Lyle 65, 99, 103−5,
  109−10, 114
Te Pass, Albert 99, 113
Thorez, Maurice 210, 216
Tobago 34, 43, 136
Toussaint L'Ouverture 20, 203,
  205, 212, 219
Trinidad and Tobago 2, 18, 46,
  48, 201−3, 227, 246
  and Sugar Protocol 7, 57−8,
    89, 91, 95, 98−101 passim
  education system 25−6, 243,
    247, 250, 253−4
  electoral system 9−10, 126,
    136−7
  politics 9, 135, 153−4
  sugar 3−4, 35−42, 51−2, 54,
    63−5
Trotskyism 204, 213−4, 220

United Nations 11, 147, 154−5,
  157, 161
United States 20, 178, 192
  and Caribbean education 25,
    252−3, 255
  and Caribbean politics 13,
    27−8, 148, 166−7
  and Caribbean sugar 8, 56,
    58, 65, 77, 94
  constitution-making in 120−1
  relations with Grenada 141,
    145, 152, 164−5, 167
  relations with Haiti 22−3,
    226−7, 230−1, 234−5
University of the West Indies
  (UWI) (formerly University
  College of the West Indies)
  24−5, 245−6, 253−5

Valdman, Albert 231
Vié, Jean-Emile 181−2
Voodoo 22−3, 204, 226, 232−7

Webster, Ronald 160
West Indies Act (1967) 157, 160
West Indies Encumbered Estates
  Act (1854) 63, 67

West Indies Federation 147,
    152–3, 157, 246
Westminster model (120–40)
    9–10, 151
    and democracy 124–37
Whiteman, Unison 133–4, 161,
    165

Wilberforce, William 222, 226
Williams, Dr Eric 10, 153–4,
    244
Workers and Farmers Party
    (Trinidad) 19, 132
World Bank 4, 147, 231